AF600577

ORDINATION IN SOCIETIES OF THE COMMON LIFE

A Historical Synopsis and a Commentary

THE CATHOLIC UNIVERSITY OF AMERICA
CANON LAW STUDIES
No. 341

Ordination in Societies of the Common Life

A HISTORICAL SYNOPSIS AND A COMMENTARY

A DISSERTATION
SUBMITTED TO THE FACULTY OF THE SCHOOL OF CANON LAW OF THE CATHOLIC UNIVERSITY OF AMERICA IN PARTIAL FULFILLMENT OF THE REQUIREMENTS FOR THE DEGREE OF DOCTOR OF CANON LAW

BY
REV. JOHN G. NUGENT, C.M., J.C.L.
PRIEST OF THE EASTERN PROVINCE

THE CATHOLIC UNIVERSITY OF AMERICA PRESS
WASHINGTON, D.C.
1958

IMPRIMI POTEST
Sylvester A. Taggart, V.C.M.
Superior Provincialis

Philadelphiae, die 28 februarii 1958

NIHIL OBSTAT
Clemens V. Bastnagel, S.T.L., J.U.D.
Censor Deputatus ad hoc

Washingtonii, die 20 maii 1958

IMPRIMATUR
Patricius A. O'Boyle, D.D.
Archiepiscopus Washingtonensis

Washingtonii, die 22 maii 1958

Printed by The Abbey Press, St. Meinrad, Indiana, U.S.A.

TO

MY MOTHER AND FATHER

FOREWORD

Of all the responsibilities that can be laid on man's shoulders in this life, perhaps the gravest is responsibility for the ordination of a priest. It is for this reason that Holy Mother Church places this responsibility only upon those whom by experience she knows to be able to bear the burden.

When a religious institute has obtained the privilege of exemption, it is automatically considered in law as ready to assume the responsibility for the ordination of its members.[1] Before this time, responsibility for the ordination of its members lies primarily on the shoulders of the bishops.[2] Experience teaches, however, that even before the Church sees fit to grant certain religious institutes the privilege of exemption, it judges that these institutes are ready to carry the responsibility for the ordination of their members. In these instances, the Holy See, by way of indult, grants to such institutes the privilege of issuing dimissorial letters.

The concern of Holy Mother Church over the ordination of priests is extended in the same way to the matter of the ordination of the members of Societies of the Common Life. Societies of the Common Life, as a canonical institute in the Church juridically distinct from Religious Congregations, date back only as far as the time when the Code went into effect.[3] It was determined by the Code, therefore, that in the matter of ordination, Societies are governed by the laws which regulate the ordination of secular clerics. This places full responsibility for the ordination of members of Societies on the shoulders of the bishops. Since, however, some clerical Societies have, as a matter of fact, proved their capabilities over a period of centuries, provision was made in the Code for opportune concessions

[1] Cf. canon 964, n. 2.
[2] Cf. canon 964, n. 4.
[3] Cf. *infra*, pp. 16-18.

to be granted to Societies in the matter of ordination, but the right to make such concessions was reserved to the Holy See. These enactments were stated in canon 678: *In iis quae ad studiorum rationem et ad suscipiendos ordines pertinent, sodales iisdem legibus tenentur ac saeculares clerici, salvis peculiaribus praescriptionibus a Sancta Sede datis.* This is all that the Code has to say about the ordination of members of Societies.

In the present dissertation, an effort has been made to outline the present law for the ordination of members of Societies in two chapters. Chapter III deals with the present common law for the ordination of members of Societies. This law is ascertained by an application to Societies of the present law for the ordination of secular clerics. Chapter IV deals with the various privileges granted to Societies by the Holy See in the matter of ordination. Throughout the dissertation, historical synopses of certain points of ordination law are inserted in those places where such synopses aid in a better understanding of those matters of the present law which are under consideration.

This work is dedicated to the Immaculate Mother of God.

The writer takes this occasion to express his sincere thanks to the Congregation of the Mission of the Eastern Province for the opportunity to pursue a course of graduate study in Canon Law; to the members of the Faculty of the School of Canon Law for their devoted assistance; to the priests of Divinity College at the Catholic University of America for their kind encouragement; and to all who have helped in any way whatsoever in the preparation of this dissertation.

TABLE OF CONTENTS

INTRODUCTION

As an introduction to the study of the law for ordination in Societies of the Common Life, some acquaintance should be made with the principal clerical Societies of the Common Life in the Church.

Societies of the Common Life may be defined as societies in which the members lead a common life after the manner of religious under the government of superiors and according to approved constitutions, but without the three usual public vows of religion.[1] A Society is a clerical Society if many of its members are priests; otherwise it is a lay Society.[2] A Society is of pontifical approval if it has obtained approbation, or at least a decree of praise, from the Holy See; a Society is of diocesan approval if it has been erected by an ordinary, but has not yet obtained the decree of praise from the Holy See.[3]

Those clerical Societies which are engaged exclusively in the work of the foreign missions are ordinarily subject to the Sacred Congregation for the Propagation of the Faith.[4] Those clerical Societies which are not engaged exclusively in the work of the foreign missions, even though some of their members are so engaged, are ordinarily subject to the Sacred Congregation for Religious.[5] And those clerical Societies which are limited to a nation with whom the Holy See has a concordat can be subject to the Sacred Congregation for Extraordinary Ecclesiastical Affairs.[6]

It seems that no exhaustive list of clerical Societies of the Common Life of pontifical approval has ever been published. It seems that the closest thing to such an exhaustive list is the list of "Ecclesiastical Congregations" (*Congregazioni Ecclesiastiche*) published in the *Annuario Pontificio*. This

[1] Canon 673, § 1.
[2] Canon 673, § 2, collated with canon 488, n. 4.
[3] Canon 673, § 2, collated with canon 488, n. 3.
[4] Canon 252, § 3.
[5] Canon 251, § 1.
[6] Canon 255.

list, however, includes both clerical Religious Congregations of pontifical approval and clerical Societies of the Common Life of pontifical approval, and no indication is given of the specific category to which each institute belongs.[7] It seems that the list is intended to be exhaustive. The institutes included in the list seem to be arranged in the chronological order in which they became institutes of pontifical approval.

A list of twelve missionary Societies subject to the Sacred Congregation for the Propagation of the Faith as of April 1, 1943, was published by Stanghetti in the year 1943.[8] The same list was published by Paventi in the year 1946.[9] And again in the year 1950, Paventi, in a commentary on the Constitutions of the Spanish Institute of Saint Francis Xavier for the Foreign Missions, published the same list of twelve Societies and added to it the Seminary for the Foreign Missions in Mexico.[10] It seems, however, that not all the Societies included in these lists are necessarily of pontifical approval, for some of them do not appear in the *Annuario Pontificio.*

Heimbucher distinguished between Religious Congregations and Societies of the Common Life. But in the section of his work which he devoted to Societies, mention of Religious Congregations is sometimes found, and the reader cannot always be sure that any given institute mentioned in this section is not a Religious Congregation unless he

[7] *Annuario Pontificio per l'Anno 1952* (Città del Vaticano: Tipografia Poliglotta Vaticana, 1952), pp. 765-793 (hereafter cited as *Annuario*).

[8] *Prassi della S. C. de Propaganda Fide,* Bibliotheca Missionalis, n. 1 (Romae: Officium Libri Catholici, 1943), pp. 34-35, nota (3) (hereafter referred to as *Prassi*).

[9] *De Iuramento ac de Titulo Missionis,* Bibliotheca Missionalis, n. 3 (Romae: Officium Libri Catholici, 1946), p. 87 (hereafter referred to as *De Iuramento*).

[10] *Organización del Instituto Español del S. Francisco Javier para Misiones Extranjeras Comentario y Exposición de las Constituciones* (Burgos: Aldecoa, 1950), p. 60 (hereafter referred to as *Organización del Instituto Español*).

has knowledge of the fact from other sources. The work of Heimbucher, nevertheless, is most helpful in view of its completeness.[11]

From the *Annuario Pontificio,* from the works of Stanghetti, Paventi and Heimbucher, and from other canonical dissertations on the law of Societies, the present writer has attempted to construct as exhaustive a list as possible of the clerical Societies of the Common Life of pontifical approval in the Church today. When the exact nature and status of an institute remained doubtful even after consultation of these works, reliable members of the institute in question were contacted by private communication.

As a result of these investigations, a list of twenty-three clerical Societies of pontifical approval was compiled. These Societies are given here in the chronological order in which they became Societies of pontifical approval, as far as this order could be determined. With each Society is given the name of the founder, the place and date of foundation, the date on which the Society became a Society of pontifical approval, the bond by which the members are united to the Society, the chief works of the Society, and the Sacred Roman Congregation to which the Society is subject. A brief bibliography is given in a footnote.

Following, then, is a list of twenty-three clerical Societies of pontifical approval. The Societies are arranged in the chronological order in which they received pontifical approbation, at least by way of a decree of praise.

1. The Institute of the Oratory of Saint Philip Neri (The Congregation of the Oratory) was founded in Rome by Saint Philip Neri (1515-1595) in the year 1564. The Society was approved by Pope Gregory XIII on July 15, 1575. The only bond existing in the Society is the bond of mutual charity. The works of the Society are threefold: prayer, preaching and the dispensing of the sacraments.

[11] *Die Orden und Kongregationen der katholischen Kirche* (3. ed., 2 vols., Paderborn: Verlag Ferdinand Schöningh, 1933-1934), II, 552-637, 660-661 (hereafter referred to as *Die Orden*).

The Society is subject to the Sacred Congregation for Religious.[12]

2. The Congregation of the Oratory of Jesus and of Mary Immaculate was founded in Paris by Cardinal Pierre de Bérulle (1575-1629) on November 11, 1611. The Society was approved by Pope Paul V on May 10, 1613. The only bond in the Society is the bond of charity. The works of the Society are the education of clerics, the administration of colleges and preaching. The Society passed out of existence as a result of the French Revolution, but was reorganized in 1852 by Fathers Gratry and Petetot. It is subject to the Sacred Congregation for Religious.[13]

[12] *Annuario,* p. 765; Holstenius, *Codex regularum monasticarum et canonicarum* (6 vols., ed. M. Brockie, Augustae Vindelicorum, 1759), VI, 234-264 (hereafter referred to as *Codex regularum*); Agnelli, *The Excellencies of the Congregation of the Oratory* (translated from the Italian and abridged by Frederick Antrobus, London, 1881); Helyot, *Dictionnaire des Ordres Religieux,* in Migne, *Encyclopédie Théologique,* I Série, Tomes XX-XXIII (4 vols., Paris, 1847-1859), III, 57-68 (hereafter referred to as *Ordres*); Heimbucher, *Die Orden,* II, 562-566; Currier, *History of Religious Orders* (New York, 1899), pp. 607-612 (hereafter referred to as *Orders*); Pisani, *The Congregations of Priests from the Sixteenth to the Eighteenth Century,* Catholic Library of Religious Knowledge, n. 14 (translated from the French by Mother Mary Reginald, O.P., London-St. Louis, 1930), pp. 55-57 (hereafter referred to as *Congregations*); Maire, *Histoire des Instituts Religieux et Missionaires* (Paris, 1930), pp. 181-191 (hereafter referred to as *Instituts*); Stanton, *De Societatibus sive Virorum sive Mulierum in Communi Viventium sine Votis* (2. ed., Halifaxiae: Apud Custodiam Librariam Maioris Seminarii a Sanctissimo Corde B. M. V., 1936), pp. 30-35 (hereafter referred to as *De Societatibus*); Ristuccia, *Quasi-Religious Societies,* The Catholic University of America Canon Law Studies, n. 261 (Washington, D.C.: The Catholic University of America Press, 1949), pp. 14-17 (hereafter referred to as *Societies*); Waters, *The Probation in Societies of Quasi-Religious,* The Catholic University of America Canon Law Studies, n. 306 (Washington, D.C.: The Catholic University of America Press, 1951), pp. 34-35, 41-42 (hereafter referred to as *Probation in Societies*); Kapsner, *Catholic Religious Orders* (Collegeville: St. John's Abbey Press, 1948), p. 184 (hereafter referred to as *Orders*).

[13] *Annuario,* p. 766; Holstenius, *Codex regularum,* VI, 529-543;

3. The Congregation of the Mission (Vincentians, Lazarists) was founded in Paris by Saint Vincent de Paul (1581-1660) on April 17, 1625. The Society was approved by Pope Urban VIII on January 12, 1632. The members pronounce private vows of poverty, chastity, obedience and stability. The principal works of the Society are the missions and the education of ecclesiastics. The Society is subject to the Sacred Congregation for Religious.[14]

4. The Society of Priests of Saint Sulpice (Sulpicians) was founded in Paris by Jean-Jacques Olier (1608-1657) in the year 1642. The Society was approved by Cardinal Flavius Chigi, Papal Legate to France, on August 5, 1664. The only bond in the Society is an agreement. The exclusive work of the Society is the education of ecclesiastics. It is subject to the Sacred Congregation for Religious.[15]

5. The Paris Foreign Mission Society was founded in Paris in the year 1660 by a group of French Vicars Apos-

Leherpeur, *L'Oratoire de France* (Paris, 1926); Helyot, *Ordres*, III, 68-90; Heimbucher, *Die Orden*, II, 566-571; Currier, *Orders*, p. 613; Pisani, *Congregations*, pp. 57-69; Maire, *Instituts*, pp. 181-191; Stanton, *De Societatibus*, pp. 57-60; Waters, *Probation in Societies*, pp. 36-37; Kapsner, *Orders*, p. 184.

[14] *Annuario*, p. 766; *Acta Apostolica, Bullae, Brevia et Rescripta in gratiam Congregationis Missionis* (Parisiis, 1876) (hereafter cited as *Acta Ap. in gratiam C. M.*); *Collectio Privilegiorum et Indulgentiarum quae S. Sedes Congregationi Missionis benigne Concessit* (3. ed., Parisiis, 1900); Helyot, *Ordres*, II, 753-769; Heimbucher, *Die Orden*, II, 574-586; Currier, *Orders*, pp. 441-445; Pisani, *Congregations*, pp. 70-93; Maire, *Instituts*, pp. 191-203; Stanton, *De Societatibus*, pp. 61-66; Ristuccia, *Societies*, pp. 21-25; Waters, *Probation in Societies*, pp. 37-38, 59; Kapsner, *Orders*, p. 347.

[15] *Annuario*, p. 767; *Constitutions of the Society of the Priests of Saint Sulpice* (There is no place or date of publication, but the decree of definitive approbation of July 8, 1931, is appended.); Monval, *Les Sulpiciens*, Collection "Les Grands Ordres Monastiques et Instituts Religieux," dirigée par Edouard Schneider (Paris: Éditions Bernard Grasset, 1934); Helyot, *Ordres*, III, 577-594; Heimbucher, *Die Orden*, II, 586-592; Currier, *Orders*, pp. 624-625; Pisani, *Congregations*, pp. 94-117; Maire, *Instituts*, pp. 203-210; Stanton, *De Societatibus*, pp. 71-74; Ristuccia, *Societies*, pp. 25-27; Waters, *Probation in Societies*, p. 40; Kapsner, *Orders*, p. 332.

tolic who were, at the time, the ordinaries of vicariates in the foreign mission fields. The Society was approved on August 11, 1664. The members of the Society, unlike the members of other missionary Societies who are incorporated by an oath, make a *propositum* (*acte de bon propos*) to serve the missions in the Society. The Society is engaged exclusively in the work of the missions and is subject to the Sacred Congregation for the Propagation of the Faith.[16]

6. The Society of Priests of Mercy (Mercy Fathers) was founded in Lyons in the year 1808 by Jean-Baptiste Rauzan (1757-1847). The Society was approved definitively by Pope Gregory XVI on February 18, 1834. The members take private vows of stability, obedience and chastity, and make a promise of following evangelical poverty. The principal works of the Society are preaching, teaching, giving retreats, instructing youth and laboring generally for the salvation of souls. It is subject to the Sacred Congregation for Religious.[17]

7. The Society of the Catholic Apostolate (Pallottine Fathers, formerly known as the Pious Society of the Missions) was founded in Rome on April 4, 1835, by the Venerable Vincent Pallotti (1795-1850). The Society was approved by Pope Gregory XVI on July 11, 1835. The members are bound by promises of poverty, chastity, obedience and stability. The principal works of the Society are catechetics, preaching, missions, retreats, administration of

[16] *Annuario*, p. 767; Launay, *Histoire Générale de la Société des Missions-Étrangères* (3 vols., Paris, 1894); Goyau, *Les, Prêtres des Missions Étrangères*, Collection "Les Grands Ordres Monastiques et Instituts Religieux," dirigée par Edouard Schneider (Paris: Éditions Bernard Grasset, 1932); Helyot, *Ordres*, IV, 873-889; Heimbucher, *Die Orden*, II, 600-606; Pisani, *Congregations*, pp. 123-139; Maire; *Instituts*, pp. 218-224; Stanton, *De Societatibus*, pp. 77-82; Kapsner, *Orders*, p. 317.

[17] *Annuario*, p. 770; *Constitutions de la Société des Prêtres de la Miséricorde* (Rome, 1928); *The Fathers of Mercy* (New York: the Paulist Press, 1920); Heimbucher, *Die Orden*, II, 634; Stanton, *De Societatibus*, pp. 83-84; Kapsner, *Orders*, p. 320.

the sacraments, the Catholic press, the foreign missions, chaplaincies, Christian education of youth, and seminaries. But in all these works it is the special aim of the Society to enlist the support of the laity. The Society is subject to the Sacred Congregation for Religious.[18]

8. The Congregation of the Most Precious Blood (Precious Blood Fathers) was founded in Umbria on August 15, 1815, by Blessed Gaspar del Bufalo (1786-1837). The Society was approved on December 17, 1841. The members are bound by a promise of fidelity to the Society. The principal works of the Society are missions, retreats, parishes, colleges and chaplaincies. It is subject to the Sacred Congregation for Religious.[19]

9. The Congregation of Jesus and Mary (The Eudists) was founded at Caën on March 25, 1643, by Saint John Eudes (1601-1680). The Society received the decree of praise on July 25, 1851. The members make a protestation of fidelity to the Society till death. The principal work of the Society is the education of ecclesiastics. It is subject to the Sacred Congregation for Religious.[20]

[18] *Annuario*, p. 770; *Constitutiones Piae Societatis Missionum* (Ratisbonae, 1922); *Constitutions of the Pious Society of Missions* (translated by order of the General Council, 1935); *Directorium Piae Societatis Missionum* (auctoritate Capituli Generalis anni 1919 a Consilio generali editum, Ratisbonae); *Promptuarium Facultatum Piae Societatis Missionum iussu Sexti Capituli Generalis Editum* (Romae: Ad. SS. Salvatorem in Unda, 1932); Helyot, *Ordres*, IV, 1627-1644; Heimbucher, *Die Orden*, II, 614-619; Currier, *Orders*, pp. 626-627; Stanton, *De Societatibus*, pp. 84-86; Ristuccia, *Societies*, pp. 31-33; Waters, *Probation in Societies*, pp. 40, 60; Kapsner, *Orders*, p. 198.

[19] *Annuario*, p. 772; *Regula et Constitutiones Congregationis Missionis a Pretioso Sanguine D. N. J. C.* (Carthagena, 1946); *Customary of the Society of the Precious Blood, American Province* (Carthagena, 1949); Helyot, *Ordres*, IV, 215-228; Heimbucher, *Die Orden*, II, 611-613; Currier, *Orders*, pp. 490-491; Stanton, *De Societatibus*, p. 86; Ristuccia, *Societies*, pp. 33-35; Waters, *Probation in Societies*, pp. 40, 60-61; Kapsner, *Orders*, p. 214.

[20] *Annuario*, p. 773; *Constitutions de la Congrégation de Jésus et Marie* (Paris, 1928); *Règles Complementaires de la Congrégation*

10. The Missionaries of Africa (The White Fathers) were founded in Algeria in the year 1868 by Cardinal Charles Lavigerie (1825-1892). The Society received the decree of praise on March 16, 1879. The members are bound by oath. The Society is a missionary Society and is subject to the Sacred Congregation for the Propagation of the Faith.[21]

11. The Society of Missionaries to Africa (The Society of African Missionaries of Lyons) was founded in Lyons on December 8, 1856, by Bishop Melchior de Marion Bresillac († 1859). The Society received the decree of praise on November 1, 1890. The members are bound by oath. The Society is a missionary Society and is subject to the Sacred Congregation for the Propagation of the Faith.[22]

12. The Society of Missionaries of Saint Joseph of Mill Hill (The Mill Hill Fathers) was founded in England on March 18, 1866, by Father Herbert Vaughan (1832-1903), later Cardinal Archbishop of Westminster. The Society received the decree of praise on January 28, 1897. The members are bound by oath. The Society is a missionary Society and is subject to the Sacred Congregation for the Propagation of the Faith.[23]

de Jésus et Marie (Paris, 1931); Helyot, *Ordres*, II, 243-253; Heimbucher, *Die Orden*, II, 592-595; Currier, *Orders*, pp. 617-619; Pisani, *Congregations*, pp. 118-122; Maire, *Instituts*, pp. 210-218; Stanton, *De Societatibus*, pp. 74-77; Ristuccia, *Societies*, pp. 28-30; Waters, *Probation in Societies*, pp. 39-40, 44-46, 61; Kapsner, *Orders*, p. 89.

[21] *Annuario*, p. 779; *Société des Missionnaires d'Afrique, Constitutions* (Namur, Grands Lacs, 1948); Heimbucher, *Die Orden*, II, 623-630; Maire, *Instituts*, pp. 295-299; Stanton, *De Societatibus*, p. 88; Waters, *Probation in Societies*, p. 40; Kapsner, *Orders*, p. 348.

[22] *Annuario*, p. 780; *The Society of African Missions, Constitutions and Directory* (Cork: Guy & Company Ltd., 1935); *Ordo Divini Officii Recitandi Missaeque Celebrandae ad usum Societatis Missionum ad Afros pro anno Domini 1951* (Lugduni: Ex Typis Missionum ad Afros, 1950); Heimbucher, *Die Orden*, II, 607-608; Maire, *Instituts*, pp. 290-295; Stanton, *De Societatibus*, p. 121; Waters, *Probation in Societies*, p. 61; Kapsner, *Orders*, p. 317.

[23] *Annuario*, p. 781; Heimbucher, *Die Orden*, II, 621-623; Currier,

13. The Society of Maryknoll for Foreign Missions (The Catholic Foreign Mission Society of America, The Maryknoll Missionaries) was founded in New York in the year 1911 by Reverend James A. Walsh (1867-1936), later Bishop Walsh, and Reverend Thomas F. Price (1861-1919). The Society received the decree of praise on July 15, 1915. The members are bound by oath. The Society is a missionary Society and is subject to the Sacred Congregation for the Propagation of the Faith.[24]

14. The Society of Saint Columban for the Missions in China (The Columban Fathers) was founded in Ireland in the year 1917 by Reverend Edward J. Galvin, later Bishop Galvin. The Society was approved by the Holy See on June 5, 1925. The members are bound by an oath. The Society is a missionary Society and is subject to the Sacred Congregation for the Propagation of the Faith.[25]

15. The Pontifical Institute of the Holy Apostles Peter and Paul and of Saints Ambrose and Charles for the Foreign Missions was formed when Pope Pius XI united the Foreign Mission Institute of Milan with the Pontifical Seminary of Saints Peter and Paul in Rome on May 23, 1926. The Foreign Mission Institute of Milan had been founded in Milan by Monsignor Angelo Ramazzotti († 1861) in the year 1850.[26] The Pontifical Seminary of Saints Peter and

Orders, pp. 631-633; Stanton, *De Societatibus*, p. 88; Ristuccia, *Societies*, pp. 38-40; Waters, *Probation in Societies*, p. 40; Kapsner, *Orders*, p. 159.

[24] *Annuario*, p. 786; *Constitutions of the Catholic Foreign Mission Society of America* (2. ed., New York: Maryknoll, 1938); Powers, *The Maryknoll Movement* (Maryknoll: Field Afar Press, 1920); Lane, *The Early Days of Maryknoll* (New York: McKay, 1951); Heimbucher, *Die Orden*, II, 609, 610; Stanton, *De Societatibus*, p. 88; Ristuccia, *Societies*, pp. 41-44; Waters, *Probation in Societies*, pp. 40, 62; Kapsner, *Orders*, p. 44.

[25] *Annuario*, p. 786; *Constitutiones Societatis Sancti Columbani pro Missionibus apud Sinenses* (Dublin: Sealy, Bryers and Walker, 1932); Heimbucher, *Die Orden*, II, 609; Stanton, *De Societatibus*, p. 88; Waters, *Probation in Societies*, p. 62; Kapsner, *Orders*, p. 49.

[26] *Costituzioni dell'Istituto delle Missioni Estere de Milano* (Mi-

Paul in Rome was founded in Rome in the year 1874 by Monsignor Pietro Avanzini († 1877).[27] The Society formed by the union of these two institutes is a missionary Society subject to the Sacred Congregation for the Propagation of the Faith. The members are bound by oath.[28]

16. The Society of Missionary Priests of Saint Paul the Apostle (The Paulist Fathers) was founded in New York in the year 1858 by Reverend Isaac Thomas Hecker (1819-1888). The Society received the decree of praise on July 13, 1929. The members make promises of poverty, chastity, obedience and perseverance in the Society. The principal work of the Society is the conversion of those who are separated from Holy Mother Church. The Society is subject to the Sacred Congregation for Religious.[29]

17. The Foreign Mission Society of the Province of Quebec was founded in Montreal on February 2, 1921, by the bishops of the civil province of Quebec in Canada. The Society was approved by the Holy See on July 15, 1929. The members, most of whom are French-speaking, are bound by oath. The Society is a missionary Society and is subject to the Sacred Congregation for the Propagation of the Faith.[30]

18. The Foreign Mission Society of Portugal was founded directly by Pope Pius XI in 1922 and was approved in the year 1930. The members are bound by oath. The Society is a missionary Society. But in virtue of the Concordat

lano, 1925), Heimbucher, *Die Orden,* II, 606-607; Kapsner, *Orders,* p. 159.

[27] Heimbucher, *Die Orden,* II, 609.

[28] *Annuario,* p. 787; Paventi, *De Iuramento,* pp. 87-93.

[29] *Annuario,* p. 788; *Constitutions of the Society of Missionary Priests of Saint Paul the Apostle* (New York: The Paulist Press, 1940); *The Register of the Paulist Fathers* (October, 1951); Gillis *The Paulists* (New York: Macmillan, 1932); Heimbucher, *Die Orden,* II, 619-621; Currier, *Orders,* pp. 628-630; Stanton, *De Societatibus,* p. 87; Ristuccia, *Societies,* pp. 35- 38; Waters, *Probation in Societies,* pp. 40, 60; Kapsner, *Orders,* p. 200.

[30] *Annuario,* p. 788; Heimbucher, *Die Orden,* II, 609; Paventi, *De Iuramento,* p. 87; Kapsner, *Orders,* p. 318.

which exists between the Holy See and Portugal,[31] the Society is subject, not to the Sacred Congregation for the Propagation of the Faith, but to the Sacred Congregation for Extraordinary Ecclesiastical Affairs.[32]

19. The Society of Saint Joseph of the Sacred Heart (The Josephite Fathers) was founded in Baltimore as an offshoot of the Society of Missionaries of Saint Joseph of Mill Hill in the year 1893. The foundation was a result of the efforts of Cardinal Herbert Vaughan (1832-1903) and Cardinal James Gibbons (1834-1921). The Society received the decree of praise on May 6, 1932.[33] The members are bound by a promise. The special work of the Society is the Negro Missions in the United States. The Society is subject to the Sacred Congregation for Religious.[34]

20. The Foreign Mission Society of Bethlehem in Switzerland (formerly called the Bethlehem Institute of Immensée) was founded in Immensée in Switzerland on May 30, 1921, by several priests. The Constitutions of the Society were approved by the Holy See on March 4, 1936. The

[31] Inter Sanctam Sedem et Rempublicam Lusitanam Sollemnes Conventiones, 7 maii 1940—*Acta Apostolicae Sedis, Commentarium Officiale* (Romae, 1909-1929; Civitate Vaticana, 1929-), XXXII (1940), 217-245 (hereafter cited as *AAS*).

[32] *Annuario,* p. 789; Kapsner, *Orders,* p. 210; cf. Pius XII, ep. encycl. *Saeculo exeunte octavo,* 13 iun. 1940—*AAS,* XXXII (1940), 249-260, cf. pp. 255-257.

The information about the oath and the subjection to the Sacred Congregation for Extraordinary Ecclesiastical Affairs was obtained by private communication.

[33] S. C. de Rel., decr. 6 maii 1932—*Constitutions of the Society of St. Joseph of the Sacred Heart* (Rome: Vatican Polyglot Press, 1932), pp. 7-9.

Although no mention of this Society appears in the *Annuario Pontificio,* it is certain that in virtue of the decree of praise it is a Society of pontifical approval. Cf. canon 673, § 2, collated with canon 488, n. 3.

[34] *Constitutions of the Society of St. Joseph of the Sacred Heart; Society of Saint Joseph of the Sacred Heart 1893-1943* (Baltimore: The Josephite Press, 1943); Heimbucher, *Die Orden,* II, 609; Currier, *Orders,* pp. 634-637; Ristuccia, *Societies,* pp. 40-41; Waters, *Probation in Societies,* pp. 40, 61; Kapsner, *Orders,* p. 139.

members are bound by oath. The Society is a missionary Society and is subject to the Sacred Congregation for the Propagation of the Faith.[35]

21. The Scarboro Foreign Mission Society was founded in Almonte, Canada, in the year 1918 by J. M. Fraser. The Constitutions of the Society were approved by the Holy See on June 11, 1940. The members, most of whom are English-speaking, are bound by oath. The Society is a missionary Society and is subject to the Sacred Congregation for the Propagation of the Faith.[36]

22. The Spanish Institute of Saint Francis Xavier for the Foreign Missions (The Burgos Foreign Mission Society) was founded in Burgos, Spain, in the year 1899 by Canon Don Gerardo Villota y Urroz as a College in which young men could be trained for the service of the Missions. The College became a National Seminary for the Foreign Missions with the blessing of Pope Benedict XV in 1919, when Cardinal Juan Benlloch y Vivó was Archbishop of Burgos. The Seminary became a national missionary Society of pontifical approval on June 18, 1947.[37] The members are bound by oath. The Society is subject to the Sacred Congregation for the Propagation of the Faith.[38]

23. The Yarumal Institute for the Foreign Missions was founded in Columbia in the year 1939. The Constitutions were approved *ad septennium* on January 16, 1953.[39] The

[35] *Annuario,* p. 790; Heimbucher, *Die Orden,* II, 609, 610; Paventi, *De Iuramento,* p. 87.

[36] *Annuario,* p. 791; *Constitutions of the Scarboro Foreign Mission Society* (Scarboro Bluffs, Ontario, 1941); Heimbucher, *Die Orden,* II, 609; Stanton, *De Societatibus,* p. 88; Waters, *Probation in Societies,* p. 62; Kapsner, *Orders,* p. 318.

[37] S. C. de Prop. Fide, decr. 18 iun. 1947—Paventi, *Organización del Instituto Español,* p. 75.

The Society is not, however, listed in the *Annuario Pontifico.*

[38] Paventi, *Organización del Instituto Español;* Heimbucher, *Die Orden* II, 609.

[39] This was learned from private communication. It seems that the Society has been a Society of pontifical approval at least since its Constitutions were approved by the Holy See *ad septennium.* It is not listed in the *Annuario Pontificio.*

members of the Society are bound by oath. The Society is a missionary Society and is subject to the Sacred Congregation for the Propagation of the Faith.[40]

In addition to these twenty-three clerical Societies of pontifical approval, there are two other clerical Societies that should be mentioned. As far as the writer has been able to find out, these Societies are not yet Societies of pontifical approval.

The Home Missioners of America (The Glenmary Missioners) were founded in Cincinnati in the year 1939 by Reverend W. Howard Bishop under the patronage of Archbishop John McNicholas. The work of the Society is the conversion of the more than one hundred million non-Catholics in the United States. The members are bound by an oath of obedience.[41]

The Mexican Seminary for the Foreign Missions was founded in Mexico in the year 1948. The members are bound by oath. The institute is subject to the Sacred Congregation for the Propagation of the Faith.[42]

[40] Paventi, *De Iuramento*, p. 87.

[41] Kapsner, *Orders*, p. 111.

[42] Paventi, *Organización del Instituto Español*, p. 60.

CHAPTER I

PRELIMINARY CONSIDERATIONS

It is a commonly admitted principle that in order thoroughly to understand a question of law, one must have a knowledge of the historical background of that law. To understand the present legislation regarding the ordination of members of Societies of the Common Life, then, it seems necessary to have a knowledge of the law for the ordination of members of such institutes before the Code. When one looks for the law regulating the ordination of members of Societies before the Code, however, one is immediately faced with one fundamental problem, one difficulty. The difficulty, however, is not one which arises only when one investigates the law for the ordination of members of such institutes. It arises whenever one investigates any phase of the law regulating such institutes before the Code. The problem is this. Before the Code, those institutes which today are called Societies of the Common Life did not constitute a juridic institute essentially distinct from those institutes which today are called Religious Congregations.

Today, Societies of the Common Life may be defined as societies in which the members lead a common life after the manner of religious under the government of superiors and according to approved constitutions, but without the three usual public vows of religion.[1] Religious Congregations, on the other hand, may be defined as societies approved by legitimate ecclesiastical authority in which the members, according to the laws of their respective institutes, pronounce simple public vows, either perpetual or temporary—but, if temporary, to be renewed upon expiration—and thus tend to evangelical perfection.[2] Members of Societies of the Common Life are not religious;[3] mem-

[1] Cf. canon 673, § 1.

[2] Cf. canon 488, nn. 1, 2.

[3] Canon 673, § 1.

bers of Religious Congregations are religious.[4] Members of Societies of the Common Life are governed by the special law[5] which is found in Title XVII of Book II of the

[4] Canon 488, n. 7.

[5] Since the authors are not in agreement in a question of terminology involving the expressions "special law" and "singular law," it will be apropos at the outset to choose the system of terminology that seems to be more correct, and to adhere to this system throughout.

Although all authors are in essential agreement on the division of law by reason of scope as to place, as to persons, and as to application, there is disagreement among them in terminology regarding the expressions "special law" and "singular law." The essential teaching may be summed up as follows: by reason of scope, law is divided as to place into universal and particular; as to persons into general and special or singular; and as to application into common and singular or special.

The following authors oppose singular to general and oppose special to common: Michiels, *Normae Generales Juris Canonici, Commentarius Libri I Codicis Juris Canonici* (2. ed., 2 vols., Parisiis-Tornaci-Romae: Desclée et Socii, 1949), I, 14-15, 205 (hereafter referred to as *Normae Generales*); Coronata, *Institutiones Iuris Canonici ad Usum Utriusque Cleri et Scholarum* (5 vols., Taurini: Marietti, Vol. I, *Normae generales, De Clericis, De Religiosis, De Laicis,* 2. ed., 1939), I, 16-17 (hereafter referred to as *Institutiones*); Cappello *Summa Iuris Canonici in Usum Scholarum Concinnata* (3 vols., Romae: Apud Aedes Universitatis Gregorianae, Vol. I, 4. ed., 1945; Vol. II, 4. ed., 1945), I, 11 (hereafter referred to as *Summa*); Regatillo, *Institutiones Iuris Canonici* (2 vols., Santander: Sal Terrae, Vol. I, *Pars Praeliminaris, Normae Generales, De Personis,* 3. ed., 1948), I, 12 (hereafter referred to as *Institutiones*).

On the other hand, the following authors, more correctly, it seems, oppose the specific to the generic, and oppose what is singular and unique to what is common and ordinary, and thus oppose special law to general law and oppose singular law to common law: Van Hove, *Commentarium Lovaniense in Codicem Iuris Canonici* (1 vol. in 5 toms., Mechliniae-Romae: H. Dessain, Tom. I, *Prolegomena,* 2. ed., 1945; Tom. II, *De Legibus Ecclesiasticis,* 1930), I, 42-43 (hereafter referred to as *Commentarium*); Wernz-Vidal, *Ius Canonicum* (7 tomi in 8 vols., Romae: Apud Aedes Universitatis Gregorianae, Tom. I, *Normae Generales,* 1938; Tom. II, *De Personis,* 3. ed. a Philippo Aguirre recognita, 1943; Tom. III, *De Religiosis,* 1933; Tom. IV, *De Rebus,* Vol. I, *Sacramenta, Sacramentalia, Cultus divinus, Coemeteria et Sepultura ecclesiastica,* 1934), I, 156, nota (14) (here-

Code.[6] Members of Religious Congregations are governed, along with members of Orders,[7] by the special law which is found in Titles IX to XVI of Book II of the Code.[8] These eight titles constitute the special law for religious in general, into which category Orders and Religious Congregations, and these institutes alone, now fall.

Before the Code, however, the relative juridic position of what are now called Orders, Religious Congregations and Societies of the Common Life was quite different. The fundamental reason for this difference was the fact that before the Code those institutes which are now called Religious Congregations did not constitute the religious state strictly so-called. Their members were not religious in the strict sense.[9] As a consequence, the special law for

after referred to as *Ius Canonicum*); Vermeersch-Creusen, *Epitome Iuris Canonici cum Commentariis ad Scholas et ad Usum Privatum* (3 tomi, Mechliniae-Romae: H. Dessain, Tom. I, *Libri I et II Codicis iuris canonici*, 7. ed., 1949; Tom. II, *Liber III Codicis iuris canonici*, 6. ed., 1940), I, 20 (hereafter referred to as *Epitome*); Beste, *Introductio in Codicem* (3. ed., Collegeville, Minn.: St. John's Abbey Press, 1946), pp. 13, 62 (hereafter referred to as *Introductio*).

The latter terminology will be used in this dissertation.

[6] Canons 673-681.

[7] Orders may be defined as societies, approved by legitimate ecclesiastical authority, in which the members, according to the laws of their respective institutes, pronounce solemn public vows, and thus tend to evangelical perfection. Cf. canon 488, nn. 1, 2.

[8] Canons 487-672.

[9] Pius XII, ap. const. *Provida mater*, 2 febr. 1947—*AAS*, XXXIX (1947), 114-124, cf. pp. 116-117; ap. const. *Sponsa Christi*, 21 nov. 1950—*AAS*, XLIII (1951), 5-21, cf. p. 7.

Wernz, writing in 1901, distinguished the various religious states by reason of essence as follows: I. *Status religiosus completus sive proprius et stricte dictus;* II. *Status religiosus completus sive proprius, sed minus stricte dictus;* III. *Status religiosus improprius atque late acceptus.* Cf. *Ius Decretalium* (6 vols., Romae et Prati, 1898-1914, Vol. I, *Introductio in Ius Decretalium*, Romae, 1898; Vol. III, *Ius Constitutionis Eccles. Catholicae*, Romae, 1899; Vol. III, *Ius Administrationis Eccl. Catholicae*, Romae, 1901), III 621-622. To constitute the essence of the religious state, he wrote, four things are required: the observance of the three evangelical counsels, per-

religious, a law generally referred to as *Jus Regularium,* was restricted, in its application as common law, to the Orders. Hence, neither Congregations with simple vows nor Societies without public vows were governed by the *Jus Regularium.*[10] Since the *Jus Regularium* was rich in

petual vows by which their observance is strengthened, a manner of living in common undertaken by a profession which is public, i.e., received in the name of the Church, and ecclesiastical approbation of the institute in which this profession is made. Cf. *Ius Decretalium,* III, 610-614. The complete and proper religious state properly so-called is found only in those institutes in which is found the complete essence of the religious state and in which the vows are public and solemn. The complete and proper religious state improperly so-called is found in those institutes in which is found the total essence of the religious state and in which the vows are public but simple. The religious state in the broad sense, which is the religious state improperly so-called, is found in those institutes which lack the total essence of the religious state because either one or another of the vows is lacking, or not all three vows are public, i.e., are not received in the name of the Church, or the vows are replaced by an oath, or there are neither vows nor an oath. Cf. *Ius Decretalium,* III, 621-622; cf. also Bachofen, *Compendium Juris Regularium* (Neo-Eboraci—Cincinnati—Chicagiae: Benziger Brothers, 1903), pp. 363-364. Such precise division of vows into public and private, and further division of public vows into solemn and simple, however, was not common in the writings of other authors before the Code. Some authors did not use the words "public" or "private" at all in their divisions of the vows. E.g., Ferraris, *Prompta Bibliotheca Canonica, Iuridica, Moralis, Theologica, nec non Ascetica, Polemica, Rubristica, Historica* (ed. novissima, 9 tomi, Romae, 1885-1899), VII 668-669 (hereafter referred to as *Bibliotheca*); André et Condis et Wagner, *Dictionnarie de Droit Canonique* (5. ed., 4 vols., Paris, 1901), III, 705; Ojetti, *Synopsis Rerum Moralium et Iuris Pontificii* (3. ed., 4 vols., Romae, 1909-1914), III, 4151-4152 (hereafter referred to as *Synopsis*). Other authors equivalated the terms "simple vow" and "private vow." E.g., Vermeersch, "Vows," *The Catholic Encyclopedia* (15 vols., 2 Supplements and Index, New York: Appleton Co., 1907-1922), XV, 511-514, cf. p. 513 (hereafter referred to as *CE*); Freriks, *Religious Congregations in Their External Relations,* The Catholic University of America Canon Law Studies, n. 1 (Washington, D.C.: Columbia Polytechnic Institute for the Blind, 1916), p. 60.

10 Mocchegiani, *Iurisprudentia Ecclesiastica ad Usum et Commoditatem Utriusque Cleri* (3 vols., Ad Claras Aquas-Friburgi Brisgoviae, 1904-1905), I, 75 (hereafter referred to as *Iurisprudentia*).

privileges,[11] and since both Congregations with simple vows and Societies without public vows did not by common law enjoy these privileges, the position of the Congregations with simple vows resembled the position of the Societies without public vows more than it resembled the position of the Orders. For the members of neither the Congregations nor the Societies were religious; and yet they imitated the life of religious. Because of this similarity, both the Holy See, in its legislation, and the canonists, in their writings, grouped together the Congregations and the Societies, and even designated the two with a common name.

Before the Code, the Holy See rarely enacted legislation which was universal and special for what are today called Religious Congregations and Societies of the Common Life. But the fact that the Holy See at that time considered both these institutes in the same juridic category is evident in the few examples of such legislation which did occur, especially in the examples involving the question of the ecclesiastical approbation necessary for the foundation of a new institute. This fact is also evident in numerous examples of responses of the Holy See involving such institutes in particular cases.

The ecclesiastical approbation necessary for the founding of a religious institute, or for the founding of institutes which today are called Religious Congregations or Societies of the Common Life, was not always papal approbation. Before the year 1215, the approval of the local bishop sufficed. Canon 13 of the IV General Council of the Lateran (1215), however, forbade the foundation of new *religiones*.[12] In view of the use attaching to the word *religiones*, some thought that the prohibition extended only to the foundation of institutes of regulars. For this reason canon

[11] Cf. Bouix, *Tractatus de Jure Regularium* (2 vols., Parisiis, 1857), II, 73-173.

[12] Mansi, *Sacrorum Conciliorum Nova et Amplissima Collectio* (53 vols. in 60, Parisiis, 1901-1927), XXII, 1002-1003 (hereafter cited as Mansi).

23 of the II General Council of Lyons (1274) forbade the foundation of *religiones* and of *ordines.*[13] The word *ordo,* as it was used by the II General Council of Lyons, was broader than the word *religio,* and included institutes which are now called Religious Congregations and institutes which are now called Societies of the Common Life.[14] Hence, from the year 1274, the approval of the Holy See was necessary for the foundation of such institutes.

Before the middle of the sixteenth century there arose various institutes of men who imitated the life of religious by living in common under voluntary obedience and with a habit distinct from that of secular priests. These men, however, did not make a solemn profession; some of them made a simple profession in such a way that they could legitimately leave the institute, and others made no profession at all. The Faithful, however, were not familiar with these technicalities, and, seeing them one day living a life which was apparently that of religious with solemn perpetual profession, and seeing them the next day walking the streets in secular garb, were scandalized. In order to avert this scandal, Pope Pius V, in his Constitution *Lubricum vitae genus,* given on November 17, 1568, commanded that all members of such institutes either make solemn profession or leave their institutes.[15] Stanton

[13] Mansi, XXIV, 96-97.

[14] C. un., *de religiosis domibus,* tit. VII, in Extravag. Ioan. XXII; Panormitanus (1386-1453) (Nicolaus de Tudeschis, Abbas Siculus, Abbas Modernus), *Commentaria in Quinque Libros Decretalium* (5 vols. in 7, Venetiis, 1588), Lib. II, tit. II, c. 2, n. 11, in fin. (hereafter cited as Panormitanus); Suarez († 1617), *Opus De Virtute et Statu Religionis,* Pars II, Liber II, Caput XVI, n. 22, in *Opera Omnia* (26 vols., Parisiis, 1856-1866 [2 Indices, 1878]), Vols. XIII-XVI, cf. XV, 204; Pirhing († 1679), *Jus Canonicum* (5 vols., Dilingae, 1722), Lib. III, tit. XXXVI, n. 33 (hereafter cited as Pirhing); Schmalzgrueber († 1735), *Ius Ecclesiasticum Universum* (5 vols. in 12, Romae, 1843-1845), Lib. III, tit. XXXVI, n. 48 (hereafter cited as Schmalzgrueber).

[15] *Bullarum Diplomatum et Privilegiorum Sanctorum Romanorum Pontificum Taurinensis Editio* (24 vols. et Appendix, Augustae Tauri-

(† 1941) showed from the context of this Constitution and from the tenor of the Constitutions by which institutes of men without solemn vows were approved after the year 1568 that the Constitution did not affect all institutes which today would be called Religious Congregations or Societies of the Common Life, but only those institutes whose members gave the impression, especially by their habit, that they were solemnly professed religious.[16]

The first indication that the major line of distinction might some day lie between Orders and Religious Congregations on the one hand, and Societies of the Common Life on the other, instead of between Orders on the one hand and Religious Congregations and Societies of the Common Life on the other, came when Pope Gregory XIII, in his Constitution *Ascendente Domino,* given on May 25, 1584, made the doctrinal declaration that simple vows *could* be accepted by the Church as sufficient to constitute one a religious in the strict sense. In this Constitution, the pope actually made this disposition with regard to those members of the Society of Jesus who do not pronounce solemn vows.[17] But this was singular law, and members of what are today called Religious Congregations never did become religious in the strict sense until the Code.[18]

In the nineteenth century a custom arose against the law requiring papal approbation for the foundation of what are today called Religious Congregations and Societies of the Common Life, whereby such institutes could be canonically erected by means of episcopal approbation alone.[19] This custom, insofar as it concerned institutes with

norum-Neapoli, 1857-1872), VII, 725-726 (hereafter cited as *Bull. Rom. Taur.*).

[16] *De Societatibus,* pp. 16-17.

[17] *Codicis Iuris Canonici Fontes,* cura Emi Petri Card. Gasparri editi (9 vols., Romae [postea Civitate Vaticana]: Typis Polyglottis Vaticanis, 1923-1939. Vols. VII-IX, ed. cura et studio Emi Iustiniani Card. Serédi), n. 153 (hereafter cited as *Fontes*).

[18] Cf. *supra,* p. 16, note 9.

[19] Bouix, *Tractatus de Jure Regularium,* I, 214; Ojetti, *Sypnopsis,*

simple vows, received official approval from Pope Leo XIII at the turn of the century, in his famous Constitution *Conditae a Christo,* the so-called *Magna Charta* of Religious Congregations, given on December 8, 1900.[20] In 1906, however, Pope Pius X demanded once again that papal permission be sought for the foundation of any institutes with simple vows or for the foundation of any institutes without vows.[21] Unity of treatment of Religious Congregations and Societies of the Common Life on this point, as also on so many other points, was retained even in the Code, where both types of institute can be erected by a decree of erection of the local bishop, provided he first obtain a *nihil obstat* from the Holy See.[22]

Following the example of the Holy See, canonists also grouped together those institutes which are now called Religious Congregations and Societies of the Common Life. There is little about such institutes in the writings of canonists before the middle of the nineteenth century, however. Where reference to such institutes is made, these institutes are usually designated by description rather than by a common name such as "Religious Congregation" or "Society of the Common Life." When these institutes became very numerous in the nineteenth century, however, canonists began to devote to them a section of their treatment of the *Jus Regularium.* The canonists began at the same time to invent common names by which all institutes in this category could be called. The most common of these names in the nineteenth century was the name "Secular Congregation," which was applied equally to institutes with simple vows and to institutes without vows. Likewise the placing together of these institutes was not limited to the matter of name. The canonists also considered that both types of institute were governed by the same body

I, 1283; Grandclaude, *Jus Canonicum* (3 vols., Parisiis, 1882-1883), II, 435.

[20] *Fontes,* n. 644.

[21] Motu propr. *Dei providentis,* 16 iul. 1906—*Fontes,* n. 675.

[22] Canons 492, 674.

of special common law. This is the case in the writings of such authors of Bouix (1808-1870),[23] the author or authors of five anonymous articles in the *Analecta Juris Pontificii,*[24] Grandclaude (1826-1900),[25] Gaspari (1852-1934),[26] Wernz (1842-1914),[27] André et Condis et Wagner,[28] and Ojetti (1862-1932).[29]

Some authors, it is true, after the turn of the century, began to treat what are now called Religious Congregations under the name "Religious Congregations," and distinctly from what are now called Societies of the Common Life. But this must be attributed to Pope Leo XIII's abovementioned Constitution, *Conditae a Christo,* of December 8, 1900, which laid the groundwork for the acceptance of these institutes which are now called Religious Congregations into the ranks of religious institutes in the strict sense,[30] a thing which occurred at the time of the Code.[31]

In 1916, an author, in his discussion of the external relations of Religious Congregations, wrote the following words:

> The basis of this treatise shall be the Religious Congregations of Simple vows, because they pos-

[23] *Tractatus de Jure Regularium,* I, 209-216.

[24] "Traité des Congrégations Séculières," *Analecta Juris Pontificii* (Rome, 1855-1869; Paris, 1872-1891), V (1861), 52-103, 147-217 (hereafter referred to as *Anal. J. P.*); "Des ordinations dans les Congrégations séculières," *Anal. J. P.*, VII (1864), 744-751; "Congrégations séculières. Privilèges. Ordinations. Direction des séminaires," *Anal. J. P.*, VII (1864), 758-764; "Congrégations Séculières," *Anal. J. P.*, XXIV (1885), 383-422; "Instituts Séculières," *Anal. J. P.*, XXVII (1887-1888), 424-446, 689-710.

[25] *Jus Canonicum,* II, 434-436.

[26] *Tractatus Canonicus de Sacra Ordinatione* (2 vols., Parisiis-Lugduni, 1893-1894), II, 87 (hereafter referred to as *De Sacra Ordinatione*).

[27] *Ius Decretalium,* II, 54-55, nota (60); III, 621-622.

[28] *Dictionnaire de Droit Canonique,* I, 533-536.

[29] *Synopsis,* I, 1283-1308.

[30] *Fontes,* n. 644.

[31] Pius XII, ap. const. *Provida mater,* 2 febr. 1947—*AAS,* XXXIX (1947), 114-124, cf. pp. 116-117; ap. const. *Sponsa Christi,* 21 nov. 1950—*AAS,* XLIII (1951), 5-21, cf. p. 7.

> sess the common element which permits of generalization, viz., the Simple vows. Those communities, however, which have not the vows as a bond of perseverance, but receive ecclesiastical approval, strive for perfection under a common rule and live after the manner of true Religious, cannot be excluded from our investigation. In virtue of these common principles, ecclesiastical law, in most regulations, considers them on an equal basis. Where limitations or extensions are necessary, explicit reference is made to the exception. This procedure, we think, has become Rome's mode of action more and more in these latter years as will be evidenced throughout the dissertation.[32]

From the foregoing considerations it seems logical to make the following practical conclusion. In investigating the historical background of the law for the ordination of members of Societies of the Common Life, one should, in trying to establish what was the jurisprudence of the Sacred Roman Congregations, look not alone to the pronouncements relative to ordination in institutes without public vows, but also to the pronouncements relative to ordination in institutes with simple public vows. This procedure has, as a matter of fact, been followed in at least four instances during the past twenty-five years by men who have investigated the problem of the ordination of members of Societies. Four different authors made reference to a pronouncement of the year 1864, in which the Sacred Congregation of Bishops and Regulars resolved four doubts which arose with regard to the ordination of members of the Congregation of Priests of the Schools of Charity.[33] This Congregation, founded in Venice by the Cavanis brothers in 1802, was an institute with simple public vows, and today is a Religious Congregation.[34] And

[32] Freriks, *Religious Congregations in Their External Relations*, p. 12.

[33] S. C. Ep. et Reg., *Tarvisina*, 6 maii 1864—*Fontes*, n. 1991.

[34] Heimbucher, *Die Orden*, II, 417; "Traité des Congrégations Séculières," *Anal. J. P.*, V (1861), 77-78; Kapsner, *Orders*, p. 215; *Annuario*, p. 770.

yet, a response involving this Congregation was used by these four authors to prove a point in the law for the ordination of members of institutes without public vows, or Societies.[35]

Another conclusion which seems to flow logically from the foregoing is the following. The doctrine of those authors who, right before the Code, wrote about the ordination of non-regulars, but limited their discussion to the ordination of members of institutes with simple public vows, can be applied, *positis ponendis,* to the question of the ordination of members of institutes without public vows. Such a discussion, limited to the ordination of members of institutes with simple public vows, is found in the works of authors such as Bastien (1866-1940),[36] Mocchegiani (1839-1905)[37] and Many (1847-1922).[38]

[35] Oesterle, "Weihekandidaten aus einer Diözesan-Priestergenossenschaft," *Theologisch-praktische Quartalschrift* (Linz, 1848-), LXXXV (1932), 563-571, cf. pp. 570-571 (hereafter referred to as *ThPrQs*); Schaaf, "Episcopus Proprius Ordinationis Religiosorum," *The Ecclesiastical Review (The American Ecclesiastical Review* [from July, 1905, to December, 1943, *The Ecclesiastical Review*], Philadelphia, 1889-1943; Washington, D.C., 1944-), XC (1934), 491-509, cf. pp. 507-508 (*The Ecclesiastical Review* will hereafter be referred to as *ER*); Moeder, *The Proper Bishop for Ordination and Dimissorial Letters,* The Catholic University of America Canon Law Studies, n. 95 (Washington, D.C.: The Catholic University of America, 1935), p. 113 (hereafter referred to as *Proper Bishop*); Rothoff, *Le Droit des Sociétés sans Voeux* (Paris: Desclée de Brouwer, 1949), pp. 172-173 (hereafter referred to as *Sociétés*).

[36] *Directoire Canonique à l'Usage des Congrégrations à Voeux Simples* (1. ed., Abbaye de Maredsous, 1904; 3. ed., Bruges, 1923), (1. ed.), pp. 235-241 (hereafter referred to as *Directoire Canonique*).

[37] *Iurisprudentia,* I, 480-482.

[38] *Praelectiones de Sacra Ordinatione* (Parisiis, 1905), pp. 409-431 (hereafter referred to as *De Sacra Ordinatione*).

CHAPTER II

THE COMMON LAW FOR THE ORDINATION OF MEMBERS OF SECULAR CONGREGATIONS BEFORE THE CODE

Essential to an understanding of the common law for the ordination of members of Secular Congregations before the Code is a brief conspectus of the history of the law for the ordination of secular clerics. Consequently, in this chapter there will be presented a brief history of the law of the proper bishop for ordination and the law of the title for ordination up until the Council of Trent. This will be followed by a summary of the legislation of the Council of Trent with reference to the ordination of secular clerics, which legislation remained essentially the same until the Code. Then the question of the common law for the ordination of members of Secular Congregations will be examined.

The early history of the proper bishop for ordination is intimately connected with the history of the title for ordination. In Rome, during the first centuries of our era, private edifices bore the names of their owners in inscriptions placed over the entrances, and these inscriptions were called *tituli*. When such buildings were turned over to the Church as places of divine worship, the *tituli* remained. The cleric assigned to such a church was known as *titulatus* or *intitulatus*. He received sustenance from his *titulus*. But the *titulus* signified principally and primarily his office or post.[1] Canon 6 of the General Council of Chalcedon (451) forbade what is called absolute ordinations, i.e., ordinations of men who were not specially affiliated with a church or a martyry or a monastery.[2] Secular clerics, therefore, had

[1] Moeder, *Proper Bishop*, pp. 3-5.

[2] Schwartz, *Acta Conciliorum Oecumenicorum* (4 tomi, Tom. II, *Concilium Universale Chalcedonense*, Vol. II, Pars II, *Rerum Chalcedonensium Collectio Vaticana. Canones et Symbolum*, Berolini et Lipsiae: Walter de Gruyter & Co., 1936), Tom. II, Vol. II, Pars II, pp. 34 [126]-35 [127].

to have a *titulus* to be ordained, unless they were assigned to take care of the shrine of a martyr. This *titulus* signified primarily an office, and only secondarily the sustenance derived from the temporal goods received in connection with the fulfillment of that office. Canon 6 of the Council of Chalcedon became the nucleus of similar legislation throughout the Western Church for the next six centuries.[3] But towards the end of the eleventh century there were many infractions of the law which forbade absolute ordinations, resulting in a large number of *clerici vagantes* or *acephali.* To correct this abuse, Pope Alexander III (1159-1181), in canon 5 of the III General Council of the Lateran (1179), enacted the following law:

> Episcopus, si aliquem sine certo titulo, de quo necessaria vitae percipiat, in diaconum vel presbyterum ordinaverit, tamdiu necessaria ei subministret, donec in aliqua ei ecclesia convenientia stipendia militiae clericalis assignet; nisi forte talis qui ordinatur, extiterit, qui de sua vel paterna haereditate subsidium vitae possit habere.[4]

Canon 5 of the III General Council of the Lateran was misunderstood. The common interpretation given it was that the sole title of ordination no longer implied a permanent service at a certain church, but meant the possession of a sufficient income for the support of the cleric ordinand. It made no difference whether this support came from a church, a cleric's private property, or a cleric's paternal inheritance.[5] Pope Innocent III (1198-1216) extended the requirement of a title to the subdiaconate.[6] This same pope also gave explicit recognition to patrimony as a legitimate title.[7]

From the beginning of the thirteenth century, the laws of the Church no longer mentioned the perpetual assignment of a cleric to a particular church as a prerequisite

[3] Moeder, *Proper Bishop*, pp. 7-8.

[4] Mansi, XXII, 220.

[5] Moeder, *Proper Bishop*, pp. 9-10.

[6] C. 16, X, *de praebendis et dignitatibus*, III, 5.

[7] C. 23, X, *de praebendis et dignitatibus*, III, 5.

for the reception of Orders. Instead, Church Law insisted on the possession of an ecclesiastical benefice or of a patrimony as a prerequisite for the reception of Orders. This became the new concept conveyed by the phrase *"titulus ordinationis."*[8]

Bearing in mind the foregoing conspectus of the history of the *titulus ordinationis,* one can better understand the history of the proper bishop for ordination. Upon the death of the Apostles, bishops ordained men who were not their subjects, or went into other cities to ordain and to govern. Because of these disciplinary disturbances, the early councils strictly forbade bishops to exercise their powers outside of their own territories or to ordain men who were not their subjects.[9] During the succeeding centuries, therefore, the proper bishop for the ordination of a layman to the clerical state was the bishop of the place where the layman lived. The proper bishop for the promotion of a cleric to higher Orders was the bishop of the church to which the cleric was assigned by his first ordination.[10]

In the twelfth century the change in the ordination title mentioned above brought about a change in the matter of the proper bishop for ordination. In the twelfth century, title connoted the idea of sustenance. The early canons forbade bishops to promote to major Orders men who were their subjects by reason of domicile without providing them with such a title. Slowly, bishops began to feel that they had a right to promote to major Orders anyone over whom they had any authority on condition that they provided him with such a title.[11] At the time of Pope Clement IV (1265-1268), bishops were considered to have authority over anyone who had a benefice in their dioceses, and anyone who had his place of origin in their dioceses.[12] A sum-

[8] Moeder, *Proper Bishop,* p. 11.

[9] Moeder, *Proper Bishop,* pp. 22-23.

[10] Moeder, *Proper Bishop,* pp. 24-29.

[11] Moeder, *Proper Bishop,* pp. 29-30.

[12] C. 1, *de temporibus ordinationum et qualitate ordinandorum,* I, 9, in VI°.

mary of the Decretal Law with reference to the proper bishop is found in a decretal of Pope Boniface VIII (1294-1303):

> Quum nullus clericum parochiae alienae praeter superioris ipsius licentiam debeat ordinare: superior intelligitur in hoc casu episcopus, de cuius dioecesi est is, qui ad ordines promoveri desiderat, oriundus, seu in cuius dioecesi beneficium obtinet ecclesiasticum, seu habet, (licet alibi natus fuerit), domicilium in eadem....[13]

At some time prior to the Council of Trent, still another bishop was considered competent to promote a man to Orders, namely, a bishop who had such a man employed in his household.[14]

To recapitulate, then, at the time immediatetly prior to the Council of Trent, a bishop could promote to major Orders anyone who had a benefice, origin or domicile in his diocese, or anyone employed in his household, provided that such an ordinand was provided with a *titulus* for his sustenance in the form of a benefice, of a pension, or of his own patrimony.

The law regulating the title and the proper bishop for ordination, as it existed right before the Council of Trent, was re-enacted in the disciplinary decrees of the Twenty-first and Twenty-third Sessions of the Council. In canon 8 of the Twenty-third Session the Council commanded that every one should be ordained by his own bishop.[15] The Council did not state explicitly that by anyone's own bishop it meant the bishop of the place in which such a person had his origin, an ecclesiastical benefice or his domicile. But this was to be understood in virtue of the Decretal Legis-

[13] C. 3, *de temporibus ordinationum et qualitate ordinandourm,* I, 9, in VI°.

[14] Moeder, *Proper Bishop,* pp. 30-31.

[15] Conc. Trident., sess. XXIII, *de ref.,* c. 8.

Use is made of the *Concilium Tridentinum. Diariorum, Actorum, Epistularum, Tractatuum Nova Collectio* (ed. Societas Goerresiana, 13 vols., Friburgi Brisgoviae: Herder, 1901-).

lation.[16] The Council did make explicit reference, however, to anyone's proper bishop by reason of household service. It stated that a bishop had to have a man in his employ for three years before he could promote him to Orders by reason of household service.[17]

No secular cleric could be ordained unless he possessed a title of benefice, patrimony or pension; and even those with a patrimony or a pension could not be ordained unless they were necessary or useful to some church or pious place, and were actually assigned there.[18]

Dimissorial letters could be granted to a secular cleric by his own bishop alone, to the exclusion of all others with the exception of the Chapter after a see had been vacant for a year, or before that time if an ecclesiastical benefice had been obtained or was about to be obtained.[19]

A secular cleric desiring promotion to minor Orders had to have good testimonials from his pastor and from his schoolmaster; and one desiring promotion to any major Order had to have good testimonials from one whom the bishop had commissioned to announce the banns publicly and to investigate personally the ancestry, age, morals and life of the ordinand. And if anyone was to be ordained by another bishop with dimissorial letters from his own bishop, his probity and morals had to be recommended by means of testimonials from his own bishop.[20]

No one could be promoted to the subdiaconate before his twenty-second, to the diaconate before his twenty-third, or to the priesthood before his twenty-fifth year of age.[21]

Interstices of one year had to be observed between minor

[16] Cc. 1, 2, 3, *de temporibus ordinationum et qualitate ordinandorum,* I, 9, in VI°.

[17] Conc. Trident., sess. XXIII, *de ref.*, c. 9.

[18] Conc. Trident., sess. XXI, *de ref.*, c. 2; sess. XXIII, *de ref.*, c. 16.

[19] Conc. Trident., sess. VII, *de ref.*, c. 10; sess. XXIII, *de ref.*, c. 10.

[20] Conc. Trident., sess. XXIII, *de ref.*, cc. 5, 8, 13, 14.

[21] Conc. Trident., sess. XXIII, *de ref.*, c. 12.

Orders and the subdiaconate, between the subdiaconate and the diaconate, and between the diaconate and the priesthood.[22]

Those to be ordained to minor Orders had to know the Latin language and give evidence of intelligence. Those to be ordained to the subdiaconate and the diaconate had to be instructed in letters and in those things that pertained to the exercise of their Orders. Those to be ordained to the priesthood had to be competent to teach the people those things which are necessary for all to know to be saved, and competent also to administer the sacraments.[23]

Before an ordination, all ordinands had to be examined by the ordaining bishop or his delegate with regard to their parentage, person, age, education, morals, learning and faith.[24]

Finally, Orders had to be conferred publicly, at the times specified by law, in the cathedral church and in the presence of the canons of the church; or, if it was a question of a place removed from the episcopal see, in the highest ranking church of the locality and in the presence of the local clergy.[25]

Such were the enactments of the Council of Trent regarding the ordination of secular clerics. This legislation constituted law which was universal, special and common. This law was special because it bound only one class of the Faithful, namely, secular clerics. Nevertheless it was universal and constituted the common law for the ordination of secular clerics all over the world.[26]

At the time the Council of Trent ended (1563), there were in existence several institutes whose members imitated the life of regulars, but who made no solemn profession. A doubt arose whether these institutes were bound by the above-mentioned enactments of the Council of Trent

[22] Conc. Trident., sess. XXIII, *de ref.*, cc. 11, 13, 14.

[23] Conc. Trident., sess. XXIII, *de ref.*, cc. 11, 13, 14.

[24] Conc. Trident., sess. XXIII, *de ref.*, c. 7.

[25] Conc. Trident., sess. XXIII, *de ref.*, c. 8.

[26] Cf. *supra*, p. 15, note 5.

which regulated the ordination of secular clerics, or whether these institutes, in the matter of the ordination of their members, enjoyed the privileges of regulars. The doubt was solved by Pope Pius V in the Constitution *Romanus Pontifex,* dated October 14, 1568.[27]

Before examining this Constitution, one may well look briefly at some of the non-regular institutes which were in existence at the time the Constitution was issued, and which, therefore, were affected by it.

The Brothers of the Common Life were founded in Holland by Gerard de Groote (1340-1384) around the year 1380. This institute, dedicated to the work of teaching and preaching, was approved by the Holy See. It flourished in the fifteenth century, languished during the Protestant Revolt, and completely disappeared as a result of the creation of diocesan seminaries, the institution of new teaching institutes, and the French Revolution. The members lived in common, but took no vows.[28]

The Hermits of Saint Mary of Gonzaga, also known as the Hermits of Saint John the Baptist of Penance, were founded by Jerome Raigni de Castelgioffre, who was aided in his undertaking by Francis de Gonzaga. A rule was composed for the Hermits by one of the bishops of Reggio, and was approved by Pope Alexander VI (1492-1503). But they later asked for the Rule of Saint Augustine. They lived in common without the ordinary vows of religion, but they wore a habit distinct from that of the secular clergy. Their general lived in their principal monastery at Gonzaga. In the latter half of the sixteenth century they had establishments in the dioceses of Reggio Emilia, Verona, Mantua, Brescia and Sinigaglia.[29]

[27] *Fontes,* n. 129.

[28] Helyot, *Ordres,* IV, 529-530; Heimbucher, *Die Orden,* II, 552-560; Stanton, *De Societatibus,* pp. 24-26; Kapsner, *Orders,* p. 32; Waters, *Probation in Societies,* pp. 33-34.

[29] Helyot, *Ordres, II,* DVJ-DVB*;* cf. S. C. Ep. et Reg., *Regien., Veronen., Mantuana, Brixien. et Senogallien.,* 15 febr. 1578—*Fontes,* n. 1333.

The Hermits of Saint Jerome of Blessed Peter of Pisa were founded by Blessed Peter Gambacarti of Pisa (1355-1435) around the year 1380. The members were admitted to the priesthood in the middle of the fifteenth century. Constitutions were drawn up in the year 1444. According to these Constitutions, the members pronounced only simple vows, but they imitated the life of regulars and wore a habit distinct from that of the secular clergy.[30]

The Institute of the Oratory founded by Saint Philip Neri (1515-1595) in the year 1564 is one of the very few Societies of the Common Life, if not the only one, founded before the year 1568. This Society was mentioned above.[31]

In addition to such institutes as the four just mentioned, there was another type of institute whose members imitated the life of regulars, but who made no solemn profession. It was exemplified in the institutes of *canonici saeculares.*

The *canonici* were secular priests who, while engaged in the parochial ministry, lived in common according to a rule of life. This mode of life was instituted by Saint Eusebius of Vercelli (286-371) and by Saint Augustine (354-430), and was reformed by Saint Chrodegang of Metz (712-766). After a second reform in the eleventh century, a division occurred. Some *canonici* took solemn vows and became *canonici regulares.* The others made no solemn profession and became known as *canonici saeculares.*[32]

Canonici saeculares were in existence at the time of Pope Boniface VIII (1294-1303).[33]

In the fifteenth century, Saint Lawrence Giustiniani (1380-1465) established in Venice an institute of *canonici saeculares* called the Canons of Saint George in Alga. The members of this institute lacked solemn vows, but imitated the life of regulars and wore a habit distinct from that

[30] Currier, *Orders,* pp. 329-330; cf. Pius V, const. *Lubricum vitae genus* 17 nov. 1568—*Bull. Rom. Taur.,* VII, 725-726.

[31] Cf. p. 3.

[32] Stanton, *De Societatibus,* pp. 5-7.

[33] Cf. c. 43, *de electione et electi potestate,* I, 6, in VI°, §5.

of the secular clergy. This institute was approved by Pope Eugene IV (1431-1447), at one time himself a member of the Canons of Saint George.[34]

Another institute of *canonici saeculares* which was in existence at the close of the Council of Trent was the Congregation of Saint John the Evangelist in Portugal. Members of this institute pronounced simple vows of poverty, chastity and obedience, which bound only as long as they remained in the institute. The members were actually referred to as *canonici saeculares* by popes in bulls in which they were granted privileges.[35]

These, then, are some of the institutes of non-regulars which were in existence on October 14, 1568, and were comprehended in the Constitution *Romanus Pontifex.* In this Constitution, Pius V stated that there were in existence certain institutes of clerics who made either a temporary profession or no profession at all. The clerics in some of these institutes were *canonici saeculares,* and were sometimes referred to as *religiosi,* although they were not religious in the strict sense, i.e., regulars. The clerics in the other institutes were secular clerics living after the manner of regulars. Some of these *canonici saeculares* and secular clerics living after the manner of regulars, said the Pope, were being ordained to sacred Orders without possessing one of the titles required by the Council of Trent for the ordination of secular clerics.[36] These clerics pretended that membership in their respective institutes was equivalent, in the matter of title, to membership in a *religio.* Difficulties arose, however, when some of them left their institutes (as they were perfectly free to do), could find

[34] Anonymous, "Traité des Congrégations Séculières," *Anal. J. P.*, V (1861), 53; Anonymous, "Congrégations Séculières," *Anal. J. P.*, XXIV (1885), 386; cf. Pius V, const. *Lubricum vitae genus,* 17 nov. 1568—*Bull. Rom. Taur.*, VII, 725-726.

[35] Anonymous, "Traité des Congrégations Séculières," *Anal. J. P.*, V (1861), 53-54; Anonymous, "Congrégations Séculières," *Anal. J. P.*, XXIV (1885), 386.

[36] Cf. Conc. Trident., sess. XXI, *de ref.*, c. 2; cf. *supra*, p. 29.

no means of support, and began to beg and to engage in unbecoming businesses. To remedy this situation, therefore, Pope Pius V explicitly extended the above-mentioned requirement of the Council of Trent, so that it included all non-professed clerics (i.e., all clerics lacking solemn profession) of any institute whatsoever, whether they were "*religiosi,*" i.e., *canonici saeculares,* or whether they were secular clerics living in common after the manner of religious. In addition, Pius V, in this same Constitution, enacted a one year's suspension from the conferral of major Orders to be incurred *ipso iure* by anyone contravening the prescripts of the Constitution.[37]

Just thirty-four days after the issuance of the Constitution *Romanus Pontifex,* Pope Pius V issued the Constitution *Lubricum vitae genus,* dated November 17, 1568. This Constitution, as seen above,[38] commanded all those who lived in common under voluntary obedience, and who, though they lacked the solemn vows of religion, nevertheless wore a habit distinct from that of the secular clergy, either to make a solemn profession or to leave their respective institutes. The Constitution named the Canons of Saint George in Alga[39] and the Hermits of Saint Jerome of Blessed Peter of Pisa[40] specifically as falling under its prescription.[41] After members of such institutes as these made a solemn profession, there was no longer any difficulty about the law regulating their ordination; for then they enjoyed the privileges of the *Jus Regularium.* The members of institutes in which the habit did not differ from that of secular clerics, however, were not comprehended under the Constitution *Lubricum vitae genus.* And thus such institutes continued to be regulated in the matter of ordination by the prescripts of the Council of Trent for

[37] Pius V, const. *Romanus Pontifex,* 14 oct. 1568—*Fontes,* n. 129.

[38] Cf. p. 19.

[39] Cf. *supra,* pp. 32-33.

[40] Cf. *supra,* p. 32.

[41] Pius V. const. *Lubricum vitae genus,* 17 nov. 1568—*Bull. Rom. Taur.,* VII, 725-726.

the ordination of secular clerics. As proof that such was actually the practice of the time, several contemporary documents and sources can be cited.

About ten years after the Constitution *Romanus Pontifex* and the Constitution *Lubricum vitae genus,* it came to the knowledge of the Sacred Congregation of Bishops and Regulars that the Hermits of Saint Mary of Gonzaga[42] in the Dioceses of Reggio Emilia, Verona, Mantua, Brescia and Sinigaglia were being ordained without a title in contravention of the prescripts of the Council of Trent[43] and of Pius V's Constitution *Romanus Pontifex* of October 14, 1568.[44] The Sacred Congregation, therefore, sent a communication to the bishops of these five dioceses, calling to their minds the enactments of the Council of Trent and of Pope Pius V, and reminding them of the penalties which they had incurred if they had knowingly acted contrary to these enactments.[45]

A decade later, on March 11, 1588, Saint Philip Neri, who objected to the suggestion that vows be pronounced in the Institute of the Oratory, gave his reasons why candidates should not despoil themselves of their possessions. Among other things he stated that those who possess a patrimony should retain it as a title of ordination for the subdiaconate.[46] It was only right that the Institute of the Oratory should follow the law of the Council of Trent regarding the title of ordination for secular clerics, for only a few years before the writing of the letter just mentioned, Pope Gregory XIII (1572-1585) wrote to Saint Philip, in-

[42] Cf. *supra,* p. 31.

[43] Conc. Trident., sess. XXI, *de ref.,* c. 2; cf. *supra,* p. 29.

[44] *Fontes,* n. 129; cf. *supra,* pp. 33-34.

[45] S. C. Ep. et Reg., *Regien., Veronen., Mantuana, Brixien.* et *Senogallien.,* 15 febr., 1578—*Fontes,* n. 1333.

[46] The wishes of Saint Philip in this matter are found expressed in a letter written at the command of Saint Philip on March 11, 1588. This letter, according to Stanton, is cited by Ponnelle and Bordet on pages 327 and 328 of their work, entitled *St. Philippe Neri et la société romaine de son temps* (Paris, 1928).—*De Societatibus,* p. 31.

sisting that the Institute of the Oratory remain a congregation of secular priests.[47]

The next evidence of what was the common law for the ordination of members of Secular Congregations is drawn from singular law, that is, from indults granting to particular institutes certain exemptions from the common law. Whenever privileges were given to superiors of Secular Congregations whereby they could issue dimissorial letters for the ordination of their own subjects, or whereby they could present their own subjects for ordination under the title of the congregation or the common table, it was evident from the wording of the privilege that the Holy See was enacting singular law, and that Secular Congregations not so privileged were still regulated by the common law for the ordination of secular clerics, as had been enacted by the Council of Trent. This will be quite evident in the privileges to be mentioned in Chapter Four of this dissertation, in which will be discussed, among other things, singular law for the ordination of members of Secular Congregations before the Code. It will suffice here to give two examples of such privileges.

The Congregation of Priests of Christian Doctrine was founded by Venerable César de Bus (1544-1607) in L'Isle, near Avignon, in the year 1592. From the time of its foundation until around the beginning of the seventeenth century, its members pronounced no vows at all. From about the beginning of the seventeenth century until 1616 its members pronounced simple vows. In 1616 the Congregation was united to the Somaschi, an institute of regulars, and its members pronounced solemn vows until this union was dissolved in 1647. In 1659 the Doctrinarians, as they are called, were again given permission to pronounce simple vows.[48] In the Constitution granting this permission,

[47] This letter, according to Stanton, is quoted by Cardinal Perraud on page 20 of his work, entitled *Oratoire de France* (Paris, 1866). —*De Societatibus*, pp. 30-31.

[48] *Annuario*, p. 765; Helyot, *Ordres*, II, 48-68 et IV, 392-395; Heimbucher, *Die Orden*, II, 571-573; Currier, *Orders*, pp. 438-440;

there was also contained the following privilege. Clerics who had pronounced the three simple vows of poverty, chastity and obedience and who had taken the oath of perseverance in the Congregation could, with the permission of their General or Provincial, be ordained to all major Orders under the title of the congregation. It is clear from the text of this Constitution that this was a privilege which derogated from the common law by which members of such congregations with simple vows had to be ordained under one of the titles required for the promotion to major Orders of a secular cleric, viz., benefice, patrimony or pension.[49]

The Secular Clerics Living in Common, or Bartholomites, were founded by Bartholomew Holzhauser (1613-1658) in Salzburg in the year 1640. One of the prinicpal aims of the institute was the promotion of zeal and piety among the clergy. The members pronounced no vows, but took an oath of obedience and an oath of stability. They wore the habit of secular priests.[50] In the year 1685, Pope Innocent XI (1676-1689) declared in a brief that the Bartholomites were not, by reason of their assuming the status of the common life, rendered incapable of holding ecclesiastical benefices either with or without the care of souls. If they could not obtain a benefice, however, the Pope, in the same brief, permitted as a privilege (*"concedimus, et indulgemus"*) the use of the title of the community or the institute (i.e., the title of the common table). For the use of this privilege, the permission of the Superior General was required. Furthermore, the stipulation was made that

Pisani, *Congregations*, pp. 42-45; Stanton, *De Societatibus*, pp. 38-41; Kapsner, *Orders*, p. 84; Anonymous, "Traité des Congrégations Séculières," *Anal. J. P.*, V (1861), 64.

[49] Alexander VII, const. *Sacrosancti*, 15 mart. 1659—*Bull. Rom. Taur.*, XVI, 445-447.

[50] Holstenius, *Codex regularum*, VI, 543-596; Helyot, *Ordres*, I, 373-379; Heimbucher, *Die Orden*, II, 595-598; Currier, *Orders*, p. 623; Stanton, *De Societatibus*, pp. 41-45; Kapsner, *Orders*, p. 14; Ristuccia, *Societies*, pp. 19-20; Waters, *Probation in Societies*, pp. 38-39.

if a cleric ordained under the title of the community should be dismissed, the institute would be responsible for his support.[51]

Witness to what was the common law can be found not only in the wording of indults such as those mentioned immediately above, but also in the refusal of the Holy See to grant or acknowledge such privileges in certain instances. Following are two cases in point.

The Oblates of Ostuni were founded by Charles Stigliani around the middle of the seventeenth century. They were modeled on the Oblates of Saint Charles Borromeo at Milan.[52] The Oblates of Saint Charles enjoyed the privilege of having their members ordained under the title of the common table. The Oblates of Ostuni claimed that this privilege was communicated to them. Late in the seventeenth century, however, one of the bishops of Ostuni challenged the Oblates on this point. The case was brought to Rome. On February 17, 1685, the Sacred Congregation of the Council decreed that the Oblates of Ostuni could not be promoted to sacred Orders under the title of the common table, even though they lacked a benefice or patrimony.[53]

The Pious Workmen were founded by Venerable Charles Caraffa (1561-1633) in Naples in the year 1600. The members pronounced no vows, but their rule was very strict.

[51] Innocentius XI, breve *Prospero felicique*, 9 febr. 1685— *Bull. Rom. Taur.*, XIX, 613-614.

[52] The Oblates of Saint Charles, also called the Oblates of Saint Ambrose, were founded by Saint Charles Borromeo, Cardinal Archbishop of Milan (1560-1584), and were approved by Pope Gregory XIII in 1578. The members took a vow of obedience to the Archbishop of Milan, and were to work with zeal and piety for the salvation of souls in the Archdiocese. Cf. *Institutionum ad Oblatos S. Ambrosii Peritinentium Epitome* (Mediolani, 1716); Helyot, *Ordres*, III, 18-25 et IV, 1020-1021; Heimbucher, *Die Orden*, II, 560-561; Currier, *Orders*, pp. 620-622; Stanton, *De Societatibus*, pp. 35-38; Kapsner, *Orders*, p. 182; Ristuccia, *Societies*, pp. 17-19; Waters, *Probation in Societies*, pp. 35-36, 42-44.

[53] S. C. C., *Ostunen.*, 17 febr. 1685—*Anal. J. P.*, VII (1864), 746-748.

The institute was approved by Pope Paul V (1605-1621) in 1606. The Pious Workmen were united to the Rural Catechists by Pope Pius XII in 1943. The new institute formed from this union is a Religious Congregation called the Pious Workmen Rural Catechists.[54] In the beginning of the eighteenth century, the Pious Workmen petitioned Pope Clement XI (1700-1721) for an indult or privilege ("*quod indulgere dignaretur*") whereby the Superior General could grant dimissorial letters for the promotion of the members of the institute to minor or major Orders. On May 20, 1708, however, a particular congregation consisting of five cardinals, together with Cardinal Petra (1662-1747), Secretary of the Sacred Congregation, which had been appointed to examine the request, rejected the petition by means of a rescript.[55]

The historical discussion which, perhaps more than any other, aids in an understanding of the law for the ordination of members of Secular Congregations before the Code, and even aids in an understanding of the law for the ordination of members of Societies of the Common Life after the Code, is Riganti's discussion of a decree issued in 1604 by the Sacred Congregation of the Council in favor of the Institute of the Oratory at Rome and Naples. This discussion, written towards the middle of the eighteenth century, is contained in Riganti's consideration of the rejection of the petition of the Pious Workmen mentioned immediately above.[56]

In the year 1604, the Sacred Congregation of the Council

[54] *Annuario*, p. 766; Holstenius, *Codex regularum*, VI, 512-529; Helyot, *Ordres*, III, 102-110; Heimbucher, *Die Orden*, II, 573-574; Currier, *Orders*, pp. 615-616; Kapsner, *Orders*, p. 207; The fact that the new institute is a Religious Congregation was learned from private communication.

[55] Riganti, *Commentaria in Regulas, Constitutiones et Ordinationes Cancellariae Apostolicae* (4 vols. in 2, Coloniae Allobrogum, 1751), in Reg. XXIV, § III, n. 324 (Vol. II, p. 380) (hereafter referred to as *Commentaria in Regulas*).

[56] Riganti, *Commentaria in Regulas*, in Reg. XXIV, § III, nn. 326-333 (Vol. II, pp. 380-381).

decreed that members of the Institute of the Oratory at Rome and Naples could be promoted to all the minor and major Orders by the local ordinaries in whose dioceses they had a domicile, and without dimissorial letters from their bishops of origin.[57] This decree was proposed as an example or precedent for the favor requested by the Pious Workmen. But, as pointed out by Riganti (1661-1735), there was no parallel between the declaration of the Sacred Congregation of the Council in favor of the Institute of the Oratory and the privilege requested by the Pious Workmen. In the first place, the decree in favor of the Institute of the Oratory did not grant anyone faculties to issue dimissorial letters. It merely declared that the local ordinaries of the dioceses in which were located the houses of the Institute of the Oratory in Rome and Milan had the right to promote to Orders on their own authority the members of these houses. This declaration was occasioned by the following circumstances. Men were coming to the Oratory at Milan and Rome from other dioceses. When the time came for their ordination, the bishops of origin were petitioned for dimissorial letters. These they refused to send, on the grounds that they wanted these ordinands for service in their own dioceses. This was leading to the disintegration of the Institute of the Oratory. The Institute of the Oratory brought its trouble to the Holy See, and the Holy See declared that it was not dependent on the bishops of origin in this matter.[58]

The second point made by Riganti is that the decree in favor of the Institute of the Oratory did not even contain

[57] S. C. C., decretum, 1604—Riganti, *Commentaria in Regulas,* in Reg. XXIV, § III, n. 326 (Vol. II, p. 380); Honorante, *Praxis Secretariae Tribunalis Eminentissimi et Reverendissimi Domini D. Cardinalis Urbis Vicarii* (2. ed., Romae, 1762), p. 130 (hereafter referred to as *Praxis*); Monacelli, *Formularium Legale Practicum Fori Ecclesiastici cum Supplemento* (4 vols., Vol. II, *Pars Secunda,* Romae, 1706), Titulus XIII, Formula IV, n. 41 (Vol. II, p. 87) (hereafter referred to as *Formularium*).

[58] Riganti, *Commentaria in Regulas,* in Reg. XXIV, § III, n. 326 (Vol. II, p. 380).

a privilege. It was simply a declaratory decree, certifying a right which was already possessed. In order to understand this second point, it is necessary to know about a change that took place in the year 1694 with regard to the four titles in virtue of which one could obtain a proper bishop for the reception of Orders.

The four titles by which a man could call a bishop his own with regard to ordination, namely, benefice, origin, domicile and three-year household service, remained the same from the Council of Trent until the Code. During the first one hundred and thirty years after the Council of Trent, however, certain unworthy clerics who had been denied Orders by bishops who knew them, sought out other bishops who did not know them, but who, nevertheless, were their own proper bishops in virtue of one of these four titles. They obtained these proper bishops in places where their unworthiness was unknown either by being promised a benefice while still laymen, or by claiming that the place where they were born while their parents happened to be travelling—if such a thing occurred in their case—was their place of origin, or by establishing domicile by means of a brief sojourn, or by becoming employed in the household of a bishop who would not take the trouble to have himself informed of the worthiness of these men through testimonial letters from the bishops who did know them. Such procedure, in conformity perhaps with the letter of the law, was against the spirit of the law and defeated its purpose. As a remedy for this state of affairs, Pope Innocent XII (1691-1700), in the Constitution *Speculatores,* dated November 4, 1694, defined and restricted the meaning of one's own bishop by reason of benefice, origin, domicile and household service.[59]

What was required in order that a man might obtain a proper bishop by reason of origin, benefice or domicile before the Constitution *Speculatores* of 1694 can be learned from the ordinary gloss on the decretal of Pope Boniface

[59] *Fontes,* n. 258.

VIII mentioned above,[60] in which origin, benefice and domicile were mentioned as titles by which a man could obtain a proper bishop for the reception of Orders.

In the ordinary gloss on this decretal, it was stated that with reference to a person's origin he retained a domicile in the place in which he was born.[61] In the Constitution *Speculatores*, however, Pope Innocent XII declared that a man could not claim as his bishop of origin the bishop of the place where he was born *ex accidente* by reason of the fact that his parents were travelling away from home when he was born.[62]

In the ordinary gloss, the following observation was made with regard to the proper bishop by reason of benefice: *intelligo sive istud sit beneficium propter quod ordinem recepit, sive non.*[63] The Constitution *Speculatores,* on the other hand, stated that no bishop could tonsure a man not subject to him by reason of origin or domicile, on the pretext namely of an ecclesiastical benefice to be conferred immediately after tonsure.[64]

The following comments were made in the ordinary gloss with regard to the proper bishop by reason of domicile. It was stated that one could have a domicile in several places,[65] provided that one lived in each to the same extent;[66] otherwise a person was said to have his domicile wherever he had the greater part of his belongings.[67] The

[60] C. 3, *de temporibus ordinationum et qualitate ordinandorum,* I, 9, in VI°; cf. p. 28.

[61] *Glossa Ordinaria* ad c. 3, *de temporibus ordinationum et qualitate ordinandorum,* I, 9, in VI°, s. v. *oriundus.*

[62] Innocentius XII, const. *Speculatores,* 4 nov. 1694, § 4—*Fontes,* n. 258.

[63] *Glossa Ordinaria* ad c. 3, *de temporibus ordinationum et qualitate ordinandorum,* I, 9, in VI°, s.v. *ecclesiasticum.*

[64] Innocentius XII, const. *Speculatores,* 4 nov. 1694, § 3—*Fontes,* n. 258.

[65] D. (50.1) (6.2); c. 15, X, *de foro competenti,* II, 2; c. 29, X, *de rescriptis,* I, 3.

[66] C. 2, *de sepulturis,* III, 12, in VI°.

[67] D. (50.1) (27.3); C. (3.24) 2.

simple possession of a house, however, was not sufficient for the constituting of a domicile.[68] The Constitution *Speculatores,* on the other hand, made the following requirements of a man desiring to obtain a proper bishop for ordination by reason of domicile. He could do so in either of two ways. First, he could live in a place for ten years and affirm under oath that he intended to live there perpetually. Secondly, he could transfer the greater part of his belongings to a certain place, build a house there, dwell there for a considerable length of time, thus demonstrating his intention of living there perpetually, and, in addition, affirm this intention under oath.[69]

Neither the decretal nor the ordinary gloss mentioned the proper bishop by reason of household service. The Council of Trent, however, required that a man be in the service of a bishop for three years before that bishop could ordain him.[70] The Constitution *Speculatores* made the further requirement that the ordaining bishop obtain testimonial letters from his servant's bishop of origin or domicile.[71]

In view of the foregoing, it is clear that the decree of 1604 of the Sacred Congregation of the Council in favor of the Institute of the Oratory was declaratory. It granted no privileges. It merely stated what was the common law of the time, namely, that secular clerics, among whom were numbered the members of the Institute of the Oratory, obtained a proper bishop for ordination in the place where they lived. No further qualification was needed in respect to the place in 1604 other than the fact that it was their home, the place where they spent most of their time. Since men who joined the Oratory at Rome and Naples made Rome and Naples their home, the proper bishops for their

[68] D. (50.1) (17.13).

[69] Innocentius XII, const. *Speculatores,* 4 nov. 1694, § 5—*Fontes,* n. 258.

[70] Conc. Trident., sess. XXIII, *de ref.*, c. 9.

[71] Innocentius XII, const. *Speculatores,* 4 nov. 1694, § 6—*Fontes,* n. 258.

promotion to Orders were the bishops of Rome and Naples, and this in virtue of the common law. The Sacred Congregation of the Council merely declared what was the common law, thus to protect the Oratory against the unjust demands of certain individual bishops.

In view of the Constitution *Speculatores,* it is also easy to see how, after its issuance in 1694, the members of institutes like that of the Oratory who came from dioceses other than the ones in which were located the houses of the institutes in which they resided, could not claim the bishops of the dioceses in which they resided as their proper bishops for ordination. To do this, after 1694, a privilege was required.

It is easy to see how Monacelli[72] and Honorante,[73] writing after the Constitution *Speculatores,* came to consider the declaration of the Sacred Congregation of the Council of 1604 as a privilege. They also reasoned, however, that this "privilege" was not revoked by universal legislation of the Constitution *Speculatores.* It is difficult to see how they came to this conclusion. For even if the Decree of 1604 had been a privilege, it would have been revoked by the Constitution *Speculatores,* which revoked all contrary privileges, indults and apostolic letters.[74]

Riganti, on the other hand, discerned the true nature of the Decree of 1604. It was, he stated, merely a declaration of the common law of the time as contained in the decretal *Quum nullus* of Pope Boniface VIII, made by the Sacred Congregation to protect the Oratory from the unjust claims of certain bishops of origin.[75] In confirmation of his claim he pointed first to the fact that the resolution of the Sacred Congregation of the Council was handed down in the form of a brief, the form which is customary for a declaration

[72] *Formularium,* Titulus XIII, Formula IV, n. 41 (Vol. II, p. 87).

[73] *Praxis,* p. 130.

[74] Innocentius XII, const. *Speculatores,* 4 nov. 1694, § 10—*Fontes,* n. 258.

[75] Riganti, *Commentaria in Regulas,* in Reg. XXIV, § III, nn. 326-327 (Vol. II, pp. 380-381).

regarding law which already exists, and not for the enactment of new law. Secondly, the learned Jesuit, Father Costa, who was consulted at the time the Sacred Congregation was examining the question, was of the opinion that the Oratorians had no need of an indult on this point. For by the very fact that they chose a domicile in any place, they became subject to the bishop of that place and could be promoted to Orders by that same bishop. Thirdly, not only did the Oratorians at Rome not use any such indult, but their superior, as well as many of the priests of the institute, upon being asked, admitted that they did not even know of the existence of such a privilege.[76] That such an indult was never used by the Oratorians in Rome was admitted even by Monacelli[77] and by Honorante.[78] The Oratorians in Rome were always ordained with dimissorial letters from their bishops of origin.

Allusion will be made to the foregoing discussion in the next chapter in connection with the problem of the proper bishop for the ordination of members of Societies of the Common Life under the present discipline. For the present, it will suffice to note that all through this discussion it is evident that the common law for the ordination of members of Secular Congregations before the Code was identical with the common law for the ordination of secular clerics. Evidence of this fact is also had in the case of two Secular Congregations which received responses from the Holy See in regard to the ordination of their members in the nineteenth century.

The Clerics of Saint Viator (The Viatorian Fathers) were founded at Lyons by Louis J. Querbes (1793-1859) in the year 1831. The institute was approved by Pope Gregory XVI in 1838. The members pronounce the simple vows of poverty, chastity and obedience, and their main work is teaching and helping the diocesan clergy in par-

[76] Riganti, *Commentaria in Regulas*, in Reg. XXIV, § III, nn. 328-329 (Vol. II, p. 381).

[77] *Formularium*, Titulus XIII, Formula IV, n. 41 (Vol. II, p. 88).

[78] *Praxis*, p. 130.

ishes.[79] In the year 1838, the Sacred Congregation of Bishops and Regulars did not accede to a request that the rectors of the various houses be given the faculty of granting dimissorial letters for the ordination of their subjects.[80]

The Congregation of Priests of the Schools of Charity was founded in Venice by the Cavanis brothers (Antonio Angelo, † 1858, and Marco Angelo, † 1853) in the year 1802. Approved by Pope Gregory XVI in 1836, its houses are subject to the jurisdiction of the local ordinaries. Its members take the three simple vows of poverty, chastity and obedience.[81] After the institute had spread into several dioceses, a question arose as to who was the proper bishop for the ordination of its members. On the one hand, the members were subject to transfer, and thus, it was said, could not acquire a domicile. If these same members were born in dioceses other than the ones in which they were stationed, the local ordinaries of the latter dioceses could not be called their proper bishops for ordination either by reason of origin or by reason of domicile. On the other hand, it seemed that these latter bishops should be their proper bishops for ordination, inasmuch as the members were subject to the authority of these bishops. The problem was brought to the Holy See. Since the institute had not been granted any privileges in this matter, its members were equivalated to secular clerics in the matter of ordination, and the case was settled in virtue of the Constitution *Speculatores*. Following are the *dubia* and responses by which the Sacred Congregation of Bishops and Regulars settled the case, as they are reported in the *Fontes*.

> 1. An et quomodo Episcopus Tarvisinus ad sacram Ordinationem admittere possit alumnos Instituti N. ex fide Superioris domus declarantis

[79] *Annuario*, p. 790; Heimbucher, *Die Orden*, II, 449; Kapsner, *Orders*, p. 53.

[80] S. C. Ep. et Reg., *Lugdunen.*, 21 sept. 1838—*Acta Sanctae Sedis* (41 vols., Romae, 1865-1908), I (1865), 364 (hereafter cited as *ASS*).

[81] *Annuario*, p. 770; Heimbucher, *Die Orden*, II, 417; Kapsner, *Orders*, p. 215; Anonymous, "Traité des Congrégations Séculières," *Anal. J. P.*, V (1861), 77-78.

> eosdem alumnos adscriptos esse eidem domui; vel potius necessariae sint litterae dimissoriae et testimoniales Episcopi originis, seu domicilii, iuxta formam Constitutionis Innocentii XII, quae incipit: *Speculatores*.
>
> 2. An et quomodo idem dici debeat quoad alumnos iam promotos ad tonsuram, vel ad aliquem Ordinem.
>
> 3. An et quomodo, haud obstante promissione obedientiae Episcopo facta in sacra Ordinatione, liceat Superioribus Instituti (praedicti) transferre eosdem alumnos in aliam provinciam quin venia a dicto Episcopo petatur.
>
> 4. An in casu egressus ab Instituto per dimissionem aut dispensationem, iidem alumni subiiciantur iurisdictioni Episcopi dioecesis in qua sita est domus cui adscripti sunt; vel potius illi Episcopo cui subiecti erant prius quam Instituto adscriberentur.
>
> R. Ad. 1. Negative ad primam partem; affirmative ad secundam.
>
> Ad 2. Affirmative in omnibus.
>
> Ad 3. Superiorem provincialem posse libere uti facultate transferendi alumnos provinciae iuxta Constitutiones a S. Sede approbatas.
>
> Ad. 4. Negative ad primam partem; affirmative ad secundam.[82]

The same decision is also reported in three other collections. In these collections, the decision is prefaced by a report of the discussion that took place in the Sacred Congregation before the decision was made. These collections are the *Acta Sanctae Sedis,*[83] the *Analecta Juris Pontificii,*[84]and the collection made by Bizzarri (1802-1877).[85] Immediately following the decision in the *Acta Sanctae Sedis* are the following observations, which may be taken

[82] S. C. Ep. et Reg., *Tarvisina,* 6 maii 1864—*Fontes,* n. 1991.

[83] I (1865), 358-366.

[84] VII (1864), 744-751.

[85] *Collectanea in Usum Secretariae Sacrae Congregationis Episcoporum et Regularium* (2. ed., Romae, 1885), pp. 706-712 (hereafter referred to as *Collectanea*).

as a summary of the canonical doctrine of the time on this point of law.

Ex iis colliges:

1. Instituta religiosa votorum simplicium vindicare alia iura sibi non posse, praeter ea, quae specialiter concessa demonstrent.

2. Facultatem concedendi literas dimissorias ad ordines recipiendos, inter specialia privilegia recenseri, eamque facultatem erui non posse ex auctoritate, quam Superiores alicuius Instituti exercent in suos alumnos independenter ab Ordinario originis seu domicilii.

3. Neque locorum Ordinarios ex unico titulo auctoritatis quam exercere possunt super iisdem alumnis, posse eosdem ordinibus initiare, posthabita Constitutione Innocentii XII *Speculatores*.

4. Per obedientiam, quam alumni promittunt Episcopo ordinanti, laedi non posse iura Instituti, quae ex Apostolica auctoritate eidem Instituto competunt.

5. In casu egressus, quo deseritur Institutum, alumnos subiici illi Ordinario, cui subiecti erant, priusquam Institutum ipsum ingrederentur. (Nota: Interdum a S. Congregatione exeunt rescripta vel indulta, in quibus, clausula reperitur, qua iniungitur eiusmodi alumnis ad ss. ordines provectis, ut benevolum Episcopum inveniant, qui eos recipiat tamquam subditos in sua dioecesi, euismodi clausula oeconomice apponi videtur ad evitandas difficultates quae oriri possent. Sed si fiat casus in quo benevolum Episcopum clericus non reperiat, ad hunc recipiendum tenetur Episcopus originis seu domicilii. Quicumque enim valor attribuatur literis, quae dantur, et dari debent, pro aggregatione ad aliquod Institutum, etiamsi dicantur excorporationis, cum tamen clericus non reperiat dioecesim cui adscribatur, consequens videtur, ut non possit a proprio Episcopo reiici.)[86]

Five years after the answers were given to the *dubia* proposed by the Congregation of Priests of the Schools of Charity, Pope Pius IX (1846-1878), in the Constitution *Apostolicae Sedis,* instituted the following penalty:

[86] *ASS,* I (1865), 366-367.

> Suspensionem [Sum. Pont. reservatam] per annum a collatione ordinum ipso iure incurrit, qui excepto casu legitimi privilegii, Ordinem Sacrum contulerit absque titulo beneficii vel patrimonii clerico in aliqua Congregatione viventi, in qua solemnis professio non emittitur, vel etiam religioso nondum professo.[87]

Here again it is evident that Secular Congregations were bound by the common law to the laws regulating the ordinations of secular clerics.

Two years after Pope Pius IX instituted this penalty, the Sacred Congregation for the Propagation of the Faith issued an Instruction on the title of the mission. In this Instruction the Sacred Congregation touched upon other titles. The title of the common table, it stated, was used by those clerics who lived in common after the manner of religious, but pronounced either simple vows or no vows at all; but this title could be used only by clerics who belonged to a congregation or institute which had received a special privilege to this effect from the Apostolic See.[88]

At the end of the nineteenth century, a very clear statement of the common law for the ordination of members of Secular Congregations who pronounced vows was issued by the Holy See itself. It was contained in a response of the Sacred Congregation of Bishops and Regulars dated February 12, 1894, which response was occasioned by a misunderstanding of the famous Decree *Auctis admodum* of November 4, 1892.

In the latter half of the nineteenth century many members of Secular Congregations were leaving their institutes after their promotion to major Orders. This created a heavy burden for the bishops who were obliged to receive these men into their dioceses. Consequently, in the year 1892, the Bishops of Germany, in their annual meeting at Fulda, petitioned the Holy See for legislation to remedy

[87] Pius IX, const. *Apostolicae Sedis,* 12 oct. 1869, V, 4—*Fontes,* n. 552.

[88] S. C. de Prop. Fide, instr. 27 apr. 1871, § 4—*Fontes,* n. 4878.

this situation.[89] In response to this petition, the Sacred Congregation of Bishops and Regulars issued the Decree *Auctis admodum,* which forbade the conferral of major Orders before perpetual profession.[90]

In reading the Decree *Auctis admodum,* some got the impression that it presupposed that all Secular Congregations with vows had the right to grant dimissorial letters for the ordination of their members. Two years later the following question was put to the Sacred Congregation of Bishops and Regulars: *Utrum nunc, post decretum,* AUCTIS, *instituta votorum simplicium libere possint, sine indulto speciali, alumnis suis dimissoriales litteras ad ordines concedere.* The Sacred Congregation replied in the negative.[91]

Six years after this response, Pope Leo XIII (1878-1903) issued his famous Constitution *Conditae a Christo,* the so-called *Magna Charta* of Religious Congregations. In this Constitution the Pope warned bishops against promoting to Orders men living in their dioceses without fulfilling the requirements of law with regard to the needed dimissorial letters and title of ordination.[92]

The case of a Precious Blood Father, which was decided by the Sacred Congregation of Bishops and Regulars in 1905, throws light on the question of the incardination of a member of a Secular Congregation who was ordained according to the common law, i.e., with dimissorial letters from his own proper bishop and not from his major superior. This priest was ordained while affiliated with the Congregation of the Most Precious Blood upon the issuance of dimissorial letters by the Bishop of Gaeta. Later, by

[89] Langogne, "Sur le Décret '*Auctis admodum*'," *Le Canoniste Contemporain* (Paris, 1878-1926), XVI (1893), 79-83.

[90] S. C. Ep. et Reg., decr. *Auctis admodum,* 4 nov. 1892—*Fontes,* n. 2020.

[91] S. C. Ep. et Reg., *Parisien.,* 12 febr. 1894—*ASS,* XXVI (1893-1894), 616-620.

[92] Leo XIII, const. *Conditae a Christo,* 8 dec. 1900, II, 6—*Fontes,* n. 644.

reason of poor health, he was permitted to live with his family in the Diocese of Gaeta, all the while remaining a member of the institute. In 1903 the Bishop of Gaeta denied the priest faculties for hearing confessions, and in 1904 denied him permission to say Mass in the Diocese, claiming that the priest pertained not to the Diocese but to the institute. This action was prompted by what turned out to be misinformation, in the light of which the Bishop had considered the priest a troublemaker. The priest had recourse to the Holy See, proving his innocence with regard to the charges levelled against him. He claimed that members of his Congregation never renounced their own dioceses, and were ordained with dimissorial letters from their own proper ordinaries under the title of patrimony. On January 27, 1905, the Sacred Congregation decided the case in favor of the priest, and stated its mind in the following terms.

> 1. Alumni Congregationum non exemptarum, secluso privilegio Apostolico, ordinari nequeunt absque litteris dimissorialibus proprii Episcopi.
> 2. Hinc ipsi semper pertinent ad suam dioecesim, ad quam redire ius habent quoties ex legitima causa et de Superiorum consensu extra Ordinem morantur.
> 3. Insuper subditi remanent proprii Ordinarii, qui non solum tamquam Apostolicae Sedis delegatus sed etiam potestate ordinaria in eos delinquentes animadvertere valet.
> 4. In themate sacerdos N. est membrum Congationis non exemptae a iurisdictione Ordinariorum, et ordinatus fuit cum dimissoriis Episcopi Caietae, cui subditus est non solum titulo originis et ordinationis sed etiam domicilii.[93]

The last series of legislative enactments before the Code which had any direct relation to the common law for the ordination of members of Secular Congregations was a series of enactments centering around the problem of the excardination of laymen.

From the time of the Council of Trent, a man could ob-

[93] *ASS*, XXXVIII (1905-1906), 11-13.

tain a proper bishop for ordination by reason of origin, benefice, domicile or household service. In the latter half of the nineteenth century, however, a custom arose in France, Germany, Italy, and even in Rome itself, whereby clerics or laymen, if they did not wish to be ordained in the place of their origin or domicile, sought and obtained excorporation by their own proper bishop and incorporation by the bishop of the place where they wished to be ordained. The latter bishops then ordained them without fulfilling the requirements of the Constitution *Speculatores*. In effect, this was the establishment of a fifth way whereby one could obtain a proper bishop for ordination, namely, the way of incardination.[94] The custom received official approbation from the Sacred Congregation of the Council in the Decree *A primis* in 1898. The Decree, nevertheless, stated the conditions that had to be fulfilled in the granting of such excardination and incardination.[95] As the result of ambiguous wording, a doubt arose whether the Decree sanctioned this usage for laymen as well as for clerics.[96] To clear up this doubt, the Sacred Congregation of the Council in 1906 stated explicitly that this usage was sanctioned even in the case of laymen, under the following conditions, however: first, the excardination had to be granted in writing, had to be given for the purpose of incardination to follow in a determinate diocese, and had to be given for a just cause; secondly, incardination had to be effected in accordance with the norms of the Decree *A primis,* and, in the case of ex-seminarians, in accordance with the norms of the Decree *Vetuit* of 1905;[97] and thirdly, an oath like the one required by the Constitution *Speculatores* (*"iura-*

[94] Many, *De Sacra Ordinatione*, pp. 170-171; McBride, *Incardination and Excardination of Secular Clerics*, The Catholic University of America Canon Law Studies, n. 145 (Washington, D.C.: The Catholic University of America Press, 1942), p. 91 (hereafter referred to as *Incardination*).

[95] S. C. C., decr. *A primis,* 20 iul. 1898—*Fontes*, n. 4307.

[96] Many, *De Sacra Ordinatione*, pp. 174-175; McBride, *Incardination,* p. 219.

[97] S. C. C., decr. *Vetuit,* 22 dec. 1905—*Fontes*, n. 4327.

mentum ad tramitem constitutionis Speculatores requisitum") had to be taken before First Tonsure.[98]

During the two decades before the Code, then, there were five ways by which secular clerics, and, consequently, members of Secular Congregations which lacked special privileges, could obtain a proper bishop for ordination, namely, origin, benefice, domicile, household service and incardination.

Up to this point, an attempt has been made in this Chapter to establish what was the common law for the ordination of members of Secular Congregations before the Code, primarily upon an examination of the legislation by which such ordinations were regulated, and upon an examination of the decisions handed down by the Holy See in this matter. It will be helpful now to turn to the writings of the pre-Code canonists in order to see if the conclusions reached thus far are in harmony with their teaching.

Up until the middle of the last century, the canonists did not usually devote a special section, in their treatment of the *Jus Regularium,* to the law regulating Secular Congregations. If they adverted to the Secular Congregations at all, they did so only in passing, e.g., by showing that they were comprehended under the terms "*religiones*" and "*ordines*" employed in the IV General Council of the Lateran and the II General Council of Lyons, which forbade the founding of new "*religiones*" and "*ordines.*"[99] The reason for their failure to devote a special section of their treatises to the law governing Secular Congregations was, no doubt, the fact that each Congregation was governed,

[98] S. C. C., decr. 24 nov. 1906—*Fontes,* n. 4330.

For further information about the question of the proper bishop for the ordination of laymen by reason of incardination, cf. Many, *De Sacra Ordinatione,* pp. 170-171, 174-175; McBride, *Incardination,* pp. 91-96, 113-116, 216-219; Moeder, *Proper Bishop,* pp. 31-32; Francia, "Animadversiones circa incardinationem," *Apollinaris* (Romae, 1928-), IX (1936), 216-218.

[99] Cf. *supra,* pp. 18-19.

in practice, primarily by its constitutions which were approved by the Holy See, since at the time there existed almost no special legislation applicable to all Secular Congregations.

From about the middle to the end of the nineteenth century, most of the authors devoted a special section of their treatises to the ever-increasing Secular Congregations. In this category they included all institutes in which the members did not profess solemn vows. It made no difference whether the members took what are now called simple public vows, or what are now called private vows, or no vows at all. Many canonists also devoted entire articles to this phase of the law in canonical periodicals. All these authors were in agreement about the fact that Secular Congregations, in matters pertaining to the ordination of their members, were governed by a common law identical with the law for the ordination of secular clerics.[100]

From about the end of the nineteenth century to the advent of the Code, and especially after the Constitution *Conditae a Christo,* many canonists treated separately and apart from all other institutes the institutes whose members took vows which indeed were perpetual but not solemn. These canonists agreed that such institutes, by the common law, followed the law for the ordination of secular clerics.[101] One of these authors, Many (1847-1922), in addition to stating the common law regarding the proper

[100] Anonymous, "Des Ordinations dans les Congrégations Séculières," *Anal. J. P.*, VII (1864), 744-751; Anonymous, "Congrégations Séculières. Privilèges. Ordinations. Direction des Séminaires," *Anal. J. P.*, VII (1864), 758-764; Anonymous, "Congrégations Séculières," *Anal. J. P.*, XXIV (1885), 383-422; Gasparri, *De Sacra Ordinatione,* II, 87; Wernz, *Ius Decretalium,* II 54-55, nota (60), III, 621-622; Mocchegiani, *Iurisprudentia,* I, 455-456; Freriks, *Religious Congregations in their External Relations,* p. 106.

[101] De Angelis, *Praelectiones Iuris Canonici* (5 tomi in 9, Romae-Parisiis, 1877-1891), Tomus II, Pars II, p. 201; Piatus Montensis, *Praelectiones Juris Regularis* (2. ed., 2 vols., Tornaci, 1898), II, 286; Bastien, *Directoire Canonique* (1. ed.), p. 236; Many, *De Sacra Ordinatione,* pp. 409-431.

bishop and the canonical title, as it has been stated all throughout the present Chapter,[102] also stated that institutes which do not enjoy the privilege of granting dimissorial letters for the ordination of their members are ruled by the common law for the ordination of secular clerics in all the other aspects of the law of ordination.[103] It will be of interest to see what Many taught about the other points of the law of ordination as applied to these institutes in detail.

What Many said about the examination that was to be undergone by the ordinands who were members of the institutes which lacked the privilege of granting dimissorial letters should be quoted exactly. It will be of great interest in the development of the next Chapter. Many stated: *Unde jus faciendi examen pertinet ad episcopum proprium ratione originis, vel beneficii.* To this sentence he appended at the foot of the page the following note: *Omitto episcopum domicilii, quia alumnus ordinandus, voto obedientiae adstrictus, non potest adimplere condiciones in bulla* SPECULATORES *requisitas ut quis subditus sit alicui episcopo ratione domicilii.*[104] It was for the bishop of origin or benefice to determine the time and the manner of this examination, as well as to designate the examiners, who might well be the superiors of the institutes.[105]

The Congregations had to observe the laws regulating the time and the place of ordination.[106]

The right to dispense from the interstices pertained to the bishop who was the proper bishop by reason of the Constitution *Speculatores.*[107]

There were required the same testimonial letters that

[102] *De Sacra Ordinatione*, pp. 409-412, 427-429.
[103] *De Sacra Ordinatione*, p. 422.
[104] Many, *De Sacra Ordinatione*, p. 422.
[105] Many, *De Sacra Ordinatione*, pp. 422-423.
[106] Many, *De Sacra Ordinatione*, p. 423.
[107] Many, *De Sacra Ordinatione*, p. 424.

were required for the ordination of secular clerics by the Constitution *Speculatores*.[108]

The question of the banns *probably* presents what is an *apparent* exception to the general principle that Secular Congregations were by the common law held to the law for the ordination of secular clerics. For, although secular clerics were bound by the law of the banns, there was a probable opinion that members of Secular Congregations were not so bound. The opinion was based on the fact that the Decree *Romani Pontifices* of the Sacred Congregation for the State of Regulars, issued in 1848, had demanded that before anyone was to be admitted into any Order, Congregation, Society, Institute, Monastery or House, testimonials be obtained both from the ordinary of his place of origin and from the ordinaries of all the places in which he had spent a year or more after becoming fifteen years of age. These ordinaries had to investigate the person in question and provide the institute with testimony concerning the candidate's ancestry, age, morals, life, reputation, condition, education and knowledge. They also had to investigate whether there was present any impediment or irregularity.[109] Inasmuch as the end of the law which required the banns was achieved through the fulfillment of the prescripts of this Decree, some authors were of the opinion that Congregations were excused from the law of the banns. This opinion appeared tenable as a solidly probable opinion before the Code.[110]

[108] Many, *De Sacra Ordinatione*, p. 424, nota 1.

[109] S. C. super Statu Regularium, decr. *Romani Pontifices*, 25 ian. 1848—*Fontes*, n. 4375.

[110] Cf. Many, *De Sacra Ordinatione*, pp. 426-427; Gasparri, *De Sacra Ordinatione*, II, 26.

CHAPTER III

THE COMMON LAW FOR THE ORDINATION OF MEMBERS OF SOCIETIES OF THE COMMON LIFE AFTER THE CODE

Article 1. Preliminary Remarks

In the discussion on the common law for the ordination of members of Societies after the Code, it seems apropos at the outset to determine exactly the places in which this law can be found.

The fundamental canon for the determination of the law for the ordination of members of Societies is canon 678: *In iis quae ad studiorum rationem et ad suscipiendos ordines pertinent, sodales iisdem legibus tenentur ac saeculares clerici, salvis peculiaribus praescriptionibus a Sancta Sede datis.*

The first body of law indicated in canon 678 as the law governing the ordination of members of Societies is the law governing the ordination of secular clerics. This body of law, in its turn, can be found in two sources, namely, on the one hand, in the Code of Canon Law, and on the other hand, in the special prescripts of the Holy See, which lie outside the Code but nonetheless are binding on all secular clerics.

Besides designating the law for the ordination of secular clerics as one of the bodies of law governing the ordination of members of Societies, canon 678 also indicates that there are peculiar prescripts of the Holy See in this regard which must be observed. The expression used is, "*salvis peculiaribus praescriptionibus a Sancta Sede datis.*" Upon first sight one may inquire what is the force of the expression "*peculiaribus praescriptionibus.*" Does it indicate special prescripts, namely, such as are intended for the members of all Societies? Or does it indicate singular prescripts, namely, privileges granted to individual Societies? Upon investigation it seems that both types of prescripts are indicated.

The Holy See has, at times, used the adjective *"peculiaris"* to convey the concept of special in regard to law, and has, at other times, used the same word to convey the concept of singular in regard to law. It was used by Pope Pius XII in the Constitution *Provida Mater* of February 2, 1947, to convey the concept of special: *"Lex peculiaris Institutorum saecularium."*[1] It was used by the Pontifical Commission for the Authentic Interpretation of the Canons of the Code in the same year to convey the concept of singular. The Commission at that time declared that it was opportune that privileges regarding ordination be given to individual Societies *"In virtù della clausola 'salvis peculiaribus praescriptionibus a Sancta Sede datis' del can. 678."*[2] It seems, however, that in canon 678 the Holy See has used the word *"peculiaribus"* in a broad sense which includes the notions both of special and of singular, for there are examples of both special prescripts and singular prescripts emanating from the Holy See as regulating the ordination of members of Societies.

Singular prescripts, by which privileges are granted, however, are not of interest in this place. These singular prescripts will be considered in Chapter IV of this dissertation, which will treat of the singular law governing the ordination of members of Societies. Here it will be sufficient to consider the special regulations of the Holy See governing the ordination of members of all Societies as a special class of persons in the Church.

The most notable special enactment of the Holy See regulating the ordination of members of all Societies is the Instruction of the Sacred Congregation for Religious,

[1] *AAS*, XXXIX (1947), 114-124, cf. p. 120.

[2] P. C. I., litt. 24 iul. 1947—*Commentarium pro Religiosis et Missionariis* ([from 1920 to 1934, *Commentarium pro Religiosis*] Romae, 1920-), XXVIII (1949), 16-18, cf. p. 17 (The *Commentarium pro Religiosis* will hereafter be referred to as *CpR;* the *Commentarium pro Religiosis et Missionariis,* as *CpRM*).

Quantum Religiones, dated December 1, 1931. This Instruction is addressed to the highest superiors of clerical religious institutes and clerical Societies and concerns the clerical and religious formation of members called to the priesthood and the examination to be made before the reception of Orders. That the Holy See by this Instruction intends to bind not only Orders and Religious Congregations but also Societies of the Common Life is clear from the heading of the Instruction: *Ad Supremos Religionum et Societatum Moderatores,* and also from explicit references made to Societies in paragraphs 1, 3, 14, 17 and 21 of the Instruction.[3]

Another argument pointing to the fact that this Instruction is intended for Societies is the fact that the corresponding Instruction on the clerical and religious training of candidates for the secular priesthood was issued by the Sacred Congregation for the Discipline of the Sacraments in 1930.[4] It had already been decided in 1919, however, that the Sacred Congregation competent for treating matters of ordination in Societies is the Sacred Congregation for Religious.[5]

Finally, the authors are in agreement that the Instruction *Quantum Religiones* is intended for Societies of the Common Life as well as for religious institutes.[6]

The body of juridic enactments regulating the common law for the ordination of members of Societies, then, may be summed up under three headings:

1. The canons of the Code which regulate the ordination

[3] *AAS,* XXIV (1932), 74-81.

[4] S. C. de Sacr., instr. *Quam ingens Ecclesiae,* 27 dec. 1930—*AAS,* XXIII (1931), 120-129.

[5] Commissio specialis Cardinalium designata ad normam canonis 245, responsum, 24 martii 1919, ad III—*AAS,* XI (1919), 251.

[6] Stanton, *De Societatibus,* pp. 158-168; Blat, *Commentarium Textus Codicis Iuris Canonici* (5 tomi in 7 vols., Tom. II, Vol. II, *Liber II, Partes II et III, Ius de Religiosis et Laicis iuxta Codicis Ordinem,* 3. ed., Romae: apud "Angelicum," 1938), Tom. II, Vol. II, p. 393; Ristuccia, *Societies,* p. 196; Rothoff, *Sociétés,* pp. 163-166.

of secular clerics. Included among these canons are the following:

a. Book II, Title I: The Enlisting (*adscriptio*) of Clerics in a Determinate Diocese, canons 111 to 117;

b. Book III, Title VI: The Sacrament of Holy Orders, canons 948 to 1011, with the exception of those canons which treat exclusively of the ordination of religious.

2. Special prescriptions of the Holy See regulating the ordination of all secular clerics, e.g., the response of the Pontifical Commission for the Authentic Interpretation of the Canons of the Code given on July 24, 1939, regarding the incardination of a cleric tonsured by his own bishop for the service of another determinate diocese.[7]

3. Special prescriptions of the Holy See regulating the ordination of all members of Societies, e.g., the Instruction of the Sacred Congregation of Religious *Quantum Religiones*, dated December 1, 1931.[8]

With the law indicated in the preceding paragraph one can set about trying to establish the common law for the ordination of members of Societies. But one does not progress far before learning that practically all Societies follow singular law with regard to perhaps two of the most important aspects of the law, namely, the granting of dimissorial letters and the question of the canonical title. It is discovered that today, ordinarily, a Society no sooner has the Decree of Praise than it also possesses indults whereby the major superiors are empowered to grant dimissorial letters, and whereby the members can be ordained to the subdiaconate under the title of the common table.[9] The question arises, therefore, to what avail would one spend time in attempting to establish at length what is the common law in this matter. A justification for these efforts, however, may be found in the fact that a knowl-

[7] *AAS*, XXXI (1939), 321.

[8] *AAS*, XXIV (1932), 74-81.

[9] Cf. P. C. I., 24 iul. 1947— *CpRM*, XXVIII (1949), 16-18.

edge of the common law is very practical for new Societies. For new Societies usually lack indults between the time of their canonical erection and the time when they receive the Decree of Praise, and experience has shown that the application of the common law during this early period in the existence of each Society presents many difficulties.

In an attempt to solve these difficulties, the writer will in the present Chapter make an effort to examine closely the common law for the ordination of members of Societies. The general outline he proposes to follow will be that of Title VI of Book III of the Code, which treats of the Sacrament of Holy Orders. In following this outline, he will treat at length those laws for the ordination of secular clerics which, in their application to members of Societies, present special difficulties. The other laws, namely, those which present no difficulty in their application, he will consider in relation to the Societies in quite general terms. For if any difficulty should arise in a Society with regard to these last mentioned laws, the solution would be the same as it would be in reference to a secular cleric; and such solutions can be readily found in the ordinary manuals.

It should be noted at the outset that consideration is given to only those Societies for which the *nihil obstat* has been obtained from the Holy See, and which have been canonically erected by means of a formal episcopal decree of erection according to the prescriptions of canon 674 collated with canons 492, § 1, and 100, § 1, and according to the *Normae* of the Sacred Congregation for Religious of March 6, 1921, describing the procedure of the Sacred Congregation in the approbation of new Religious Congregations.[10] For until such a decree of erection is issued, a Society has no moral personality in the Church, and

[10] *AAS*, XIII (1921), 312-319.

Stanton asserts that these *Normae* apply to Societies of the Common Life as well as to Religious Congregations. *De Societatibus*, p. 101.

thus there can be no question of the ordination of its members. A bishop is free to ordain men who have gathered together to prepare the groundwork for a new Society. But until this Society has been canonically erected, these men are not members of any Society, and therefore are governed by the laws regulating the ordination of secular clerics with no reference to such law as applies to Societies whatsoever.[11]

Finally, it should be noted that in the present Chapter any reference made to a Society will always be a reference to a non-exempt Society. For in the present Chapter the common law for the ordination of members of Societies is being treated, and Societies by common law are non-exempt.[12] In like manner, therefore, any reference to an ordinary will always be a reference to a local ordinary, because only major superiors in exempt clerical Societies enjoy the status of an ordinary.[13]

ARTICLE 2. THE MINISTER OF HOLY ORDERS IN SOCIETIES

SECTION 1. STATE OF THE QUESTION

In discussing the law regulating the minister of Holy Orders in non-exempt Societies of the Common Life, one may well at the very outset distinguish those things which are certain from those things which are doubtful, and distinguish also those things about which the authors are in agreement from those things about which they disagree. Actually, there are two fundamental points on which there is agreement, and three on which there is disagreement.

The first point on which there is agreement does not concern exclusively the law for the ordination of mem-

[11] Cf. Oesterle, "Weihekandidaten aus einer Diözesan-Priestergenossenschaft," *ThPrQs*, LXXXV (1932), 563.

[12] Canon 675 collated with canon 500, § 1; canon 680 collated with canons 615 and 618, § 1. Cf. Stanton, *De Societatibus*, pp. 111, 149; Ristuccia, *Societies*, pp. 105, 227; Rothoff, *Sociétés*, pp. 115, 186-187.

[13] Canon 675 collated with canons 500, § 1, and 198, § 1, § 2. Cf. Stanton, *De Societatibus*, p. 111.

bers of Societies. Rather, is it a fundamental principle of the law for the ordination of secular clerics, which is necessary as a premise for the solution of certain questions regarding the law for the ordination of members of Societies. This fundamental principle concerns the distinction between the proper bishop for the promotion of a layman to First Tonsure and the proper bishop for the promotion of a secular cleric to higher Orders.

In the years immediately following the promulgation of the Code, there seems to have been little doubt about the fact that a man tonsured by his own proper bishop for the service of another determinate diocese with the consent of the bishop of that other diocese was incardinated in that other diocese, and not in the diocese of the bishop who tonsured him, even though he had never set foot in that other diocese. This was evident from the clear wording of canon 111, § 2,[14] and from a private response of the Pontifical Commission for the Authentic Interpretation of the Canons of the Code given on August 17, 1919, soon after the promulgation of the Code.[15] This doctrine was confirmed by a public response of the Commission given on July 24, 1939.[16]

There was disagreement, however, during the two decades that followed the promulgation of the Code, as to who was the proper bishop for the promotion to higher Orders of such a cleric as the one mentioned in the previous paragraph, namely one who was incardinated in a diocese in which he did not have a domicile. In other words, there was disagreement whether the primary factor in determining the proper bishop for the advancement to higher Orders of an incardinated cleric was the factor of domicile or the factor of incardination. Some authors held that the

[14] Per receptionem primae tonsurae clericus adscribitur seu, ut aiunt, *incardinatur* dioecesi pro cuius servitio promotus fuit.

[15] Bouscaren, *The Canon Law Digest* (2 vols. and Supplement through 1948, Milwaukee, Wis.: The Bruce Publishing Co., 1934-1943-1949), I, 89 (hereafter cited as *Digest*).

[16] *AAS*, XXXI (1939), 321.

bishop of the place where a cleric had his domicile was the sole proper bishop for that cleric's promotion to higher Orders, even though that cleric was incardinated in another diocese. These authors held that a cleric's incardination in a particular diocese, if unaccompanied with that cleric's possession of a domicile in that same diocese, did not give the bishop of that diocese any right to promote that cleric to higher Orders.[17] Other authors who wrote during these two decades, however, held that the bishop of the diocese of incardination is the sole proper bishop for the promotion of incardinated clerics to higher Orders.[18] Those of the latter group who wrote after the year 1931 could deduce a strong argument to support their contention from a private response of the Code Commission given in that year. The Bishop of Santa Fé in Argentina had asked:

> Whether one who has been promoted to first tonsure by his proper Bishop, but for the service of another diocese, and who has by that very fact become incardinated in the latter diocese in accordance with c. 111, § 2, and the Reply of the Code Commission, of 17 Aug., 1919, *ad II,* should receive the higher orders from the former Bishop or rather from the Bishop of the diocese in which he is now duly incardinated, even though he be

[17] Towards the end of the second decade following the promulgation of the Code, this opinion was defended at length by Schaaf in an article entitled "Episcopus Proprius Ordinationis," *ER,* XC (1934), 352-365, cf. pp. 356-365.

For lists of other authors who defended this opinion during these twenty years, c. Schaaf, "Episcopus Proprius Ordinationis," *ER,* XC (1934), 365, note 18; Moeder, *Proper Bishop,* p. 57, note 36; McBride, *Incardination,* p. 356, note 140.

[18] Towards the end of the second decade following the promulgation of the Code, this opinion was defended by Moeder, *Proper Bishop,* pp. 55-75.

For lists of other authors who defended this opinion during these twenty years, cf. Schaaf, "Episcopus Proprius Ordinationis," *ER,* XC (1934), 360, note 11; Moeder, *Proper Bishop,* p. 57, notes 37 and 38; McBride, *Incardination,* p. 359, note 149.

> obliged to finish his theological studies in another diocese.

On December 7, 1931, the Commission responded in the negative to the first part, and in the affirmative to the second.[19] This response, however, did not definitively settle the dispute, because in the question proposed it was not explicitly stated that the cleric in question lacked a domicile in the diocese in which he was incardinated.

Eight years later, the Commission authoritatively settled the dispute with a public response. It was asked:

> I. Whether a layman who is advanced to first tonsure by his own Bishop for the service of another determinate diocese with the consent of the Bishop of that diocese, is incardinated in that diocese according to canon 111, § 2.
>
> II. Whether the Bishop of the diocese for whose service a layman has been advanced to first tonsure by his own Bishop, can in his own right and to the exclusion of others confer orders on him or give dimissorial letters according to canon 955, § 1, even though the subject has not yet acquired a domicile in that diocese.

On July 24, 1939, the Commission replied in the affirmative to both questions.[20]

Since this response, there has been unanimity among the authors in asserting that while the proper bishop for the promotion of a layman to First Tonsure is always the bishop of domicile, the proper bishop for the promotion of a tonsured secular cleric to higher Orders, when the cleric's bishop of domicile and his bishop of incardination are distinct, is the bishop of incardination. Although it is immediately deducible from this statement that the proper bishop for the promotion of a tonsured cleric to higher Orders is always the bishop of incardination, the authors disagree, in the case wherein the bishop of domicile and the bishop of incardination are identical, by reason of which fact, domicile or incardination, the bishop

[19] *Digest,* II, 51.

[20] *AAS,* XXXI (1939), 321. The quotation is taken from *Digest,* II, 52, 237-238.

in question is the proper bishop. Nevertheless, it may be stated that, in the practical sphere, it is the unanimous opinion of contemporary canonists that the proper bishop for the promotion of a layman to First Tonsure is *always* the bishop of domicile, and that the proper bishop for the promotion of a secular cleric to higher Orders can *always be identified with* the bishop of incardination.[21]

The second point on which all the authors agree directly concerns the law governing the ordination of members of Societies itself. Canon 678 states that in matters regarding ordination members of Societies are governed by the laws regulating the ordination of secular clerics, with due compliance accorded to the specific prescriptions enacted by the Holy See. Now the two fundamental canons regulating the law concerning the minister of Holy Orders for the secular clergy are canons 955 and 956. Canon 955 commands that each one be promoted to Orders by his own

[21] Fallon, "Proper Bishop for Ordination—Reply of Code Commission," *The Irish Ecclesiastical Record* (Dublin, 1864-), 5. series, LIV (1939), 409-413 (hereafter referred to as *IER*); Coussa, "De Episcopo Proprio Sacrae Ordinationis," *Apollinaris*, XII (1939), 321-325; McBride, *Incardination*, pp. 355-370; Wernz-Vidal, *Ius Canonicum*, II, 87-88; Heneghan, "Episcopus Proprius," *The Jurist* (Washington, D.C.: The Catholic University of America, 1941-), III (1943), 326-330; Martin, "Seminarian Changing Domicile," *The Jurist*, V (1945), 448-450; Coronata, *Institutiones Iuris Canonici ad Usum Utriusque Cleri et Scholarum, De Sacramentis Tractatus Canonicus* (3 vols., Vol. II, *De Ordine*, Torino: Marietti, 1945), II, 28 (hereafter referred to as *De Sacramentis*); Cappello, *Tractatus Canonico-Moralis de Sacramentis* (5 vols., Vol. IV, *De Sacra Ordinatione*, 2. ed., Augustae Taurinorum-Romae: Marietti, 1947), IV, 218-225 (hereafter referred to as *De Sacramentis*); Woywod, *A Practical Commentary on the Code of Canon Law* (revised by Callistus Smith, revised and enlarged edition, 2 vols., New York: Wagner-London: Herder, 1948), I, 570 (hereafter referred to as *Commentary*); De Naurois, "Le 'Propre Évêque' pour l'ordination dans le clergé séculier," *Bulletin de Littérature ecclésiastique* (Paris, 1899-1908; Toulouse, 1909-), LI (1950), 15-40 (hereafter referred to as *BLE*); Bouscaren-Ellis, *Canon Law, A Text and Commentary* (2. ed., Milwaukee: Bruce, 1951), p. 417 (hereafter referred to as *Canon Law*).

proper bishop.[22] Canon 956 determines which bishop is one's proper bishop in matters of ordination. It states that the proper bishop for the ordination of seculars is the bishop of the place where they have a domicile.[23] The authors are unanimous in asserting that in virtue of canon 678 the ordination of members of Societies is governed by canons 955 and 956. Consequently they are unanimous in asserting that the proper bishop for the ordination of members of Societies is the bishop of the place where the members have a domicile.[24] Some authors, in consequence

[22] § 1. Unusquisque a proprio Episcopo ordinetur aut cum legitimis eiusdem litteris dimissoriis.

§ 2. Episcopus proprius, iusta causa non impeditus, per se ipse suos subditos ordinet; sed subditum orientalis ritus, sine apostolico indulto, licite ordinare non potest.

[23] Episcopus proprius, quod attinet ad ordinationem saecularium, est tantum Episcopus dioecesis in qua promovendus habeat domicilium una cum origine aut simplex domicilium sine origine; sed in hoc altero casu promovendus debet animum in dioecesi perpetuo manendi iureiurando firmare, nisi agatur de promovendo ad ordines clerico qui dioecesi per primam tonsuram iam incardinatus est, vel de promovendo alumno, qui servitio alius dioecesis destinatur ad normam can. 969, § 2, vel de promovendo religioso professo, de quo in can. 964, n. 4.

[24] Badii, *Institutiones Iuris Canonici* (2 vols., Vol. I, 3. ed., Florentiae, 1921), I, 282; Bastien, *Directoire Canonique* (3. ed.), p. 345; Goyeneche, "Consultationes," *CpR*, VIII (1927), 113-115; idem, *Iuris Canonici Summa Principia, Libri II, Pars II, De Religiosis, Libri II, Pars III, De Laicis* (Roma: Commentarium pro Religiosis, 1938), p. 236 (hereafter referred to as *Summa Principia*); Oesterle, "Weihekandidaten aus einer Diözesan-Priestergenossenschaft," *ThPrQs*, LXXXV (1932), 564, 566; Schaaf, "Episcopus Proprius Ordinationis Religiosorum," *ER*, XC (1934), 505; Moeder, *Proper Bishop*, pp. 111-112; Berutti, *Institutiones Iuris Canonici* (6 vols. in 7, Vol. II, Pars I, *De Personis et de Clericis in Genere*, Taurini-Romae: Marietti, 1943; Vol. III, *De Religiosis*, Taurini-Romae: Marietti, 1936), III, 370; Stanton, *De Societatibus*, p. 137; Claeys Bouuaert-Simenon, *Manuale Juris Canonici ad Usum Seminariorum* (3 vols., Vol. I, *Introductio, Libri I et II Codicis*, 5. ed., Gandae et Leodii: in Seminariis Gandavensi et Leodiensi, 1939), I, 433 (hereafter referred to as *Manuale*); Crnica, *Commentarium Theoretico-Practicum Codicis Iuris Canonici* (2 vols., Vol. I, *Normae Generales et De Personis*, Sibenik: Typis Typographiae "Kačić,"

perhaps of the brevity with which they treat this matter, do not explicitly mention canons 955 or 956, nor do they mention the requirement of domicile for the obtaining of a proper bishop. But they do assert that the proper bishop for the ordination of members of Societies is the local ordinary, and that without an indult the superiors of Societies are incompetent to issue dimissorial letters.[25] Not one of the other authors consulted contradicts this doctrine, but rather they remain silent on the matter.[26] Finally, on July 24, 1947,

1940), I, 465; Romani, *Institutiones Juris Canonici* (2 vols., Vol. I, *Ius Constitutionale,* Romae: Schola Typographica "Pio X," 1941), I, 411; McBride, *Incardination,* pp. 343-344; Stanghetti, *Prassi,* p. 42; Coronata, *De Sacramentis,* II, 27; Beste, Introductio, p. 461; Cocchi, *Commentarium in Codicem Iuris Canonici ad Usum Scholarum* (8 vols., Vol. IV, *Liber II, De Personis, Pars II, De Religiosis-Pars III, De Laicis,* 4. ed., Augustae Taurinorum: Marietti, 1946), IV, 242 (hereafter referred to as *Commentarium*); Paventi, *De Iuranmento,* p. 96; Brys, *Juris Canonici Compenduim* (2 vols., olim. a De Brabandère et Van Coillie et De Meester editum, Vol. I, 10 ed., 2. ed. post Codicem, Brugis: Desclée et Brouwer et Sii, 1947), I, 597; Schaefer, *De Religiosis ad Normam Codicis Iuris Canonici* (4. ed., Roma: Editrice "Apostolato Cattolico," 1947), pp. 993-994 (hereafter referred to as *De Religiosis*); Cappello, *De Sacramentis,* IV, 211; Ristuccia, *Societies,* pp. 199-200; Rothoff, *Sociétés,* p. 166; Vermeersch-Creusen, *Epitome,* I, 631; Gil, "Studium," *CpRM,* XXVIII (1949), 18-29, cf. p. 20; De Carlo, *Jus Religiosorum* (Parisiis-Tornaci-Romae: Desclée, 1950), p. 512; Abbo-Hannan, *The Sacred Canons* (2 vols., St. Louis and London: Herder, 1952), I, 685.

[25] Sipos, *Enchiridion Iuris Canonici* (Pécs: Haladá R. T., 1926), p. 398; Naz, *Traité de droit canonique* (4 vols., Vol. I, *Livres I et II, Introduction, Règles générales, des Personnes,* Paris: Letouzey et Ané, 1946), I, 713; Ramstein, *A Manual of Canon Law* (Hoboken: Terminal Printing and Publishing Co., 1948), p. 394; Fanfani, *De Iure Religiosorum ad Normam Codicis Iuris Canonici* (3. ed., Rovigo: Istituto Padano di Arti Grafiche, 1949), p. 714 (hereafter referred to as *De Iure Religiosorum*).

[26] Cance, *Le Code de Droit Canonique* (3 vols., Vol. II, 7. ed., Paris: J. Gabalda et Fils, Éditeurs, 1946), II, 168; Wernz-Vidal, *Ius Canonicum,* III, 499; Gester a Zeil, *Ius Religiosorum in Compendium Redactum* (Taurini: Marietti, 1935), p. 312; Blat, *Commentarium Textus Codicis Iuris Canonici,* Tom. II, Vol. II, 420; Regatillo, *Institutiones,* I, 438; Woywod, *Commentary,* I, 338; Bouscaren-Ellis, *Canon Law,* p. 328.

the Pontifical Commission for the Authentic Interpretation of the Code of Canon Law, in a letter directed to the Sacred Congregation of Extraordinary Ecclesiastical Affairs and bearing the approval of Pope Pius XII, stated that the right to grant dimissorial letters for the ordination of members of Societies pertained to the local ordinary.[27]

All the authors are today in agreement on the two principles stated above. There are three further questions regarding the minister of Orders in Societies, however, on which the authors are at present in disagreement. These three questions concern the concepts of the proper bishop, of incardination, and of the oath required by canon 956 of those who have a domicile not identical with the place of origin. In regard to these three questions, it should be noted at the outset that the majority of the authors pass over these problems in silence. The following conflicting opinions are those of the few authors who express their opinions on these questions.

The first point of disagreement regards the determination of which local ordinary is the proper bishop for the ordination of members of Societies. The disagreement is rooted in disagreement on a more fundamental question, namely, that of the domicile of members of Societies. As seen above,[28] all the authors are agreed that the proper bishop for the ordination of members of Societies is the bishop of the place where the members have a domicile. But since the authors disagree as to where the members of Societies have a domicile, they also disagree in their efforts to determine which of several bishops is the proper bishop for the ordination of members of Societies. Six authors hold that members of Societies retain the domicile they had in the world before their entry into their Societies, and that consequently the bishop of that place is their proper bishop for promotion to Orders.[29] In essen-

[27] *CpRM*, XXVIII (1949), 16-18.

[28] *Supra*, pp. 66-69.

[29] Schaaf, "Episcopus Proprius Ordinationis Religiosorum," *ER*,

tial agreement with these six authors are two others who simply deny that the proper bishop is the bishop of the place in which is located the house to which the ordinands are attached.[30] One author denies that *any* bishop is competent to ordain members of Societies according to a common law, and that there is a *lacuna* in the law in this regard.[31] One author claims that the proper bishop for those who are only temporarily incorporated is the bishop of the place from which they came, and that the proper bishop for those who are perpetually incorporated is the bishop of the place in which is located the house to which they are attached.[32] Finally, three authors claim that the proper bishop is the bishop of the place in which is located the house to which the ordinands are attached.[33]

The second point of disagreement regards the matter of incardination. Eight authors hold that clerical members of Societies must be incardinated in some diocese.[34] Four authors deny that all clerical members of Societies must be incardinated in some diocese.[35]

XC (1934), 504-509; Stanton, *De Societatibus*, p. 138; McBride, *Incardination*, p. 344; Paventi, *De Iuramento*, pp. 100-101; Ristuccia, *Societies*, p. 200; Gil, Studium," *CpRM*, XXVIII (1949), 20-21.

[30] Oesterle, "Weihekandidaten aus einer Diözesan-Priestergenossenschaft," *ThPrQs*, LXXXV (1932), 566-569; Moeder, *Proper Bishop*, pp. 112-113.

[31] Stanghetti, *Prassi*, p. 38.

[32] Rothoff, *Sociétés*, pp. 166-169.

[33] Goyeneche, "Consultationes," *CpR*, I (1920), 144-145, 177-178, cf. pp. 177-178; idem, "Consultationes," *CpR*, VIII (1927), 113-114; Abbo-Hannan, *The Sacred Canons*, II, 88; Hannan, "The Ordination of Quasi-Religious," *The Jurist*, XII (1952), 443-456, cf. pp. 450-451.

[34] Moeder, *Proper Bishop*, pp. 112-114; Stanton, *De Societatibus*, p. 139; Beste, *Introductio*, p. 461; Ramstein, *A Manual of Canon Law*, p. 394; Ristuccia, *Societies*, p. 200; Rothoff, *Sociétés*, pp. 172-173; Gil, "Studium," *CpRM*, XXVIII (1949), 21-22; De Naurois, "Le 'Propre Évêque' pour l'ordination dans le clergé séculier," *BLE*, LI (1950), 15.

[35] McBride, *Incardination*, p. 345; Stanghetti, *Prassi*, pp. 38-39; Abbo-Hannan, *The Sacred Canons*, II, 88; Hannan, "The Ordination of Quasi-Religious," *The Jurist*, XII (1952), 448-454.

The third point of disagreement regards the oath required by canon 956 of those who have a domicile distinct from their place or origin. Eight authors contend that members of Societies are held to this oath in the same way as other secular clerics.[36] Three authors hold that members of Societies are excused from this oath.[37]

SECTION 2. THE DOMICILE OF MEMBERS OF SOCIETIES

It has been seen that in virtue of canon 678 members of Societies are bound by the laws governing the proper bishop for the ordination of secular clerics as contained in canons 955 and 956. According to canon 956, the fundamental requirement for obtaining a proper bishop for ordination is the requirement of domicile. It seems proper, therefore, to preface any treatment of the proper bishop for the ordination of members of Societies with a treatment of the question of the domicile of members of Societies.

It is forbidden to promote to Orders members of Societies during the period of their probation.[38] Since the purpose of examining the question of the domicile of members of Societies is to determine which bishop is the proper bishop for ordination, the discussion of domicile in this section will be limited to a discussion of the domicile of members of Societies who have completed their period of probation.

In order properly to understand the question of the domicile of members of Societies, it is necessary first to

[36] Bastien, *Directoire Canonique* (3. ed.), p. 345; Goyeneche, "Consultationes," *CpR*, VIII (1927), 113-114; Schaaf, "Episcopus Proprius Ordinationis Religiosorum," *ER*, XC (1934), 505-507; Stanton, *De Societatibus*, pp. 137-138; Vermeersch-Creusen, *Epitome*, I, 631; Rothoff, *Sociétés*, pp. 170-172; Gil, "Studium," *CpRM*, XXVIII (1949), 21; De Carlo, *Jus Religiosorum*, p. 512.

[37] McBride, *Incardination*, p. 345; Ristuccia, *Societies*, p. 201; Hannan, "The Ordination of Quasi-Religious," *The Jurist*, XII (1952), 448-449.

[38] S. C. de Rel., instr. "*Quantum Religiones*," 1 dec. 1931, n. 14—*AAS*, XXIV (1932), 74-81, cf. pp. 79-80; cf. Waters, *Probation in Societies*, p. 104.

examine the question of the domicile of religious. The law distinguishes two kinds of domicile, namely, voluntary or free[39] and necessary or legal.[40] This distinction forms a convenient basis for a division of the treatment of the question of the domicile of religious.

It is the certain and unanimous teaching of canonists that religious are completely incapable of possessing a domicile which is voluntary or free.[41] The fundamental reason for this is that in virtue of religious profession religious lose their *"velle et nolle,"*[42] or, more correctly, their own will in matters such as this is deprived of juridical efficacy.[43] This incapacity is absolute. That is to say, religious are incapable of possessing a voluntary domicile even though they might claim that its acquisition is voluntary in the sense that they have voluntarily subjected themselves to the will of their superior. Likewise they cannot acquire a voluntary domicile by way of a ten years' residence, for such a duration of residence is not a matter of their own volition. This doctrine applies to all cases, whether it be a question of diocesan domicile or parochial domicile; whether it be a question of the temporarily professed or of the perpetually professed; whether it be a question of religious of pontifical approval or religious of diocesan approval; or whether it be a question of religious who are in their majority or religious who are in their minority.[44]

The reason for the incapacity of religious to possess a voluntary domicile is the fact that they have subjected themselves by religious profession to the dominative power of their superiors.[45] Now, although members of Societies

[39] Canon 92, § 1.

[40] Canon 93, § 1.

[41] Michiels, *Principia Generalis de Personis in Ecclesia* (Lublin, Polonia: Universitas Catholica-Brasschaat, Belgium: De Bievre, 1932), p. 145 (hereafter referred to as *Principia*).

[42] C. 27, *de electione et electi potestate*, I, 6, in VI°.

[43] Michiels, *Principia*, p. 145.

[44] Michiels, *Principia*, pp. 145-146; Schaefer, *De Religiosis*, p. 985.

[45] Michiels, *Principia*, pp. 146; Schaefer, *De Religiosis*, p. 985;

do not make a religious profession, nevertheless, at the time of their incorporation in their respective Societies at the end of the period of their probation, they make an act of submission to their respective superiors by the tradition of their persons, and thus they become subject to the dominative power of their superiors in essentially the same way in which religious become subject to the dominative power of their superiors. It makes no difference whether this tradition of their persons be made by private vow, by oath, by promise, or by tacit agreement.[46] It follows, therefore, that just as religious are incapable of possessing a voluntary domicile, so, too, members of Societies are incapable of possessing a voluntary domicile. This conclusion is confirmed by the teaching of many canonists.[47] If, therefore, members of Societies can have any domicile, it must be a domicile which is necessary or legal.

From the teaching of canonists on the question of the domicile of religious, the following facts are discovered with reference to necessary or legal domicile. Before the Code, religious were considered to have a necessary domicile in the diocese in which was located the house to which they were attached. Pope Benedict XIV, in the Constitution *Impositi Nobis* of February 27, 1747, while discussing the ordination of regulars, made explicit reference

Coronata, *Institutiones*, I, 146; Vermeersch-Creusen, *Epitome*, I, 194; Wernz-Vidal, *Ius Canonicum*, II, p. 16, nota 12.

[46] Canon 675 collated with canon 501, § 1: cf. Stanton, *De Societatibus*, pp. 111-112; Ristuccia, *Societies*, pp. 113-114; Rothoff, *Sociétés*, pp. 116-117; Schaefer, *De Religiosis*, pp. 990-991; Wernz-Vidal, *Ius Canonicum*, III, pp. 498-499, nota (4); Coronata, *Institutiones*, I, p. 646, nota 5; Vermeersch-Creusen, *Epitome*, I, 629; Cappello, *Summa*, II, 99; Goyeneche, "Consultationes," *CpR*, I (1920), 177-178; Hannan, "The Ordination of Quasi-Religious," *The Jurist*, XII (1952), 451-452.

[47] Coronata, *Institutiones*, I, 146-147; Vermeersch-Creusen, *Epitome*, I, 194-195; Cappello, *Summa*, II, 160; Berutti, *Institutiones Iuris Canonici*, Vol. II, Pars I, 15; Abbo-Hannan, *The Sacred Canons*, II, 88; Goyeneche, "Consultationes," *CpR*, I (1920), 178; Hannan, "The Ordination of Quasi-Religious," *The Jurist*, XII (1952), 451.

to the domicile of religious as being the diocese or the place in which the religious staped.[48] That religious obtained a true and necessary domicile in the houses of which they were members was the teaching of the great canonists of the seventeenth and eighteenth centuries, e.g., Passerini (1595-1677),[49] Pirhing (1606-1679),[50] Schmalzgrueber (1663-1735),[51] and Petra (1662-1747).[52] At the time immediately prior to the Code, this was still the common teaching, as is evident from the works of two authors who at that time treated *ex professo* the question of the domicile of religious, namely, Vermeersch (1886-1936)[53] and d'Angelo (1885-1930).[54]

Today, the authors are almost unanimous is asserting that, in consequence of their subjection to the dominative power of their superiors, religious have a necessary domicile in the diocese in which is located the house to which they are attached.[55]

[48] N. 2: ".... eorum Domicilii, nimirum illius Dioecesis, ac Loci, in quo ipsi Ordinandi commorantur."—*Fontes,* n. 376.

N. 12: "Quod si aliquis Antistes Regularem virum, in sua Dioecesi proprium domicilium non habentem,... sine adiuncta praefata..., ad Ordines promovere praesumpserit:..."—*Fontes,* n. 376.

[49] *De Hominum Statibus et Officiis* (3 tomi, Lucae, 1732), Q. 189, art. 10, n. 817.

[50] Lib. II, tit. II, n. 17.

[51] Lib. II, tit. II, n. 14.

[52] *Commentaria ad Constitutiones Apostolicas* (5 tomi, Venetiis, 1729), Urbanus II, const. unica *Cum Universi,* sectio II, nn. 11-13.

[53] "De Domicilio Regularium," *De Religiosis et Missionariis Supplementum et Monumenta Periodica (Periodica de Re Morali, Canonica, Liturgica* [from 1905 to 1919, *De Religiosis et Missionariis Supplementum et Monumenta Periodica;* from 1921 to 1927, *Periodica de Re Canonica et Morali utilia praesertim Religiosis et Missionariis*], Brugis et Romae, 1905-1936; Romae, 1937-), Vol. IV, 2. ed., 1913), 189-195 (hereafter referred to as *Periodica*).

[54] *Del domicilio ecclesiastico e dei suoi effetti* (Giarre, 1916), p. 37.

[55] Maroto, *Institutiones Iuris Canonici* (2 vols., Vol. I, 3. ed., Romae: Apud Commentarium pro Religiosis, 1921), I, p. 474, nota (2); Voltas, "De Domicilio quoad Ordinationem Religiosorum," *CpR,* II (1921), 299-307; Vermeersch, "De Domicilio Religiosorum," *Periodica,* IX (1921), (7)-(8); idem, "De ordinatione religiosorum qui

Now, since the underlying reason why religious are said to possess a necessary domicile is their subjection to the dominative power of their superiors, and since members of Societies are subject to the dominative power of their superiors in the same way as religious,[56] it follows that members of Societies also have a necessary domicile in the place in which is located the house to which they are attached. This conclusion is supported by the explicit teaching of the following authors: Goyeneche,[57] Prümmer (1866-1931),[58] Coronata,[59] Berutti,[60] Cappello,[61] Vermeersch-Creusen,[62] Abbo-Hannan,[63] and Hannan.[64]

'iure saecularium' reguntur," *Periodica,* IX, (1921), (16)-(18); Toso, *Ad Codicem Juris Canonici... Commentaria Minora* (2 libri in 5 toms., Liber II, *De Personis,* Tom. I, Taurini-Romae, 1922; Tom. IV, Romae, 1927), Liber II, Tom. I, 21; Sägmüller, *Lehrbuch des katholischen Kirchenrechts* (4. ed., 1 Band in 4 Teile, Freiburg im Breisgau, Teil I, 1925; Teil II, 1926; Teil III, 1930; Teil IV, 1934), p. 292 (in Teil III); Sipos, *Enchiridion Iuris Canonici,* p. 78; Vindex, "Domicilium et quasi-Domicilium Eorumque Effectus in Codice Juris Canonici," *Jus Pontificium* (Romae, 1921-1940), VI, (1926), 34-55, 112-126, 154-158, cf. p. 47 (hereafter referred to as *JP*); Prümmer, *Manuale Iuris Canonici* (4. et 5. ed., Friburgi Brisgoviae, 1927), pp. 73-74; Coronata, *Institutiones,* I, 146-147; idem, *De Sacramentis,* II, 35; Claeys Bouuaert-Simenon, *Manuale,* I, 145; Chelodi, *Ius Canonicum de Personis* (3. ed. curavit Pius Ciprotti, Vicenza: Società Anonima Tipografica-Trento: Libreria Moderna Editrice, 1942), p. 155, nota 3; Wernz-Vidal, *Ius Canonicum,* II, p. 16, nota 12; Berutti, *Institutiones Iuris Canonici,* Vol. II, Pars I, 15; Cappello, *Summa,* II, 160; Beste, *Introductio,* p. 93; Brys, *Juris Canonici Compendium,* I, 192; Ramstein, *A Manual of Canon Law,* p. 128; Regatillo, *Institutiones,* I, 129; Woywod, *Commentary,* I, 576; Jombart, *Manuel de Droit Canon* (Paris: Beauchesne et ses fils, 1949), p. 66; Vermeersch-Creusen, *Epitome,* I, 194-195; Bouscaren-Ellis, *Canon Law,* p. 81.

[56] Cf. *supra,* pp.72-73. [57] "Consultationes," *CpR,* I (1920), 178.

[58] *Manuale Iuris Canonici,* pp. 73-74.

[59] *Institutiones,* I, 146-147.

[60] *Institutiones Iuris Canonici,* Vol. II, Pars I, 15.

[61] *Summa,* II, 160. [62] *Epitome,* I, 194-195.

[63] *The Sacred Canons,* II, 88.

[64] "The Ordination of Quasi-Religious," *The Jurist,* XII (1952), 451-452.

One might take issue with the validity of the conclusion reached in the preceding paragraph by denying one of the premises on which it rests, that is, by denying that religious have a necessary domicile in the place in which is located the house to which they are attached. Actually, that religious have such a necessary domicile is denied by Oesterle,[65] Kinane,[66] Costello,[67] and Michiels.[68] Schaefer († 1948), after stating the common opinion, conceded that the opposite opinion was not without merit, but did not indicate which doctrine he himself favored.[69]

Michiels recapitulates the arguments employed by Oesterle, Kinane and Costello in defense of their position.[70] They are three in number. First, a legal or necessary domicile, since it is founded on a fiction of law, can be admitted only in the cases expressely designated by the law itself. But nowhere in the Code is it stated that religious have a legal or necessary domicile properly so-called. Secondly, religious have no need of a domicile, because the juridic effects that accrue to others in virtue of prescripts of the law in which domicile is the determining factor, accrue to religious in virtue of prescripts of the law which avoid the use of the word "domicile." In these latter prescripts of law, the following expressions are used: *"in loco Domus suae," "in loco ubi Domus sita est," "in loco, in quo sita est Domus Religiosa ad cuius familiam Religiosus pertinet."*[71] Thirdly, a domicile requires stability in one place; but, with the exception of members of monastic orders, re-

[65] "De domicilio Religiosorum," *CpR,* V (1924), 167-168.

[66] "Necessary Domicile," *IER,* 5 series, XXVII (1926), 647-648.

[67] *Domicile and Quasi-Domicile,* The Catholic University of America Canon Law Studies, n. 60 (Washington, D.C., 1930), pp. 170-173.

[68] *Principia,* pp. 149-150.

[69] Schaefer expressed himself thus: *"Sunt auctores, qui merito opinantur . . ."—De Religiosis,* pp. 985-986.

[70] *Principia,* p. 149.

[71] Cf., e.g., canons 850 and 938, § 2, collated with canon 514, § 1; canon 956 collated with canon 965; canons 1216 ff. collated with canon 1221, § 1; and canon 1561 collated with canon 1563.

ligious do not generally enjoy such a stability.

The first objection rests on the assertion that a legal or necessary domicile is founded on a fiction of law. The classical definition of a fiction of law is that given by Alciatus: *Fictio est legis adversus veritatem in re posibili ex justa causa dispositio.*[72] This definition was adopted by Reiffenstuel (1642-1703), who, in a full treatment of the question of fiction of law laid the groundwork for the doctrinal treatment of the subject by subsequent canonists.[73] Following the doctrine of Reiffenstuel, canonists of the present day, in discussing the matter of fiction of law, are agreed on the following points. A fiction of law is *always* contrary to fact. It is the considering as true something which is *certainly* false. Secondly, the motive behind the institution of a fiction of law is the desire that natural equity be achieved. Thus, for example, canon 422, § 2, states that a canon who is a jubilarian is considered as present with regard to the *distributiones . . . inter praesentes,* even though in truth he be absent; and canon 1116 states that a child who is in reality illegitimate, because conceived out of lawful wedlock, is considered legitimated through the subsequent marriage of its parents, provided that they were free to marry at the time of conception, pregnancy or birth.[74] With this understanding of fiction of law in mind, one finds it difficult to see how Oesterle, Kinane, Costello and Michiels says that legal or necessary domicile is founded on a fiction of law. For canon 93, which

[72] *Parergon Iuris,* Liber VI, Caput I, in *D. Andreae Alciati Mediolanensis Iurecos. Opera Omnia* (4 tomi, Basileae, 1582), Tomus IV, cols. 279-582, cf. col. 435.

[73] *Ius Canonicum Universum* (5 vols. in 7, Parisiis, 1864-1870), Lib. I, tit. II, nn. 176-196 (hereafter cited as Reiffenstuel).

[74] Maroto, *Institutiones Iuris Canonici,* I, 225-227; Wernz-Vidal, *Ius Canonicum,* I, 214-215; Coronata, *Institutiones,* I, 33-34; Cicognani-Staffa, *Commentarium ad Librum Primum Codicis Iuris Canonici* (2 vols., Vol. I, Romae: Ex Officina Typographica Romana "Buona Stampa," 1939), I, 142-143; Chelodi, *Ius Canonicum de Personis,* p. 116; Regatillo, *Institutiones,* I, 71; Vermeersch-Creusen, *Epitome,* I, 103; Michiels, *Normae Generales,* I, 435-437.

establishes certain necessary domiciles, states that a wife necessarily retains the domicile of her husband, as long as she is not lawfully separated from him; an insane person necessarily retains the domicile of his curator; and a minor necessarily retains the domicile of the person to whose power he is subject. Now, if these necessary domiciles are founded on a fiction of law, if they are founded on the consideration of something as true which is certainly false, what is that fiction? what is that consideration? Is it considering a person to be living where he is not living? Hardly. For this would be very exceptional, since most wives live with their husbands, most insane people live with their curators, and most minors live with the persons to whom they are subject. And even those wives, insane people and minors who live away from their husbands, curators and parents or guardians are usually considered as "living away from home." Would the fiction, then, perhaps consider that the wives, the insane and the minors have placed the acts required for the obtaining of a domicile as described in canon 92, § 1, when in fact they have not placed these acts? Hardly. For these acts are required, according to the unanimous teaching of canonists, for the acquisition of a *voluntary* domicile, whereas here the question is that of a necessary domicile. Finally, the constitution of necessary domiciles in canon 93, § 1, is not an exceptional measure taken by the lawmaker to guarantee that the wives, the insane and the minors be treated equitably in instances in which they would not otherwise be so treated. It seems proper to conclude, therefore, that although it is true that a fiction of law can be admitted only in the cases expressly stated in the law itself, nevertheless, since a necessary domicile does not seem to be founded on a fiction of law, the fact that a necessary domicile is not expressly granted to religious in the Code does not necessarily militate against the possession of a necessary domicile by religious.

The second objection is that religious have no need of a domicile, since the juridic effects that accrue to others in virtue of prescripts of the law in which domicile is the determining factor accrue to religious in virtue of prescripts of the law which avoid the use of the word "domicile." Schaefer summed up this argument as follows:

> Hoc sequitur etiam ex variis Codicis Iuris Canonici textibus. Per speciale iuris statutum Religioso professo in loco Domus suae iidem agnoscuntur iuridici effectus, qui aliis in loco domicilii (quasi-domicilii) competunt.
>
> Sic quoad receptionem Viatici Eucharistici et Extremae Unctionis (in cano 514, § 1, coll. can. 850 et 938, § 2; quoad ministrum sacrae ordinationis (in can. 905 [certainly 965 is intended] coll. can. 956); quoad sepulturam ecclesiasticam (in can. 1221, § 1, coll. can. 1216 ss.); quoad forum (in can. 1563 coll. can. 1561).
>
> Legislator loco formulae: in loco domicilii (quasi-domicilii) semper adhibet in Codice Iuris Canonici alteram formulam: in loco Domus suae; in loco ubi Domus sita est; in loco, in quo sita est Domus religiosa ad cuius familiam Religiosus pertinent.[75]

In this argument there is question of the laws regulating the reception of Holy Viaticum, the reception of Extreme Unction, the reception of Holy Orders, the concession of ecclesiastical burial, and the granted use of the ecclesiastical forum in reference to religious and "others" (*"aliis"*) respectively. In the laws regulating the reception of Holy Viaticum and Extreme Unction by "others," as well as in the laws regulating the burial of "others," however, the word domicile is not even mentioned, and the fact of domicile plays only a partial role. In these instances (canons 850; 938, § 2; 1216 ff.), reference is made respectively to one's *"parochus,"* the *"parochus loci, in quo degit infirmus,"* and the *"ecclesia propriae defuncti paroeciae."* In the first place, reference is made to one's *"parochus."* Now, it is clear from canon 94, § 2, that even a *vagus,* who by definition has neither a domicile nor a quasi-domicile, has his own *"parochus."* With regard to the *"parochus loci,*

[75] *De Religiosis,* pp. 985-986.

in quo degit infirmus," this pastor could very easily be the pastor of a place where a person holding a domicile or a quasi-domicile elsewhere happens to be residing as a *peregrinus* with neither a domicile nor a quasi-domicile in the place of temporary abode. Finally, with regard to the *"ecclesia propriae defuncti paroeciae,"* again it may be stated that, in virtue of canon 94, § 2, a *vagus* has his own pastor, and, consequently, his own parish. In these three instances, therefore, domicile (and even quasi-domicile) is not only not mentioned, but also plays only a partial role. The reference to the law regulating the ecclesiastical forum of "others" is a reference to canon 1561, and this canon does mention domicile and quasi-domicile. But the canons immediately following canon 1561 institute many other grounds in virtue of which one can obtain an ecclesiastical forum. Again domicile plays only a partial role.[76] Furthermore, the non-use of the word "domicile" by the lawmaker when providing for the spiritual ministrations to be exercised in behalf of religious argues only to the fact that the lawmaker desires that these ministrations be attended to in the religious house, and does not argue to a lack of domicile on the part of religious. Finally, the one remaining reference made in the argument against religious' possessing a domicile is a reference to canon 956, which does demand that "others" have nothing less than a true domicile in order to obtain a proper bishop for ordination. But this very same canon, in conjunction with canon 964, n. 4, makes the very same demand of non-exempt religious. And this is the strongest proof there is that religious possess domiciles.

The third objection is that the possession of a domicile requires stability in one place; but, with the exception of members of monastic Orders, religious do not generally enjoy such a stability. In answer to this objection, it must first be pointed out that the only kind of domicile claimed for religious is a necessary or legal domicile. The basis for

[76] Cf. canons 1562, 1563, 1564, 1565, 1566.

the objection, therefore, must be understood in this sense: a necessary or legal domicile requires stability in one place. The heart of the objection, therefore, lies in the contention that a religious usually enjoys less stability in one place than is enjoyed by those who enjoy a necessary or legal domicile according to the norm of canon 93, § 1. But is this true? Is it true that a religious enjoys less stability in the house to which he is attached than a wife or an insane person or a minor enjoys in the place where they have a necessary domicile? It seems that he surely enjoys no less stability. For although a religious may remain in one house only one year, on the other hand he may remain in one house for twenty years, or even all his life. In the same way, a wife, an insane person and a minor may retain their necessary domiciles for one year, or for twenty years, or for life. It may be objected that a religious is always in a precarious position with regard to his stability in one place, for even if he were led to believe that he would not be moved for three or six years, still he would have no guarantee that he would not be moved after one day. But in answer it may be said that a wife, an insane person or a minor is always in the same position.

From these considerations it seems clear that the objections of Oesterle, Kinane, Costello and Michiels are not strong enough to outweigh the reasoning and the authority on the side of the more common opinion, by which it is claimed that religious have a necessary domicile in the place in which is located the house to which they are attached.

SECTION 3. THE PROPER BISHOP FOR THE PROMOTION OF MEMBERS OF SOCIETIES TO FIRST TONSURE

It is certain that in virtue of canon 678 members of Societies are governed, in matters pertaining to ordination, by the law regulating the ordination of secular clerics.[77] Now, it is a cardinal principle of the law governing the

[77] Cf. *supra*, pp. 66-69.

ordination of secular clerics that the proper bishop for the promotion of laymen to First Tonsure is the bishop of the place where the laymen have a domicile, while the proper bishop for the promotion of a secular cleric to higher Orders is the bishop of the diocese in which the secular cleric is incardinated.[78] It seems to be a reasonable method of procedure, therefore, in examining the question of the proper bishop for the ordination of members of Societies, to find out first of all who is their proper bishop for promotion to First Tonsure, then to find out if they are incardinated by First Tonsure into any diocese, and finally to find out who is their proper bishop for promotion to higher Orders. The present section is devoted to an attempt to find out who is the proper bishop for the promotion of members of Societies to First Tonsure.

It is certain that in virtue of canon 678 the proper bishop for the promotion of members of Societies to First Tonsure is regulated by the prescripts of canon 956.[79] This canon states that the proper bishop for the ordination of secular clerics is the bishop of the diocese in which the ordinand has either a domicile together with his place of origin, or a domicile apart from his place of origin. There is no problem about the place of origin, which is determined by the prescript of canon 90. The question of who must, and who need not, take the oath required by canon 956 when the place of origin does not coincide with the domicile will be discussed in the next section. For the present, in order to determine one's proper bishop, it will suffice to consider domicile, which is the common element in all cases.

It seems certain, as seen in the previous section,[80] that members of Societies, after their incorporation in their institutes, have a necessary domicile in the diocese in which is located the house to which they are attached.

[78] Cf. *supra*, pp. 62-66.
[79] Cf. *supra*, pp. 66-69.
[80] Cf. *supra*, pp. 73-75.

Since the proper bishop for the promotion of members of Societies to First Tonsure is the bishop of the place in which the members have a domicile, and since the members of Societies have a necessary domicile in the place in which is located the house to which they are attached, it follows that the proper bishop for the promotion of members of Societies to First Tonsure is the bishop of the place in which is located the house to which they are attached.

This conclusion is reasonable, as can be seen from a brief consideration of the notion of jurisdiction. The promotion of a man to Orders, whether the episcopal ordinary do this immediately by ordaining on his own authority, or mediately by authoritatively issuing dimissorial letters, can be lawfully achieved only by a person who has jurisdiction over the ordinand in the external forum.[81] That is the fundamental reason why major superiors in Societies cannot, by the common law, grant dimissorial letters to their subjects; for Societies, by the common law, are not exempt, and major superiors in Societies do not, by the common law, have jurisdiction over their subjects in the external forum.[82] If a major superior of a non-exempt Society should be empowered by way of apostolic indult to grant dimissorial letters for the ordination of his subjects, the jurisdiction necessary for such a grant is considered to be delegated through the apostolic indult.[83] Ordinary jurisdiction over Societies in the external forum, however, is possessed by the local bishops in whose dioceses the houses of such Societies are located. Each bishop, by the common law, has jurisdiction over the houses located within his diocese, and consequently has jurisdiction over the members attached to these houses. Since the issuing of a call for the reception of Orders connotes the possession of public jurisdiction, it seems natural to expect to find

[81] Wernz-Vidal, *Ius Canonicum,* Tom. IV, Vol. I, 236-238; Coronata, *De Sacramentis,* II, 41; Moeder, *Proper Bishop,* p. 95.

[82] Cf. *supra,* p. 62.

[83] Voltas, "De Domicilio Ordinationem Religiosorum," *CpR,* II (1921), 301.

the right to issue that call invested in the bishop, who indeed possesses such jurisdiction.

The opinion whereby it is claimed that the proper bishop for the ordination of members of Societies is the bishop of the place in which is located the house to which they are attached is, however, the less common opinion. It is the opinion of Goyeneche, of Abbo-Hannan, and, with qualifications, of Rothoff.

In the year 1927, the Congregation of the Most Precious Blood, a non-exempt Society, consulted Goyeneche about the problem. The Society possessed no indult whereby the superiors were empowered to grant dimissorial letters for the ordination of their subjects. The scholastics of the Society were studying their Theology while stationed in the Seminary of Saint Charles, which was the Motherhouse of the Society and which was located in the Archdiocese of Cincinnati. The Precious Blood Fathers asked Goyeneche whether their scholastics in the Seminary of Saint Charles obtained a domicile in the Archdiocese of Cincinnati, and whether the proper bishop for their promotion to Orders would, as a consequence, be the Archbishop of Cincinnati. Goyeneche answered that since the proper bishop of religious—to whom must be equivalated members of Societies like the Congregation of the Most Precious Blood[84]—is, in virtue of canon 965,[85] the bishop of the place in which is located the house to which the religious are attached, so the proper bishop for the ordination of the scholastics of the Congregation of the Most Precious Blood is the Archbishop of Cincinnati, in whose Archdiocese is located the Seminary of Saint Charles, in which the scholastics are stationed.[86] Seven years previous to this answer, Goyeneche,

[84] This equivalation must be understood only with regard to the matter about which Goyeneche was consulted, vis., domicile as a determining factor of the proper bishop for ordination.

[85] Episcopus ad quem Superior religiosus litteras dimissorias mittere debet, est Episcopus dioecesis, in qua sita est domus religiosa, ad cuius familiam pertinet ordinandus.

[86] "Consultationes," *CpR*, VIII (1927), 113-115.

in answer to a question about the domicile of members of Societies, explained the reason for equivalating members of Societies to religious in this matter. The reason given was that members of Societies, just like religious, are subject to the dominative power of their superiors; and since religious, in virtue of the fact that they are subject to the dominative power of their superiors, possess a necessary domicile in the place in which is located the house to which they are attached, so, too, do members of Societies possess the same kind of a necessary domicile.[87]

Abbo-Hannan also state that the proper bishop for the ordination of members of Societies is determined by the necessary domicile which the members possess in the place in which is located the house to which they are assigned.[88]

Rothoff († 1942) agreed with this opinion to the extent of including simply those members who are perpetually affiliated with their Society.[89] His opinion will be discussed more in detail below.[90]

As seen above,[91] most of the canonists do not concern themselves with the problem of the proper bishop for the ordination of members of Societies further than to indicate that the proper bishop is to be determined, according to canons 678 and 956, by the domicile of the members, but they withhold the specific indication of where that domicile might be. Of those authors who attempt to determine specifically which bishop is the proper bishop, the majority deny that it is the bishop of the place in which is located the house to which the members are attached. The opinion of these authors must, at the present time, be labeled as the more common one. The opinion of Goyeneche and of Abbo Hannan is, at present, the less common one. The latter opinion, however, seems to the present writer to offer the true interpretation of the law. The positive rea-

[87] "Consultationes," *CpR*, I (1920), 177-178.

[88] *The Sacred Canons*, II, 88.

[89] *Sociétés*, pp. 166-167, 168.

[90] Cf. pp. 94-96.

[91] Cf. pp. 66-70.

sons for this belief have been stated above in the present section: the argument from the common teaching on the domicile of members of Societies; the argument from the notion of jurisdiction, and the authority of the canonists who have been cited thus far. The writer will now attempt to show the invalidity of the arguments of those who deny that the proper bishop is the bishop of the place where the house is located.

The majority of the authors who have written on the problem at hand claim that the proper bishop for the ordination of members of Societies is the bishop of the place where they had their domiciles before their entrance into the Societies. And the argument upon which most of these authors base their contention is an argument which seems to originate with Schaaf (1883-1946). In the year 1934, Schaaf expressed this argument in the following terms:

> Even those who have bound themselves perpetually to their society by the final oath or promise do not lose the domicile they had in the world; for canon 585 is not among those canons referring to religious which are extended to them; and this is all the more significant because of the fact that while the Code was in preparation its extension to them was repeatedly requested but denied.
>
> If then members of such societies never lose the proper diocese they had in the world and for ordination must follow the same rules as secular clerics, the proper bishop to ordain them will be according to canon 956 the bishop in whose diocese they were born and still had their domicile or in whose diocese they had their domicile without origin at the time they joined the society: for that diocese remains forever their proper diocese and its bishop, therefore, their proper bishop for ordination.[92]

Stanton († 1941), writing two years later, used the same argument, and cited Schaaf.[93] McBride used the same

[92] "Episcopus Proprius Ordinationis Religiosorum," *ER*, XC (1934), 505.

[93] *De Societatibus*, p. 138.

argument about five years later, but cited no one.[94] Paventi, writing in 1946, used the same argument, and cited both Schaaf and Stanton.[95] Soon afterwards, Ristuccia used the same argument, and cited both Schaaf and McBride.[96] Finally, in 1949, Gil used the same argument, but with one qualification. Gil claimed that when a non-tonsured member of a Society lacked a domicile, with origin or without origin, in the place from which he came when he entered the Society (as would be the case, e.g., with anyone in his majority who had only a quasi-domicile in the world), the proper bishop for such a member's promotion to First Tonsure would be the ordinary of the place in which is located the house to which such a member is attached. Gil would call such an ordinary an *"Ordinarius domicilii quasi-religiosi,"* and he claims that such an ordinary would be the proper ordinary for promotion to Orders, *"in sensu revera improprio mereque formali."*[97]

In the attempt to show the fallacy in this argument, let it be said at the outset that the major premise of the argument is absolutely correct: canon 585 is not among those canons referring to religious which are extended to members of Societies. Ever since 1920, many authors have cited Goyeneche[98] as their authority for saying that, while the Code was in preparation, it was asked several times that canon 585 be applied to Societies, and that this petition was denied.[99] In 1946, Paventi, in his work entitled *De Iuramento ac de Titulo Missionis,* incorporated the actual text of canon 585 as it appeared in the Schema of the Code of 1914. He stated that the canon, as it stood there, differed little from the same canon as it appeared in the Schemata of 1912 and of 1916. It enumerated the groups who were

[94] *Incardination,* p. 344.

[95] *De Iuramento,* pp. 100-101.

[96] *Societies,* pp. 200-201.

[97] "Studium," *CpRM,* XXVIII (1949), 20-21.

[98] "Consultationes," *CpR,* I (1920), 178.

[99] E.g., Bastien, *Directoire Canonique* (3. ed.), pp. 345-346; Cocchi, *Commentarium,* IV, 242; Vermeersch-Creusen, *Epitome,* I, 631.

ipso iure to lose the diocese which they had in the world. Members of Societies were not among those groups. Paventi, however, also reported certain suggestions for revision made by certain bishops and regular superiors. Some of these bishops and superiors proposed the following addition to those who would *ipso facto* lose their proper dioceses: *Sacris initiati in societate virorum in communi viventium sine votis.* Others would have added: *Religiosi qui vota temporaria vel iuramentum perseverantiae vel peculiares quasdam promissiones ad normam suarum constitutionum ediderunt, si per sex integros annos eisdem ligati fuerint.*[100] Since there is no mention of Societies in canon 585 as it stands in the Code today, and since no canon of Title XVII of Book II of the Code applies canon 585 to Societies, it is clear that canon 585, in the present discipline, does not, by the common law, apply to members of Societies.

Granted, then, that the major premise of Schaaf and of those who hold the same opinion as Schaaf be correct, and that canon 585 does not apply to members of Societies, it seems that these authors give a too broad interpretation to canon 585. According to them, when canon 585 says that when a man makes perpetual profession he *ipso iure* loses the diocese which he had in the world, it implies that all religious, whether they be clerics or laymen at the time of their entrance into religion, can retain as a proper diocese—at least up until the time of perpetual profession—the diocese in which they lived prior to their entrance into religion. They claim that these proper dioceses are retained in virtue of the fact that the religious in question retain their domiciles in the dioceses from which they come.[101] Their reasoning may be summed up thus. A man cannot lose something which he does not have. Therefore, if by perpetual profession *all* religious—whether they were clerics or laymen at the time of their entrance into religion—

[100] Paventi, *De Iuramento*, pp. 100-101.
[101] Cf. canon 94, § 1.

lose their proper dioceses at the time of perpetual profession, they must *all* have retained their proper dioceses up until the time of perpetual profession. They further reason that since canon 585 has not been applied to members of Societies, members of Societies—*all* members of Societies, whether they were clerics or laymen at the time of their entrance into their Societies—retain the domiciles and proper dioceses which they had in the world not only before their perpetual affiliation with their Societies, but also after such perpetual affiliation.

In answer to this argument, it must be stated that canon 585 seems to refer *only* to those religious who were clerics at the time of their entrance into religion. The Code, it is true, speaks of the proper bishop or the proper ordinary in two senses. Used in one sense, the phrase has reference to the general power of jurisdiction which a bishop or ordinary enjoys over all the Faithful subject to him. Used in another sense, the phrase has reference to that special jurisdiction enjoyed by a bishop or an ordinary whereby he is competent to promote a subject to Orders, and whereby he has a special power over a man so promoted if the man has been incardinated in his diocese. When the Code speaks of a proper diocese, however, in no other place does the expression have a meaning other than the diocese of incardination.[102] To justify giving it another meaning in canon 585, there should be adduced positive arguments in favor of such an interpretation. There is to be found, however, not one such argument in the works of Schaaf and of those who follow him in this matter. On the other hand, positive arguments can be adduced in favor of the opinion by which the words "*propriam . . . dioecesim*" in canon 585 are restricted in meaning to the concept of the diocese of incardination. These arguments are taken, according to the norm of canon 18, from the context and from parallel passages.

The first positive argument in favor of according a re-

[102] Cf. canon 115.

strictive meaning—namely the diocese of incardination—to the words *"propriam . . . dioecesim"* in canon 585 is taken from context. In its context, canon 585 appears at the very end of eight canons which treat of the effects of profession (canons 578-585). The first six of these canons treat of effects which, in general, concern *all* religious. In the seventh canon, canon 584, the Code speaks of the effects of religious profession upon a very special group of religious, namely, those who possessed benefices at the time of their entrance into religion. It seems only natural to expect that in the next and last canon, canon 585, the Code will continue to speak of the effects of profession on a *special group* of religious, and not revert to a discussion of its effects on all religious in general. Furthermore, with canon 584 the Code began to discuss the effects of profession on a group who of necessity had to be clerics.[103] It is only natural to expect that the very next canon is still referring only to clerics.

Additional positive arguments in favor of according the restrictive meaning of the diocese of incardination to the words *"propriam . . . dioecesim"* in canon 585 are taken from parallel passages, namely, from canons 115 and 641. Canon 115 states: *"Etiam per professionem religiosam quis a propria dioecesi excardinatur, ad normam can. 585."* Since the enactment of the Code, there has never been any such things as the "excardination" of laymen, such as there was from the end of the nineteenth century until the advent of the Code.[104] The excardination spoken of in canon 115, effected *"ad normam can. 585,"* therefore, must be understood of incardinated clerics alone. Canon 641, § 1, too, speaks of excardination *"ad normam can. 585."* Canon 641 deals with the status of clerics in major Orders who have left the religious state. It begins with the following clause: *"Si religiosus in sacris constitutus propriam dioecesim ad normam can. 585 non amiserit, . . ."* But the only religious who could at the same time be in sacred

[103] Cf. canon 118.

[104] Cf. *supra*, pp. 51-53.

Orders and not have lost their proper diocese by perpetual profession according to the norm of canon 585 are, when generally considered, only those religous who were already in sacred Orders at the time of their entrance into religion.[105]

This interpretation of canon 585 seems also to have in its favor the authority of canonists. Among twenty-nine authors whose treatment of canon 585 has been consulted, only one, Blat († 1943), stated explicitly that the proper diocese spoken of in canon 585 includes not only the diocese of incardination, but also the diocese in which a religious had his domicile before his entrance into religion, even though at the time he was only a layman.[106] Three authors seem to express the same opinion in an implicit manner.[107] Against the contention of these authors, however, Abbo-Hannan state explicitly that the proper diocese mentioned in canon 585 refers only to the diocese in which a religious was incardinated as a cleric before his entrance into religion.[108] Eight authors, when speaking of the effects of perpetual profession as established by canon 585, speak *only* of excardination.[109] Six authors, after restating canon 585 in a non-committal fashion, speak of excardination alone.[110] Finally, ten authors simply restate canon

[105] Cf. canon 964, n. 3, collated with canon 574; canon 964, n. 4; S. C. de Rel., instr. *Quantum Religiones*, 1 dec. 1931, n. 15—*AAS*, XXIV (1932), 74-81, cf. p. 80.

[106] *Commentarium Textus Codicis Iuris Canonici*, Tom. II, Vol. II, 88.

[107] [Bachofen] Augustine, *A Commentary on the New Code of Canon Law* (8 vols., St. Louis-London: Herder, Vol. III, *Religious and Laymen*, 2. ed., 1919), III, 288; Naz, *Traité de droit canonique*, I, 627; Bouscaren-Ellis, *Canon Law*, p. 276.

[108] *The Sacred Canons*, I, 600-601.

[109] Badii, *Institutiones Iuris Canonici*, I, 303; Sipos, *Enchiridion Iuris Canonici*, p. 362; Prümmer, *Manuale Iuris Canonici*, p. 290; Claeys Bouuaert-Simenon, *Manuale*, I, 395; Romani, *Institutiones Juris Canonici*, I, 372; Cocchi, *Commentarium*, IV, 139; Regatillo, *Institutiones*, I, 407; Ramstein, *A Manual of Canon Law*, p. 352.

[110] Toso, *Ad Codicem Iuris Canonici ... Commentaria Minora*, Liber II, Tom. IV, 159; Wernz-Vidal, *Ius Canonicum*, III, 317; Goyeneche,

585 in a non-committal way, and then remain completely silent about the problem at hand.[111]

The final argument against the interpretation given to canon 585 by Schaaf, Stanton, McBride, Paventi, Ristuccia and Gil is this: it runs counter to the common teaching with regard to ecclesiastical domicile. Every domicile must be either necessary or voluntary. Now, a religious in temporary profession cannot have the necessary domicile of a minor in the place which he left at the time of entering religion, i.e., in the domicile of his parents or of those who took the place of his parents. The reason for this is that canon 93, § 1, states that a minor has a necessary domicile in the domicile of the person to whose *potestas* he is subject. But after temporary profession a religious, even though he be a minor, is withdrawn from the *potestas* of his parents or of those who took the place of his parents, and is subjected to the *potestas* or dominative power of his superiors in religion. Furthermore, canon 95, which states that a domicile is lost by departure plus the intention of not returning, ends with the expression: *"salvo praescripto can. 93."* The only other kind of domicile that a religious might be thought to possess in the place he left at the time of entering religion is a voluntary domicile. But it is the certain teaching of canonists that no religious, whether he be perpetually professed or only temporarily professed, can have any voluntary domicile whatsoever.[112]

The conclusion of this discussion on canon 585 may be summed up as follows. As to members of Societies who were incardinated clerics at the time they entered their

Summa Principia, p. 122; Schaefer, *De Religiosis,* p. 574; Brys, *Juris Canonici Compendium,* I, 560; Woywod, *Commentary,* I, 277.

[111] Berutti, *Institutiones Iuris Canonici,* III, 224-225; Coronata, *Institutiones,* I, 766; Crnica, *Commentarium Theoretico-Practicum Codicis Iuris Canonici,* I, 409; Cappello, *Summa,* II, 65; Beste, *Introductio,* p. 403; Cance, *Le Code de Droit Canonique,* II, 102; Vermeersch-Creusen, *Epitome,* I, 550; Fanfani, *De Iure Religiosorum,* p. 414; Jombart, *Manuel de Droit Canon,* p. 194; De Carlo, *Jus Religiosorum,* p. 242.

[112] Michiels, *Principia,* p. 145.

respective Societies, *no one* denies that canon 585 does not apply to them, and no one denies that they are *never* excardinated by prescript of the common law. As to members of Societies who were laymen at the time they entered their respective Societies, the fact that canon 585 does not apply to them is inconsequential, for not only does canon 585 have nothing to do with laymen or their loss of domicile, but also the domiciles which laymen had before their entrance into their Societies are lost a number of years before their perpetual affiliation with their Societies. That is to say, members of Societies lose their domiciles at the time of their temporary affiliation immediately after the period of their probation, just as religious, when they make their temporary profession immediately after their novitiate, lose the domiciles they had before their entrance into religion. The reason is the fact that they are then subjected to the dominative power of their superiors.

Besides Schaaf, Stanton, McBride, Paventi, Ristuccia and Gil, there are two other authors who disagree with the contention that the proper bishop for the ordination of members of Societies is the bishop of the place in which is located the house to which they are attached. These authors are Moeder and Oesterle.

Moeder, writing one year after Schaaf, stated: "There is no need of bringing into this discussion the matter of *domicilium necessarium seu legale* in order to ascertain who is the proper bishop for ordination." But the only reason given is this: "The canons referred to by Schäfer (in the above quotation) do not speak of a necessary or legal domicile in a house of the society." That is all that Moeder stated in support of his contention. The quotation from Schaefer referred to is the following quotation from n. 605 of the 1927 edition of *De Religiosis: "Relate ad ordines valent can. 955, 956, 979, 976, 993 ideoque omnino reguntur jure Clericorum saecularium salvis privilegiis apostolicis."*[113] It seems evident, however, that Schaefer

[113] Moeder, *Proper Bishop,* pp. 111-112.

did not intend this to be an exhaustive enumeration of the canons by which the ordination of members of Societies is governed.

Oesterle, in an article written two years prior to the article of Schaaf, also denied that the proper bishop for the ordination of members of Societies is the bishop of the place in which is located the house to which they are attached. The reason given is that members from other dioceses cannot have a domicile in the sense of canon 92 in the diocese in which they are stationed. For none of these members, during the period of their studies for the priesthood, live for ten years in the diocese in which they study; neither do they have the intention of remaining there perpetually.[114] In answer it may be said that no one claims that members have a domicile in the diocese in which they are stationed according to the norm of canon 92; that is to say, no one claims that the members have a voluntary domicile. What is claimed for the members is a necessary domicile, and this for reasons stated above.[115]

Different from the opinions of all the authors cited thus far is the opinion of Rothoff, who died in 1942, and whose work was published posthumously in 1949. Rothoff distinguished between lay members of Societies who are perpetually affiliated with their Societies, and lay members who are only temporarily affiliated. He stated that lay members who are perpetually affiliated are subject to the dominative power of their superiors in the same way as religious, and thus obtain a necessary domicile in the place in which is located the house to which they are attached. Consequently, the bishop of that place is the proper bishop for their promotion to First Tonsure.[116] This is in harmony with the doctrine of Goyeneche and of Abbo-Hannan, as it is stated above.[117]

[114] Oesterle, "Weihekandidaten aus einer Diözesan-Priestergenossenschaft," *ThPrQs*, LXXXV (1932), 566-567.

[115] Cf. *supra*, pp. 71-81.

[116] Rothoff, *Sociétés*, pp. 166-167, 168.

[117] Cf. *supra*, pp. 83-85.

With regard to members of Societies who are only temporarily affiliated with their Societies, however, Rothoff rejected the opinion which states that even these members obtain a necessary domicile in the place in which is located the house to which they are attached, and that consequently the bishop of this place is their proper bishop for their promotion to First Tonsure. Following a line of argument used by Schaaf in Schaaf's treatment of the question of the proper bishop for the ordination of members of non-exempt religious with temporary profession,[118] Rothoff stated that during their period of temporary incorporation, the intention of members of Societies not to return to their paternal homes or to their former domiciles is only conditional, i.e., dependent upon their being perpetually incorporated. In the same way, their intention of remaining in their Societies is also conditional. But, so stated Rothoff, a conditional intention suffices to create a domicile only after the condition is fulfilled.[119]

In order, then, to determine the proper bishop for the promotion to First Tonsure of temporarily affiliated members, Rothoff invoked a further distinction. He distinguished temporarily affiliated members who are still in their minority from temporarily affiliated members who have reached their majority. The minors, he said, retain the necessary domiciles which they had before their entrance, and consequently their proper bishop is the bishop of the place in which the retained necessary domiciles are located. On the other hand, said Rothoff, those who have reached their majority acquire or lose their domiciles in the same way as anyone of the Faithful who is in a similar juridical status of majority.[120]

The argument of Rothoff, however, seems to fall short before he gets to the distinction between persons in their

[118] Schaaf, "Episcopus Proprius Ordinationis Religiosorum," *ER*, XC, (1934), 501.

[119] "Or une intention conditionelle ne peut suffire à créer un domicile tant que la condition n'est pas réalisée."—*Sociétés*, p. 167.

[120] *Sociétés*, pp. 167-168.

minority and persons in their majority. It seems to fall short when he says that a conditional intention does not suffice to create a domicile. It falls short for the reason that in the case at hand there is no question of *any kind of intention whatsoever,* since there is no question of a *voluntary* domicile. It is a *necessary* domicile that is claimed for those who are temporarily incorporated. It is claimed for them because while they remain incorporated they are subject to the dominative power of their superiors in the same way as those members who are perpetually incorporated. Furthermore, once those who are still in their minority are temporarily incorporated, they lose the necessary domicile which they had with their parents without formulating *any* intention. For canon 93, § 1, states that persons in their minority necessarily retain the domicile of those *to whom they are subject.* But with temporary incorporation, such persons are *removed* from the power of their parents. Furthermore, canon 95, which speaks of the loss of domicile by departure plus the intention of not returning, ends with the phrase *"salvo praescripto can 93."*

The final opinion to be discussed is that of Stanghetti, who states that candidates who enter a Society as laymen have *no* domicile and therefore *no* proper bishop for ordination.[121] An opinion such as this, however, implies that there is a serious *lacuna* in the Code. Now, while it must be admitted that the Code is a human work with human imperfections, nevertheless such a *lacuna* should not be admitted until it is shown that there is no other reasonable explanation at hand to account for the apparent defect in the law. But in the case at hand there is a reasonable explanation. It is the explanation whereby a necessary domicile is attributed to the members in the place in which is located the house to which they are attached. The opinion

[121] "Sono chierici secolari, ma non hanno domicilo in una diocesi, quindi non hanno un proprio Ordinario. . . ." "Coloro che entrano a far parte definitivamente di un Istituto perdono il loro domicilio in una diocesi, quindi il proprio Ordinario."—*Prassi,* p. 38.

which attributes such a domicile to members of Societies is, as was seen above, the more common opinion among the authors who mention members of Societies when they *ex professo* treat of domicile.[122]

Four of the authors who deny that the proper bishop is always the bishop of the place in which is located the house to which the members of Societies are attached[123] cite in support of their contention a response given by the Sacred Congregation of Bishops and Regulars in 1864. This response, reported in full above,[124] settled a doubt about the proper bishop for the ordination of the members of the Congregation of Priests of the Schools of Charity.[125] Let it be said at the outset that issue is not taken with these authors for citing a decision intended to settle a doubt of pre-Code law in a case involving members of an institute of simple vows as an argument in support of an interpretation of law governing Societies without vows after the Code.[126] These authors, however, have failed to consider that the Sacred Congregation of Bishops and Regulars judged the case at hand according to the norms of the Constitution *Speculatores,* which was then in force, but which is now abrogated by virtue of canon 6, nn. 1 and 6.[127] The Constitution *Speculatores* is opposed to the law of the Code because it provides for a proper bishop for ordina-

122 Cf. *supra,* p. 75.

123 Oesterle, "Weihekandidaten aus einer Diözesan-Priestergenossenschaft," *ThPrQs,* LXXXV (1932), 570-571; Schaaf, "Episcopus Proprius Ordinationis Religiosorum," *ER,* XC (1934), 507-508; Moeder, *Proper Bishop,* p. 113; Rothoff, *Sociétés,* pp. 172-173.

124 Cf. *supra,* pp. 46-47.

125 S. C. Ep. et Reg., *Tarvisina,* 6 maii 1864—*Fontes,* n. 1991.

126 Cf. *supra,* pp. 16-24.

127 Leges quaelibet, sive universales sive particulares, praescriptis huius Codicis oppositae, abrogantur, nisi de particularibus legibus aliud expresse caveatur;

Si qua ex certeris disciplinaribus legibus, quae usque adhuc viguerunt, nec explicite nec implicite in Codice contineatur, ea vim omnem amisisse dicenda est, nisi in probatis liturgicis libri reperiatur, aut lex sit iuris divini sive positivi sive naturalis.

tion in virtue of any one of four titles: origin, benefice, domicile or household service, whereas the Code allows for proper bishop in virtue of only one title, viz., domicile. Likewise it cannot be said that the requirement of domicile in the Code is to be interperted, in virtue of canon 6, n. 3,[128] in the light of what the Constitution *Speculatores* stated about domicile. For the Code law on the proper bishop does not agree with part of the law of the Constitution *Speculatores,* namely that part of the Constitution *Speculatores* which deals with domicile. For the law concerning domicile in the Constitution *Speculatores* is much stricter than the law concerning the domicile necessary to obtain a proper bishop for ordination in the Code.[129] Rather must it be said that the law treating domicile in the Constitution *Speculatores* is a disciplinary law which has not been repeated in the Code, and which is, therefore, in virtue of canon 6, n. 6, abrogated.[130] Consequently the entire pre-Code law regulating the proper bishop for the ordination of secular clerics must be considered abrogated by the law of the Code regulating the proper bishop for the ordination of secular clerics. In like manner, the law regulating the proper bishop for the ordination of members of Secular Congregations before the Code, which was identical with the law regulating the proper bishop for the ordination of secular clerics before the Code, must also be con-

[128] Canones qui ex parte tantum cum veteri iure congruunt, qua congruunt, ex iure antiquo aestimandi sunt; qua discrepant, sunt ex sua ipsorum sententia diiudicandi.

[129] The following is from the Constitution *Speculatores,* n. 5: Subditus autem ratione domicilii ad effectum suscipiendi ordines is dumtaxat conseatur, qui, licet alibi natus fuerit, illud tamen adeo stabiliter constituerit in aliquo loco, ut vel per decennium saltem in eo habitando, vel maiorem rerum, ac bonorum suorum partem cum instructis aedibus in locum huiusmodi transferendo, ibique insuper per aliquod considerabile tempus commorando, satis superque suum perpetuo ibidem permanendi animum demonstraverit, et nihilominus ulterius utroque casu se vere et realiter animum huiusmodi habere iureiurando affirmet.—*Fontes,* n. 258.

[130] Cf. Coronata, *De Sacramentis,* II, 32.

sidered abrogated by the law of the Code regulating the proper bishop for the ordination of members of Societies, because this law in the Code is identical with the Code law for the proper bishop for the ordination of secular clerics.

The Sacred Congregation of Bishops and Regulars said in 1864 that for the ordination of members of the Congregation of Priests of the Schools of Charity dimissorial letters from the bishop of origin or domicile according to the Constitution *Speculatores* were necessary. As seen above,[131] the requirements for obtaining a domicile which would suffice for obtaining a proper bishop were so demanding according to the Constitution *Speculatores,* that a member of a Society could hardly be expected to obtain such a domicile in the place in which was located the house to which he was attached. It was possible *before* the Constitution *Speculatores,* as is evident in the discussion entered into above of the declaration of the Sacred Congregation of the Council in relation to the proper bishop for the ordination of members of the Institute of the Oratory at Rome and Naples.[132] In like manner is it *again* possible, now that the more strict requirements of the Constitution *Speculatores* have been abrogated by the Code. Furthermore, since the Code, not only is it that members of Societies *need not* obtain dimissorial letters from the bishops of their place of origin (in the cases wherein the bishops of origin are not identical with the bishops of domicile), but the members of Societies since the Code *may not* be ordained in consequence of the issuance of dimissorial letters from these bishops alone.

A final argument is adduced by Stanton as confirmation of the opinion that the bishop of the diocese in which is located the house to which the members of Societies are attached is *not* the proper bishop for their promotion to Orders. Stanton claims that this opinion is confirmed by

[131] Cf. supra, pp. 41-43. [132] Cf. *supra,* pp. 39-45.
[133] P. C.I., 3 iun. 1918—*AAS,* X (1918), 347.

a response of the Code Commission in 1918. The Code Commission was asked whether the penalty of canon 2410 is applicable to Societies without vows. Canon 2410 states that religious superiors who, contrary to the prescripts of canons 965, 966 and 967, presume to send their ordinand subjects to an outside bishop are *ipso facto* suspended from the celebration of Mass for a month. The Code Commission replied that canon 2410 is applicable to Societies without vows in the measure that these Societies have the privilege of granting dimissorial letters to their members.[133] It is evident, however, that the Code Commission has no reference to the proper bishop for ordination in the strict sense according to the norm of canon 955, i.e., to the bishop who has the authority to *promote to Orders,* either immediately by ordaining personally and on his own authority, or mediately by issuing dimissorial letters. For this is a matter of the common law, whereas the response concerns only cases wherein superiors have privileges. Rather, there is question of the *iura pontificalia,* i.e., the right of a bishop to perform pontifical ceremonies in his own diocese, the right that entered so much into question in the history of the exemption of regulars, as will be seen below.[134]

Upon this consideration of the various opinions with regard to the proper bishop for the ordination of members of Societies, it seems apropos to conclude this section with a consideration of the possible reasons why the opinion of Schaaf became the more common one. It seems that the principal reason why the opinion of Schaaf, which, at first sight, seems quite reasonable, was so readily accepted, was that the opposite opinion of Goyeneche was looked upon as an opinion which put a tremendous burden on a bishop in whose diocese was located a house of studies of a Society which lacked an indult to grant dimissorial letters. Such a bishop would, it was thought, be responsible for the ordination of *all* the members of that Society.

[134] Cf. *supra,* pp. 153-164.

He would also be obliged, it was thought, to receive every member who left the Society while in Sacred Orders and to provide for his support. It was not altogether clear, before the question was settled by the Code Commission in 1939, that such a bishop could share the burden by promoting some of the members to First Tonsure for another diocese with the consent of the bishop of that diocese. By so doing he would incardinate these members in that other diocese, and these men would become the responsibility of the bishop of that other diocese.[135] There was not any common knowledge, at first, of the *praxis curiae,* whereby release was granted to members of Societies in Sacred Orders on condition that they remained suspended from the exercise of their Orders until they found an *episcopus benevolus receptor.*[136] Finally, it was thought that the opinion of Goyeneche would lead to this situation. A man stationed in one diocese would be tonsured by the bishop of that diocese; and then, after being transferred, would have as his proper bishop for promotion to minor Orders the bishop of another diocese. Thus a man could have a total of eight successive proper bishops, all of whom would have promoted him to Orders.[137] But this misinterpretation of the application of the opinion of Goyeneche was due to a failure to distinguish between the proper bishop for the promotion of a layman to First Tonsure and the proper bishop for the promotion of a tonsured cleric to higher Orders—a distinction which itself was not abundantly clear before the above-mentioned response of the Code Commission in 1939.[138] In view of these considerations, it is easily understood why the opinion of Schaaf, which sounded

[135] Cf. P. C. I., 24 iul. 1939—*AAS,* XXXI (1939), 321. Cf. *supra,* pp. 62-65.

[136] Cf. S. C. C., 17 iul. 1933—*AAS,* XXVI (1934), 234-236; Beste, *Introductio,* p. 461; Vermeersch-Creusen, *Epitome,* I, 631-632.

[137] This objection to Goyeneche's opinion is presented by Schaaf, "Episcopus Proprius Ordinationis Religiosorum," *ER,* XC (1934), 506.

[138] P. C. I., 24 iul. 1939—*AAS,* XXXI (1939), 321. Cf. *supra,* pp. 62-66.

reasonable, should have been readily accepted, and the opinion of Goyeneche, which seemed to put too great a burden on some bishops, should have been rejected.

SECTION 4. THE INCARDINATION OF MEMBERS OF SOCIETIES AND THE PROPER BISHOP FOR THEIR PROMOTION TO HIGHER ORDERS

It has been seen above that before the Code Secular Congregations, in matters pertaining to ordination, were, by the common law, governed by the laws regulating the ordition of secular clerics.[139] One juridical matter which is part of the law of ordination is the matter of the enrollment of clerics in a diocese or their affiliation with a religious institute. It is logical to expect, therefore, that the enrollment—or incardination, as it is called today in reference to secular clerics—of members of Secular Congregations before the Code would also follow the laws regulating the enrollment of secular clerics in their dioceses, and not the laws regulating the affiliation of regulars with their Orders. This logical deduction is verified by the facts. For in 1864, in the case of the Congregation of Priests of the Schools of Charity reported above,[140] the Sacred Congregation of Bishops and Regulars decided that a member who left the institute was subject, not to the bishop of the diocese in which was located the house to which he had been attached, but to the bishop to whom he was subject before he entered the institute, i.e., to the bishop who, in accord with the Constitution *Speculatores* then in force, had issued dimissorial letters for his ordination, and to whom he had promised obedience in the ordination ceremony. While the member remained in the institute, the canonical obedience which he owed to his bishop was limited to this extent, that his bishop could not prevent the superiors of the institute from exercising such authority as was granted to them by Constitutions approved by the

[139] Cf. *supra*, pp. 25-56.
[140] Cf. pp. 46-48.

Holy See. When the member left the institute, however, he was fully subject to the bishop in virtue of whose authorization he was promoted to Orders.[141] Again in 1905, in the case of a Precious Blood Father reported above,[142] the Sacred Congregation of Bishops and Regulars stated explicitly that members of non-exempt Congregations, when ordained upon the issuance of dimissorial letters by their own bishop, never cease to pertain to the diocese of that bishop, and always have the right to return to that diocese whenever they remain outside of their institute with the permission of their superiors.[143]

Just as Secular Congregations were bound by the law regulating the ordination of secular clerics before the Code, so, too, Societies of the Common Life, in virtue of canon 678, are bound to the present law regulating the ordination of secular clerics. One of the most important aspects of this legislation is that which looks to the matter of incardination. The law regulating the incardination of secular clerics, as found in Title I of the Second Book of the Code[144] and in certain special prescriptions of the Holy See applicable to all secular clerics,[145] must, therefore, be included in that body of law which is applicable, in virtue of canon 678, to the ordination of members of Societies.[146]

Canon 111, § 1, states that every cleric must be enrolled either in a diocese or affiliated with a religious institute (*"religioni"*). Now, it is abundantly clear both from canon 488, n. 1, and from canon 673, § 1, that no Society of the Common Life whatsoever can come under the name "religious institute" (*"religio"*). Since, therefore, the tenor of canon 111, § 1, allows no third possibility by the common law (*"Quemlibet clericum oportet esse vel alicui dioecesi*

[141] S. C. Ep. et Reg., *Tarvisina*, 6 maii 1864—*Fontes*, n. 1991.

[142] Cf. *supra*, pp. 50-51.

[143] S. C. Ep. et Reg., 27 ian. 1905—*ASS*, XXXVIII (1905-1906), 11-13.

[144] Cc. 111-117.

[145] Cf., e.g., P. C. I., 24 iul. 1939—*AAS*, XXXI (1939), 321.

[146] Cf. *supra*, pp. 57-60.

vel alicui religioni adscriptum"), it is to be concluded that members of Societies must, by the common law, be enrolled, i.e., incardinated,[147] in some diocese.

Proof of the validity of the argument presented in the paragraph above may be drawn from the fact that the Sacred Congregation of the Council, in deciding a case involving a member of a Society, used the same line of argument with regard to another aspect of the law of incardination. In 1919, a priest of the Society of African Missionaries of Lyons, who had been ordained in 1910, asked to be dispensed from his oath and to leave the Society. The Sacred Congregation for the Propagation of the Faith, to which he had first sent his petition, replied that he would be dispensed on condition that he found a benevolent bishop who was willing to receive him. The priest was allowed to work in the diocese of Sion (or Sitten) in Switzerland from 1924 to 1931. In 1932 he brought his case before the Sacred Congregation of the Council and claimed that he had been incardinated in the Diocese of Sion (or Sitten) in virtue of canon 641, § 2.[148] The Sacred Congregation of the Council decided that canon 641 had no application in the case whatsoever, because canon 641 had reference to religious institutes and to religious according to the norm of canon 488, nn. 1 and 7, respectively, while the case at hand involved neither a religious institute nor a religious. The priest was a member of a Society which, according to canon 673, § 1, was not a religious institute, and he himself, according to the same canon, was not a religious. Furthermore, stated the Sacred

[147] Canon 111, § 2, equivalates the word "enrolled," when used in reference to diocesan clerics, to the word "incardinated." *Per receptionem primae tonsurae clericus adscribitur seu, ut aiunt, incardinatur dioescesi pro cuius servitio promotus fuit.*

[148] Episcopus religiosum recipere potest sive pure et simpliciter, sive pro experimento ad triennium: in priore casu religiosus eo ipso est dioecesi incardinatus; in altero, Episcopus potest probationis tempus prorogare, non ultra tamen aliud triennium; quo etiam transacto, religiosus, nisi antea dimissus fuerit, ipso facto dioecesi incardinatus manet.

Congregation, in those things which pertain to the reception of Orders, members of Societies are, according to the norm of canon 678, held to the same laws as secular clerics.[149] Evidently the Sacred Congregation considered that the matter of incardination was one of those things which pertained to the reception of Orders. If this be true, so, too, then must those canons which treat of incardination in Title I of Book II[150] be considered as applying to members of Societies in the same way in which they apply to secular clerics, and not in the way in which they apply to religious.[151]

A corroborative argument in favor of the contention that the laws of incardination apply to members of Societies in the same way in which they apply to secular clerics is the fact that canon 585 has not been applied, by the common law, to members of Societies. No one questions the fact that canon 585 has not been applied to Societies, and that, as a consequence, those who enter Societies as incardinated clerics never lose their incardination.[152] This proves that it is *possible* for members of Societies to remain members and at the same time to remain incardinated in a diocese. True, it does not, in itself, *prove* that those who are not incardinated in a diocese at the time of their entrance become incardinated in some diocese at the reception of First Tonsure; but it does show the reasonableness of this contention.

The final argument in favor of this contention is the argument from authority. Of twelve authors who explicitly state an opinion in this matter—the majority of the authors remain silent—eight state that members of Societies must be incardinated in a diocese,[153] and four

[149] S. C. C., *Sedunen.*, 15 iul. 1933— *AAS*, XXVI (1934), 234-236.

[150] Canons 111-117.

[151] Cf. Stanton, *De Societatibus*, p. 152.

[152] Cf. *supra*, pp. 87-88.

[153] Moeder, *Proper Bishop*, pp. 112-114; Stanton, *De Societatibus*, p. 139; Beste, *Introductio*, p. 461; Ramstein, *A Manual of Canon Law*, p. 394; Ristuccia, *Societies*, p. 200; Rothoff, *Sociétés*, pp. 172-

deny that members of a Society must be incardinated in a diocese.[154] The authors who deny that members of Societies must be incardinated in a diocese are, generally taken, the same as those who deny that, if the members are ordained by a bishop of their domicile distinct from their place of origin, they must take the oath mentioned in canon 956. A stand will be taken against this opinion about the oath below;[155] and since the question of the oath and the question of incardination are so closely related, the answers to the objections of those who contend that incardination is unnecessary will be given together with the answers to the objections of those who contend that the oath is also unnecessary.

Posited then, for the moment, the necessity of incardination, this incardination can be effected by the proper bishop in any one of three ways. First, the proper bishop can incardinate the member in his own (the proper bishop's) diocese. In this case, if the member has a domicile apart from his place of origin, he must, according to the more common opinion (to be discussed immediately), strengthen with an oath his intention of remaining in the diocese perpetually (. . . *animum in dioecesi perpetuo manendi iureiurando firmare, . . .*).[156] Secondly, the proper bishop can incardinate the member in his (the proper bishop's) own diocese with the intention of later excardinating him and having him incardinated in some other diocese.[157] In this case, should the member have a domicile distinct from the place of his origin, the oath is unnecessary.[158] Thirdly, the proper bishop can incardinate the member immediately in

173; Gil, "Studium," *CpRM,* XXVIII (1949), 21-22; De Naurois, "Le 'Propre Évêque' pour l'ordination dans le clergé séculier," *BLE,* LI (1950), 15.

[154] McBride, *Incardination,* p. 345; Stanghetti, *Prassi,* pp. 38-39; Abbo-Hannan, *The Sacred Canons,* II, 88; Hannan, "The Ordination of Quasi-Religious," *The Jurist,* XII (1952), 448-454.

[155] Cf. *supra,* p. 107.

[156] Canon 956.

[157] Canon 969, § 2.

[158] Canon 956.

the diocese of some other determined bishop, having first obtained this other bishop's consent.[159] In this case, again, should the member have in the diocese a domicile distinct from the place of his origin, the oath is unnecessary.[160] The bishop, then, in whose diocese is located the house to which the ordinand member is attached, as the proper bishop,[161] can follow any one of these three courses.[162]

In the first mode of action stated in the preceding paragraph, if the member has a domicile other than the place of his origin, he would, it is contended by the writer, have to strengthen by oath his intention of remaining perpetually in the diocese of the ordaining bishop. The foundation for this contention is that such an oath is demanded by canon 956, to which members of Societies are, by the common law, certainly bound.[163] Of eleven authors who explicitly state their opinion on the matter—the majority of the authors remain silent—eight state that members of Societies are not excused from the oath,[164] and three state that members of Societies are excused from the oath.[165]

159 P. C. I., 24 iul. 1939—*AAS*, XXXI (1939), 321.

160 Coronata, *De Sacramentis*, II, 34; Abbo-Hannan, *The Sacred Canons*, II, 81.

161 Cf. *supra*, pp. 81-102.

162 To those who deny that the proper bishop is the bishop of the place where the house is, on the grounds namely that this opinion would put too much of a burden on that bishop, the latitude allowed such a bishop in the matter of incardination may be pointed out as a fact which removes the grounds for their objection. For once a member is incardinated in another diocese, any special responsibility for that cleric *qua talis* would cease on the part of the bishop who promoted him to First Tonsure.

163 Cf. *supra*, pp. 66-69.

164 Bastien, *Directoire Canonique* (3. ed.), p. 345; Goyeneche, "Consultationes," *CpR*, VIII (1927), 113-114; Schaaf, "Episcopus Proprius Ordinationis Religiosorum," *ER*, XC (1934), 505-507; Stanton, *De Societatibus*, pp. 137-138; Vermeersch-Creusen, *Epitome*, I, 631; Rothoff, *Sociétés*, pp. 170-172; Gil, "Studium," *CpRM*, XXVIII (1949), 21; De Carlo, *Jus Religiosorum*, p. 512.

165 McBride, *Incardination*, p. 345; Ristuccia, *Societies*, p. 201;

The first author chronologically to deny that members of Societies must, by the common law, be incardinated in some diocese, and to deny that members who have a domicile apart from the place of their origin must, by the common law, take the oath required by canon 956, was McBride.[166] On page 343 McBride states that non-exempt religious, as far as the laws of ordination are concerned, include members of: a) non-exempt Religious Congregations in which perpetual vows are pronounced; b) non-exempt Religious Congregations in which only temporary vows are pronounced; and c) Societies of the Common Life. McBride then states that the words *"ceterorum omnium alumnorum cuiusvis religionis"* in canon 964, n. 4,[167] refer to members of all the institutes in the non-exempt group. On page 345 McBride states that when anyone in the non-exempt religious category spoken of in canon 964, n. 4, receives First Tonsure, he does not thereby become incardinated in the diocese of his place of domicile, since he is already by temporary profession, or by something similar, such as an oath or promise in Societies without vows, affiliated with his respective Religious Congregation or Society. Such affiliation, he claims, satisfies the requirement of canon 111, § 1.[168] Next, McBride recognizes the fact that when canon 964, n. 4, states that the ordination of those in the non-exempt group is regulated *"iure saecularium,"* reference is had, in the matter of the proper bishop, to canon 956, by which the proper bishop for the ordination of secular clerics is determined. McBride then states that if a member has a domicile other than the place of his origin, the oath mentioned in canon 956 is

Hannan, "The Ordination of Quasi-Religious," *The Jurist, XII* (1952), 448-449.

[166] *Incardination,* pp. 342-346.

[167] Ordinatio ceterorum omnium alumnorum cuiusvis religionis regitur iure saecularium, revocato quolibet indulto Superioribus concesso dandi professis a votis temporariis litteras dimissorias ad ordines maiores.

[168] Quemlibet clericum oportet esse vel alicui dioecesi vel alicui religioni adscriptum, ita ut clerici vagi nullatenus admittantur.

useless,[169] because as long as he remains in the Religious Congregation or Society, his superiors can send him outside the diocese.

To this objection it may be answered that McBride, who in this place is commenting on the words *"vel nisi agatur de promovendo religioso professo, de quo in can. 964, n. 4,"* of canon 956, includes Societies in the ambit of canon 964, n. 4, without justification. Canon 964 is clearly speaking of the ordination of religious. This is evident from the words with which it begins: *"Quod attinet ad ordinationem religiosorum."* It is also evident from the context. Chapter I of Title VI of Book III deals with the minister of sacred ordination and embraces canons 951 to 967. Canon 951 distinguishes between the ordinary and the extraordinary minister. Canon 952 speaks of those ordained by the Roman Pontiff. Canons 953 and 954 speak of episcopal consecration. Canon 955 lays down a general principle affecting the ordination of everyone, whether secular or religious. The rest of the chapter is dedicated to two separate considerations: the first, the ordination of secular clerics, from canon 956 to canon 963; the second, the ordination of religious, from canon 964 to canon 967. There are no grounds, therefore, for understanding the reference to religious in canon 964 as extending to members of Societies, especially since the ordination of members of Societies is provided for in the title of the Code which is devoted exclusively to Societies, namely, Title XVII of Book II,[170] and it cannot be claimed that there is any such treatment of ordination in that part of the Code that is devoted exclusively to the treatment of religious.[171] It may also be said that the words *"nisi agatur de promovendo religioso professo, de quo in can. 964, n. 4,"* as found in canon 956, contain an exception to the law, and that therefore these

[169] Canon 956 exempts from the oath those who have a domicile apart from the place of their origin, if they are religious ordinands to whom reference is made in canon 964, n. 4.

[170] Cf. canon 678.

[171] Cf. Titles IX to XVI of Book II, canons 492 to 672.

words must, according to canon 19,[172] be given a strict interpretation. But it is evident that a member of a Society can by no means be said to be included in the words *"religioso professo"* taken in the strict sense.[173]

With regard to the objection that the superiors of Societies can send their subjects away from the dioceses in which the subjects would be required to declare under oath their intention to remain, it must be pointed out first of all that the oath of canon 956 is not a promissory oath. The oath of canon 956 is assertory. By reason of this oath the obligation which the ordinand has to conform his words to his mind binds not only under the virtue of fidelity, but also under the virtue of religion. The words which he utters, however, merely give expression to his present intention.[174]

In the second place, there is question of the intention *to remain,* and there is no question of the intention *to serve.* The utilization of the title of the service of the diocese or the mission requires a manifestation under oath of the intention *to serve.*[175] The same must be said in regard to the oath required of a cleric before formal excardination and incardination (as opposed to initial incardination),[176] as well as in regard to the oath to serve in a diocese or a mission, which, by a prescript of the Holy See, would invalidate entrance into a religious novitiate.[177]

Finally, as to the apparent conflict between the obligation to obey a possible, or even probable, call by the superiors of a Society to come away from a diocese, and the intention to remain in that same diocese, the following must be said. The intention to remain in the diocese must mean either one of two things. It must mean either to

[172] Leges quae ... exceptionem a lege continent, strictae subsunt interpretationi.

[173] Cf. canons 488, n. 7; 673, § 1.

[174] De Naurois, "Le 'Propre Évêque' pour l'ordination dans le clergé séculier," *BLE,* LI (1950), pp. 28-29, note 32; McBride, *Incardination,* p. 551.

[175] Canon 981, § 1.

[176] Canon 117, n. 3.

[177] Canon 542, n. 1.

remain *physically present in* the diocese, or to remain *incardinated in* the diocese. But in either case the intention to remain would not be incompatible with the obedience owed to the superiors of a Society. For if the intention was to remain physically present in the diocese, this would have to be qualified with the condition "unless lawful authority should call me elsewhere." Even a diocesan priest would have to qualify his intention to this extent to provide for the case in which he might be called upon by lawful authority to do work outside of his own diocese. It may be objected that the intention would be meaningless, since a member of a Society would almost certainly be called away. But in answer it must to be stated that the element of probabilities is purely accidental. The intention is just as valid no matter how probable may be some contingency *provided for in the intention.* On the other hand, the meaning intended by canon 956 may be the intention to remain incardinated in the diocese of the ordaining bishop. If this be the meaning, there is no difficulty whatsoever, for absence from a diocese with the permission of or under the command of lawful authority, on the one hand, and incardination in that same diocese, on the other, have never been considered incompatible. And so in either case there is no conflict. And not only is there no conflict, but the oath takes on special significance when one considers the case in which an ordained man would leave a Society. The common law requires that such a man return to the diocese in which he is incardinated.[178] It is not illogical to presume that the lawmaker wanted to provide for the bishop's being assured at the time of the ordination of such a man that, *if* the latter should at some future date leave the Society, he would not be averse to remaining perpetually in the diocese in which he was incardinated at the time of his ordination.

Stanghetti, writing in 1943, may be considered to agree with McBride when the latter denies that members of So-

[178] Cf. *infra*, pp. 119-120.

cieties must be incardinated. Actually, however, Stanghetti goes farther than McBride. Stanghetti denies that members of Societies who enter as laymen have any domicile whatsoever, and, consequently, also denies that they have any proper bishop for ordination whatsoever. He claims that once the members have been promoted to Orders in the Society (he does not say by whom they are promoted) they are secular clerics who are *vagi* or *acephali*.[179] This objection is more fundamental than the objection of McBride, and has been answered above.[180]

Ristuccia, writing about six or seven years after McBride, disagrees with McBride by stating that members of Societies must, on the reception of First Tonsure, be incardinated in a diocese. But in the matter of the oath, he follows the argumentation of McBride, whom he cites, and states that the oath need not be taken by members of Societies when they are ordained by the bishop of the place in which they have their domicile apart from the place of their origin.[181]

Abbo-Hannan, whose work appeared in 1952, claim that the reception of First Tonsure by a member of a Society affiliates him as a cleric in his institute, and does not incardinate him in the diocese of the local ordinary who was his proper bishop for ordination. Abbo-Hannan also cite McBride. Like McBride, they treat members of Societies in the non-exempt group of canon 964, n. 4.[182] Abbo-Hannan remain silent on the question of the oath.

The answers to the objections of Ristuccia and of Abbo-Hannan seem to be contained in the answers to the objection of McBride.[183] Arguments still to be answered, however, are found in an article written by Hannan in 1952 and entitled "The Ordination of Quasi- Religious."[184] This

[179] *Prassi*, p. 38.
[180] Cf. *supra*, pp. 102-106.
[181] *Societies*, pp. 200-201.
[182] *The Sacred Canons*, II, 88-89.
[183] Cf. *supra*, pp. 108-111.
[184] *The Jurist*, XII (1952), 443-456.

article was occasioned by an article written by Gil in 1949.[185] Gil's article is a study occasioned by a letter of the Code Commission dated July 24, 1947, and treating the problem of the ordination of members of Societies without vows.[186]

Hannan begins to attack the problem of incardination and the oath by admitting that the words *"de promovendo religioso professo, de quo in can. 964, n. 4,"* in canon 956, and the words *"alicui religioni"* in canon 111, § 1, refer, in their explicit context, only to members of religious institutes and not to members of Quasi-Religious Societies.[187] In this admission Hannan seems to cast a shadow of doubt on the validity of the arguments proposed by McBride.

Having made this admission, however, Hannan questions the way in which Gil reconciles the oath with the obedience owed to the superiors. Gil claims that the ordaining bishop tacitly renounces the exercise of his right over the ordinand as long as the latter remains in the Society.[188] Hannan thinks rather that the ordaining bishop claims no right, not even a right whose exercise is suspended, since he has no intention of providing his diocese with an additional cleric (such an intention would result in incardination),[189] but rather the intention of supplying "an instrumentality made necessary by the lack of a provision in the law for the authority competent to proceed to the ordination of a quasi-religious."[190] Here one finds oneself at the very heart and center of the problem, and the fundamental point upon which the disagreement seems to depend begins to appear. It seems that the fundamental point of disagreement lies in a double understanding of the purpose

185 "Studium," *CpRM*, XXVIII (1949), 18-29.

186 P. C. I., litt., 24 iul. 1947—*CpRM*, XXVIII (1949), 16-18.

187 "The Ordination of Quasi-Religious," *The Jurist*, XII (1952), 448.

188 "Studium," *CpRM*, XXVIII (1949), 21.

189 Cf. canon 111, § 2.

190 "The Ordination of Quasi-Religious," *The Jurist*, XII (1952), 448.

behind the Church's laws regulating a cleric's enrollment. One school of thought, it seems, feels that the primary reason for demanding that all clerics be either incardinated in some diocese or affiliated with some religious institute is the guaranteeing for that diocese or religious institute of the services of the ones enrolled therein or affiliated therewith. It is very natural to draw this conclusion from the words of canon 111, § 2: *"Per receptionem primae tonsurae clericus adscribitur seu, ut aiunt, incardinatur dioecesi pro cuius servitio promotus fuit."* Another school of thought, it seems, feels that the primary purpose of incardination in a diocese or of affiliation with a religious institute is the guaranteeing of the fact that every tonsured cleric will be subject to authority. It is very natural to draw this conclusion from the words of canon 111, § 1: *"Quemlibet clericum oportet esse vel alicui dioecesi vel alicui religioni adscriptum, ita ut clerici vagi nullatenus admittantur."*

It seems that the latter view regarding incardination may prove the more acceptable one.[191] For it is not a rare occurrence to see men who are incardinated in one diocese spending the greater part of their lives laboring in another diocese. On the other hand, these same men who labor outside the diocese in which they are incardinated never cease to be subject to the bishop of their diocese of incardination.[192] The authority of this bishop of incardination is sometimes limited, but this limitation is imposed only by the higher authority of the Holy See. Thus, for example, when an incardinated cleric joins a religious institute, his proper bishop remains his proper bishop as long as the cleric is only temporarily professed;[193] and yet, even during this time, the bishop cannot exercise such authority over the cleric as would encroach upon the right

[191] Piontek, *De Indulto Exclaustrationis necnon Saecularizationis*, The Catholic University of America Canon Law Studies, n. 29 (Washington, D.C., 1925), p. 222.

[192] Canon 127. Cf. Abbo-Hannan, *The Sacred Canons*, I, 181.

[193] Canon 585.

of authority over the cleric which the Constitutions of the religious institute give to the cleric's superiors in religion.[194]

Another reason why the opinion which states that the primary purpose of incardination is the guaranteeing of the fact that every cleric will be subject to authority seems the more tenable one is the following. The Code itself provides for a case in which a man upon the reception of First Tonsure is incardinated in the diocese of the ordaining bishop, who, at the very time of ordination, intends to promote the candidate to First Tonsure *not* for the service of his own diocese—this, in apparent contradiction to canon 111, § 2, which states: *"Per receptionem primae tonsurae clericus adscribitur seu, ut aiunt, incardinatur dioecesi pro cuius servitio promotus fuit."* The case here contemplated is the case provided for in canon 969, § 2: *"Non prohibetur tamen Episcopus proprium promovere subditum, qui in futurum, praevia legitima excardinatione et incardinatione, servitio alius dioecesis destinetur."*

For these reasons it seems that Hannan's objection to the argument of Gil cannot be sustained.

Hannan offers one further consideration which merits attention. As a possible solution to the difficulties that remain when one rejects the solution of Gil, Hannan makes the following suggestion. Granted that members of Societies cannot be excused from the oath by any explicit statement of canons 956 and 964, n. 4; and granted that members of Societies cannot be said to be affiliated with their institutes by any explicit statement of canon 111, § 1; could it not be said that members are excused from the oath and are affiliated with their Societies through an application of the principles of the supplementary norms of law as contained in canon 20?[195] Hannan feels that there is

[194] Cf. canon 593; S. C. Ep. et Reg., *Tarvisina,* 6 maii 1864, ad III—*Fontes,* n. 1991.

[195] Si certa de re desit expressum praescriptum legis sive generalis sive particularis, norma sumenda est, nisi agatur de poenis applicandis, a legibus latis in similibus; a generalibus iuris principiis

lacking an express prescript of law covering the question of the incardination of members of Societies and overcoming the discrepancy which he sees existing between the oath mentioned in canon 956 and the obedience owed to the superiors. He therefore feels that a norm might well be taken from laws intended to provide for similar situations, viz., the law of canon 111, § 1, by which religious clerics escape the status of *vagi* through affiliation with their religious institutes, and the law of canon 956, whereby professed religious are exempted from the oath.[196]

It seems, however, that there is not lacking an express prescript of law by which is determined the position of members of Societies in relation to incardination and the oath of canon 956. It seems that this determination is made *expressly* in the prescript of canon 678: *"In iis quae . . . ad suscipiendos ordines pertinent, sodales iisdem legibus tenentur ac saeculares clerici. . . ."* True, the determinations are not expressed *explicitly* in this canon; but they are expressed *implicitly* when the canon states that members of Societies are to follow the same laws as secular clerics. It may be countered that non-exempt religious, too, are advised to follow the law of secular clerics in this matter in canon 964, n. 4, and yet they are excused from the oath and are affiliated with their institutes. But it must be answered to this objection that the *law itself* makes exceptions for religious clerics in canon 111, § 1, and in canon 956; the law makes no exceptions, however, for members of Societies.

By way of summary, then, it seems that when members of Societies are promoted to First Tonsure they must be incardinated in some diocese. It also seems that if members of Societies have a proper bishop by reason of a domicile possessed as distinct from the place of origin and are to be incardinated by First Tonsure in the diocese of their

cum aequitate canonica servatis; a stylo et praxi Curiae Romanae; a communi constantique sententia doctorum.

[196] "The Ordination of Quasi-Religious," *The Jurist*, XII (1952), 448-454.

proper bishop, and are to be thus incardinated with no view to future excardination according to the norm of canon 969, § 2, they must strengthen by oath their intention to remain in the diocese of incardination as long as they are not called elsewhere by lawful authority.

A member of a Society, then, may be, or become, incardinated in a diocese in any one of four ways. First, he may have been an incardinated cleric at the time of his entrance. In this case he remains incardinated in his original diocese. Secondly, he may be incardinated permanently in the diocese of the bishop who promotes him to First Tonsure while he is a member of a Society. In this case, if he has a domicile other than the place of his origin, he must take the oath mentioned in canon 956. Thirdly, he may be incardinated temporarily in the diocese of the bishop who promotes him to First Tonsure while he is a member of a Society, and be so incardinated with a view to future formal excardination and incardination according to the norm of canon 969, § 2. In this case, if he has a domicile distinct from the place of his origin, he need not take the oath mentioned in canon 956. Fourthly, he may, already a member of a Society, be incardinated in any diocese whatsoever by action of the bishop who promotes him to First Tonsure, provided that the bishop who promotes him has obtained beforehand the consent of the bishop in whose diocese the member is to be incardinated.[197]

With regard to the proper bishop for promotion to higher Orders, posited the incardination, by the common law, of all members of Societies, there must be followed the now universally accepted principle by which the proper bishop for the promotion of incardinated secular clerics to higher Orders is always identified with the bishop in whose diocese such secular clerics are incardinated.[198] Thus, the proper bishop for the promotion to higher Orders of a clerical member of a Society is, by the common law, the

[197] P. C. I., 24 iul. 1939—*AAS*, XXXI (1939), 321.
[198] Cf. *supra*, pp. 62-66.

bishop of the diocese in which such a clerical member is incardinated. This bishop is the proper bishop for his promotion to higher Orders, even though the clerical member has no domicile in this bishop's diocese.[199] Furthermore, this bishop can promote such a cleric to higher Orders either immediately, by direct conferral of the higher Orders on his own authority, or mediately, by issuance of dimissorial letters for the conferral of such Orders, as will be seen below in the sixth section of this article.[200]

With regard to the canonical status of members of Societies who leave their Societies as clerics, a distinction must be made between those who leave legitimately and of their own free will (e.g., at the expiration of a temporary oath or promise, or with a dispensation from an oath), and those who are dismissed.

With regard to those who are dismissed, canon 681 applies to them the prescripts of Title XVI of Book II (canons 646 to 672), which deal with the dismissal of religious. There should be no difficulty in the application of these canons to members of Societies. In order to avoid whatever confusion might have arisen from the fact that canons 646 to 672 distinguish between religious who have temporary vows and religious who have perpetual vows, the Code Commission in 1921 stated that, if the bond joining members to Societies is temporary, the canons dealing with the dismissal of religious in temporary vows are to be observed, whereas if the bond is perpetual, the canons dealing with the dismissal of religious in pereptual vows are to be observed.[201] Thus, for example, if a clerical member of a Society is dismissed according to the norm of canon 647 while under a temporary bond, a distinction must be made, according to the norm of canon 648, with reference to whether he be in sacred Orders or in minor Orders. If he be in Sacred Orders, he will have to follow the prescripts of canon 641, § 1, and of canon 642. If he

[199] P. C. I., 24 iul. 1939—*AAS*, XXXI (1939), 321.

[200] Cf. *supra*, pp. 125-128.

[201] P. C. I., 1 mart. 1921—*AAS*, XIII (1921), 177.

be in minor Orders, he will be reduced to the lay state. The status of a member of a Society who is dismissed while under a perpetual bond, on the other hand, is provided for by the application of canons 669 to 672, which deal with the status of religious dismissed while under perpetual vows.

With regard to the status of those clerical members who leave their Societies legitimately and of their free will, canon 681 makes no provision. Canon 641, § 1, is not applicable to such clerics, nor does it refer to them of itself, for it speaks only of religious.[202] Nevertheless, reduction to the lay state would seem to have the nature of a penalty for one who leaves legitimately, and thus could not, it seems, be imposed according to the principles of supplementary law, even on clerics in minor Orders.[203] Therefore it must be said that clerics who leave their Societies legitimately and of their own free will, whether they be in major or in minor Orders, remain incardinated clerics, and as such must return to their proper bishops.[204] With regard to those who are in minor Orders, however, their proper ordinary can reduce them to the lay state by decree, if he prudently judge that they cannot be promoted to sacred Orders with due respect for the clerical state.[205]

Just as ex-members of Societies who have not been dismissed do not fall under the first paragraph of canon 641 for the reason simply that they are not ex-religious, so, too, they do not fall under the second paragraph of this canon, which provides for the automatic incardination of an ex-religious in a diocese after six years' service there-

[202] Cf. *supra*, pp. 104-105.

[203] Cf. canon 20.

[204] Piontek, *De Indulto Exclaustrationis necnon Saecularizationis*, p. 224; Schaaf, "Episcopus Proprius Ordinationis Religiosorum," *ER*, XC (1934), 509, note 50; Stanghetti, *Prassi*, p. 38 (at least with reference to those members who were incardinated at the time of their entrance; the others, he contends, are not incardinated in any diocese); Rothoff, *Sociétés*, pp. 171, 178; Gil, "Studium," *CpRM*, XXVIII (1949), 21.

[205] Canon 211, § 2.

in. This disposition of law has been declared officially by the Sacred Congregation of the Council.[206]

There is one canon in Title XV of Book II (the title regulating egress from religious institutes), however, which does itself mention ex-members of Societies. This is canon 642. The first paragraph of this canon puts limitations on the offices which a secularized religious can hold. The second paragraph of the same canon applies the first paragraph to those members of Societies who have been dispensed from an oath of perseverance or from promises after having been bound by such an oath or by such promises for six years.[207]

SECTION 5. LOCAL ORDINARIES OTHER THAN RESIDENTIAL BISHOPS AND THEIR POWER TO PROMOTE TO ORDERS MEMBERS OF SOCIETIES

The discussion of the competency of the minister of Holy Orders in Societies has thus far been confined to a discussion of the competency of residential bishops to promote to First Tonsure members of Societies who have a domicile in their dioceses, and to promote to higher Orders members of Societies who are incardinated in their dioceses. Members of Societies, however, follow the laws established for the ordination of secular clerics.[208] But secular clerics can be incardinated not only in dioceses, but also in abbacies and prelacies *nullius*[290] and in vicariates and prefectures apostolic.[210] It follows therefore that members of Societies, too, can be incardinated in abbacies and prelacies *nullius* and in vicariates and prefectures apostolic. It may be asked, therefore, what is the competency of the local ordinaries in these ecclesiastical jurisdictional territories other than dio-

[206] S. C. C., *Sedunen.*, 15 iul. 1933—*AAS*, XXVI (1934), 234-236. Cf. *supra*, pp. 104-105.

[207] Cf. Goyeneche, "Consultationes," *CpR*, VIII (1927), 113-115.

[208] Canon 678.

[209] Canon 215, § 2, collated with canon 111.

[210] Vermeersch-Creusen, *Epitome*, I, 217; McBride, *Incardination*, pp. 294-295; Paventi, *De Iuramento*, pp. 82, 111-112.

ceses in regard to members of Societies who have domiciles in, or who are incardinated in, these territories? The same question may be asked in reference to the vicars of local ordinaries, or in reference to those who take charge when jurisdiction is impeded or ceases. It is the purpose of this section to try to answer these questions.

In general it may be said that in virtue of canon 678, which states that in those things which pertain to the reception of Orders, members of Societies follow the laws regulating the ordination of secular clerics, those local ordinaries other than residential bishops who are competent for the ordination of secular clerics are also competent for the ordination of members of Societies.

In dealing with this question, it is important to have an exact understanding of the meaning of the expression "to promote to Orders." To promote to Orders means more than performing an ordination ceremony. It means authoritatively to effect the ordination of a subject, whether this be done immediately by means of the direct conferral of Orders, or mediately by means of the issuance of dimissorial letters.

No local ordinary may, without the permission of the Apostolic See, promote to higher Orders a member of a Society who has been ordained by the Roman Pontiff.[211]

Aside from this exceptional case, local ordinaries (other than residential bishops) who are competent to promote secular clerics to Orders, and who are, consequently, competent to promote members of Societies to Orders, may be divided, by reason of the limitations placed by law on the exercise of their competency, into three groups: first, those who need neither a mandate nor the consent of the Cathedral Chapter (or of the corresponding body in those places where there in no Cathedral Chapter), and who need not ordinarily wait until they have been in office a year before acting; second, those who are vicars general or vicars delegate and need a mandate from those whose

[211] Canon 952.

vicars they are, but who need the consent of no one else and who need not wait before acting; third, those who both need the consent of the Cathedral Chapter (or of the corresponding body in those places where there is no Cathedral Chapter), and who have to wait a year before acting unless the ordinand must receive Orders quickly because of a benefice received or to be received, or because of an office in the diocese or territory which must be filled.

In the enumeration of the various local ordinaries which is to follow, it is to be noted first, that anyone who has the power lawfully to confer Orders immediately, by that very fact has the power to issue dimissorial letters,[212] provided that he is impeded from a direct conferral by a just cause, or provided that he is of a rite different from that of the ordinand,[213] and secondly, that anyone who has the power to issue dimissorial letters for the reception of Orders may lawfully confer those same Orders immediately if he possesses the necessary power of Orders.[214]

In the first group, which includes those who need neither a mandate nor consent from others, and who need not ordinarily wait until they have been in office a year before acting, are (besides residential bishops) the following local ordinaries. Abbots and prelates *nullius,* if they lack the episcopal character, can, within their own territories and during their tenure of office, promote to First Tonsure and to minor Orders with a direct conferral of Orders those members of Societies who are subject to them according to the norm of canon 956, and also those members of Societies who are not so subject to them but who possess the dimissorial letters required by law for such promotion.[215] They can also, even though they lack the episcopal character, issue dimissorial letters for the promotion to all Orders, even to major Orders, of those members of Societies who are subject to them according to the norm

[212] Reg. 68, R. J., in VI°: "Potest quis per alium, quod potest facere per seipsum"; Coronata, *De Sacramentis,* II, 44.

[213] Canon 955, § 2.

[214] Canon 959.

[215] Canon 957, § 2.

of canon 956.[216] If they possess the episcopal character, they are, in reference to their powers to promote members of Societies to Orders, equal to residential bishops.[217] What has been said of abbots and prelates *nullius* with reference to the ordination of members of Societies is applicable also to vicars and prefects apostolic.[218] Pro-vicars and pro-prefects apostolic, when their respective vicars and prefects apostolic have vacated their offices or have been impeded in the exercise of their jurisdiction within the situation contemplated in canon 429, § 1, can issue dimissorial letters for the promotion to all Orders of those members of Societies who are subject to them according to the norm of canon 956.[219] The same can be said of both the administrator provisionally appointed by the pro-vicar or pro-prefect apostolic according to the norm of canon 309, § 3, and of the senior missionary who is, according to the norm of canon 309, § 4, to take charge of the vicariate or prefecture during a vacancy if no other missionary has been appointed.[220] Finally, apostolic administrators constituted as such in a permanent capacity have the same rights in reference to the ordination of members of Societies as residential bishops.[221]

The second group includes those vicars who need only the mandate of the ordinaries whose vicars they are. Vicars general of residential bishops can grant dimissorial letters

[216] Canon 958, § 1, n. 4.

[217] Canon 957, § 1; canons 215, § 2, and 323, § 1, collated with canons 955 and 956.

[218] Canons 294, § 2, and 957, § 2; canon 958, § 1, n. 4; canon 957, § 1; canon 294, § 1, collated with canons 955 and 956.

[219] Canon 309, § 2, collated with canon 958, § 1, n. 4; P. C. I., 20 iul. 1929, I—*AAS*, XXI, (1929), 573; Coronata, *De Sacramentis*, II, 43.

[220] Capello, "De Litteris Dimissoriis," *Periodica*, XVIII (1929), 249-251; Toso, "De Litteris Dimissoriis," *J. P.*, IX (1929), 193; Maroto, "De Litteris Dimissoriis," *Apollinaris*, III (1930), 232-236; Schaaf, "Episcopus Proprius Ordinationis," *ER*, XC (1934), p. 353, footnote 4.

[221] Canon 315, § 1, collated with canons 955 and 956.

for the promotion to all Orders of members of Societies for whom the respective residential bishops are the proper bishops for ordination.[222] The same must be said, *positis ponendis,* for the vicars general of abbots and prelates *nullius,*[223] for the vicars delegate of vicars and prefects apostolic,[224] and for the vicars general of apostolic administrators constituted as such in a permanent capacity.[225]

The third group includes most of those local ordinaries who are chosen to administer an ecclesiastical jurisdictional territory when the jurisdiction of its ordinary has ceased, has been impeded, or has been suspended. The ordinaries in this group may grant dimissorial letters for the promotion to Orders of a member of a Society only with the consent of the Cathedral Chapter (or of the corresponding body where the Cathedral Chapter is lacking), and only after a year from the cessation, impeding or suspension of the jurisdiction of the previous ordinary, except, as regards the latter limitation, in those cases where the member of a Society must be promoted to Orders quickly because of some benefice received or to be received, or because of some office in the jurisdictional territory which must be filled. This group includes vicars capitular of a diocese,[226] diocesan administrators elected in the place of vicars capitular in dioceses in which there are no Cathedral Chapters,[227] vicars capitular of an abbacy or a prelacy *nullius,*[228] and apostolic administrators constituted as such in a temporary capacity.[229]

[222] Canon 958, § 1, n. 2. Cf. canon 368, § 1.

[223] Canon 323, § 3, collated with canons 368, § 1, and 958, § 1, n. 2.

[224] S. C. de Prop. Fide, litt., 8 dec. 1919—*AAS*, XII (1920), 120, collated with canons 368, § 1, and 958, § 1, n. 2.

[225] Canon 315, § 1, collated with canons 366, § 1; 368, § 1; and 958, § 1, n. 2.

[226] Canon 958, § 1, n. 3.

[227] Canon 427 collated with canons 432, § 1, and 958, § 1, n. 3.

[228] Canon 327, § 1, collated with canons 432, § 1, and 958, § 1, n. 3.

[229] Canon 315, § 2, n. 1, collated with canon 958, § 1, n. 3.

SECTION 6. DIMISSORIAL LETTERS FOR THE PROMOTION TO ORDERS OF MEMBERS OF SOCIETIES

Essentially, dimissorial letters are letters in which one who is competent lawfully to promote a subject to Orders grants permission for the ordination of that subject by a prelate who is not, in his own name, competent to promote that ordinand to Orders.[230] Dimissorial letters issued by local ordinaries, however, differ from dimissorial letters issued by religious superiors by reason of the amount of testimony as to the fitness of the candidate which the law requires these dimissorial letters to contain. A local ordinary is bound only to give testimony to the fitness of the ordinand in a general way.[231] A religious superior who has the authority to issue dimissorial letters, on the other hand, must be much more detailed in the testimony which he is to render in regard to the fitness of the ordinand. He must testify in the dimissorial letters that the ordinand has made his religious profession and is a member of the religious house of which the author of the dimissorial letters is superior, and that the ordinand has completed the necessary studies and has fulfilled all the other requirements made by law.[232] Cappello states that express testimony must be given with regard to the candidate's morals and with regard to the spiritual retreat to be made before the reception of

[230] Riganti, *Commentaria in Regulas*, in Reg. XXIV, § III, n. 167 (Vol. II, p. 363); Hallier, *De Sacris Electionibus et Ordinationibus* (2. ed., 3 vols., Romae, 1739-1740), Pars II, Sectio V, Caput III, Art. XI, § 1 (Vol. II, pp. 411-412); Reiffenstuel, Lib. I, tit. XI, n. 109; Gasparri, *De Sacra Ordinatione*, II, 124-126, 161; Many, *De Sacra Ordinatione*, p. 150; Cappello, *De Sacramentis*, IV, 231; Coronata, *De Sacramentis*, II, 40.

[231] Coronata, *De Sacramentis*, II, 40; Quinn, *Documents Required for the Reception of Orders*, The Catholic University of America Canon Law Studies, n. 266 (Washington, D.C.: The Catholic University of America Press, 1948), pp. 132-133.

Moeder does not mention any testimony as to the fitness of the candidate among the essential contents of dimissorial letters. Cf. *Proper Bishop*, p. 98.

[232] Canon 995, § 1.

Orders.[233] Quinn mentions that testimony should be given with regard to the fulfillment of other laws, but states that a general statement that the requirements of the Code and of the Constitutions have been fulfilled suffices.[234]

It may be asked what amount of testimony a local ordinary is bound to include in the dimissorial letters he issues for the promotion to Orders of members of Societies. Will a general testimony regardng the member's fitness suffice? Or must the ordinary incorporate detailed testimony such as that which is required of a religious superior issuing dimissorial letters for the promotion to Orders of his subjects?

It seems that the local ordinary is bound only to give general testimony to the fitness of the members of Societies for whom he issues dimissorial letters. For members of Societies are, by the common law, regulated by the laws enacted for the ordination of secular clerics,[235] and a local ordinary is not bound by law to give detailed testimony concerning the fitness of his own secular clergy when he issues dimissorial letters for their promotion to Orders. Canon 960, § 1, states merely that he must *have* the testimonials demanded by canons 993 to 1000 *before issuing* dimissorial letters. Furthermore, the canon which requires that detailed testimony be inserted in dimissorial letters[236] is binding only on the superiors of religious. But members of Societies are not religious.[237]

In strict warrant, the competent local ordinary could give permission for the ordination of members of Societies orally; but writing is strongly advised in every case.[238]

[233] *De Sacramentis*, IV, 234.

[234] *Documents Required for the Reception of Orders*, p. 159.

[235] Canon 678.

[236] Canon 995, § 1.

[237] Canon 673, § 1.

[238] Moeder, *Proper Bishop*, pp. 82-83; Coronata, *De Sacramentis*, II, 40; Cappello, *De Sacramentis*, IV, 232; Quinn, *Documents Required for the Reception of Orders*, p. 131.

The dimissorial letters should contain, in addition to the actual permission to ordain, the name of the local ordinary issuing them, the name of the prelate to whom they are addressed (or, if permission is given in a general way, e.g., "to any bishop in communion with the Holy See," the statement of that fact), the Order or Orders for which permission is given, a general attestation to the fitness of the ordinand or ordinands, and a notation of the place and date of issuance as well as the signature and seal of the grantor. A vicar general should make mention of his mandate, and a vicar capitular (or his counterpart) should make a notation of the fulfillment of the conditions demanded in canon 958, § 1, n. 3.[239]

The dimissorial letters may be sent to any bishop in communion with the Apostolic See except, apart from an apostolic indult, to a bishop of a Rite different from that of the ordinand.[240]

The bishop receiving the dimissorial letters need only make sure of their authenticity before ordaining.[241] He may, however, in the case where the examinations preceding ordination have been conducted by the local ordinary who issued the dimissorial letters, or by a delegate of the latter ordinary (i.e., in any case in which the ordinary issuing dimissorial letters has not commissioned the bishop to whom the dimissorial letters are addressed to make the examination), refuse to acquiesce in the attestations made by the examiners,[242] and institute his own examination, not only with regard to the knowledge of the candidate, but also in regard to any of the requirements for lawful ordination.[243]

Dimissorial letters given for the ordination of members of Societies can be limited or revoked by the local ordinary

239 Quinn, *Documents Required for the Reception of Orders*, pp. 131-133.

240 Canon 961.

241 Canon 962.

242 Canon 997, § 2.

243 Coronata, *De Sacramentis*, II, 236.

granting them or by his successor, but once they have been issued they do not become void by loss of office of the ordinary who issued them.[244]

Article 3. The Subject of Holy Orders in Societies

Section 1. The Obligations of Others in Reference to Ordinands in Societies

The obligations of others in reference to ordinands in Societies may be summed up under two headings: the obligation to provide for the intellectual and spiritual training of the candidates, and the obligation of passing judgment as to the fitness of the candidates for the priestly state.

The first obligation is that of providing for the intellectual and spiritual training of the candidates. Canon 678 states that in those things which pertain to their program of studies (*"studiorum rationem"*), members of Societies are bound by the same laws as secular clerics, the full binding force of the specific prescripts given by the Holy See being of course duly safeguarded. In virtue of this canon, Societies are bound by the rulings enacted in canons 1364, 1365 and 1366, which regulate the program of studies in secular seminaries, minor and major.[245]

If a Society is able to have its own house of studies, this house is to be governed neither according to the norms established in canons 587, 588 and 589, which treat of the government of religious houses of study, nor according to the norms established in canons 1357 to 1363 and 1367 to 1371, which treat of the government of diocesan seminaries. It is to be governed according to the norms established in the Constitutions of the Society and according to canons 499 to 530, *congrua congruis referendo.*[246]

When dealing with the question of studies and ordination in Societies, authors usually treat of the obligations

[244] Canon 963.

[245] Rothoff, *Sociétés*, pp. 156-160.

[246] Canon 675; Rothoff, *Sociétés*, p. 157.

of junior clergy examinations and of clerical conferences. All authors are agreed that members of Societies are not bound by canons 590 and 591, which treat of these obligations in religious institutes. All are agreed that members of Societies are bound rather by canons 130 and 131, which treat of these obligations as obligations of secular clerics.[247] Thus, priest members of Societies are bound to undergo junior clergy examinations for three years after the completion of their studies. The manner of conducting the examinations is to be determined by the local ordinary, who may for good reasons grant exemption from the examinations.[248] Since canon 130 makes no distinction between the ordinary of incardination and any other local ordinary, it seems that if a member of a Society was stationed outside of his diocese of incardination, the ordinary of the place where he was stationed, in addition to his ordinary of incardination would be competent by reason of his ordinary jurisdiction over all who have a domicile in his diocese. Furthermore, priest members, regardless of their years in ordination, are bound, ordinarily, to attend the diocesan clerical conferences which are held several times a year.[249] If, however, the Constitutions of a particular Society call for clerical conferences to be held in the houses of the Society, the members are excused from the diocesan conferences.[250]

Although most authors indicate that members of Societies are bound by the law enacted in canons 130 and 131 in virtue of canon 678, it seems that the obligation derives rather from the prescript of canon 679. For canon 678 seems to refer only to the program of studies to be followed in preparation for the reception of Orders, whereas canon

[247] Stanton, *De Societatibus*, p. 136; Schaefer, *De Religiosis*, p. 993; Ristuccia, *Societies*, pp. 194-196; Rothoff, *Sociétés*, p. 158; et alii.

[248] Canon 130.

[249] Canon 131, § 1.

[250] Canon 131, § 3; Stanton, *De Societatibus*, p. 136: Ristuccia, *Societies*, p. 195; Cocchi, *Commentarium*, IV, 241.

679 imposes on members of Societies the obligations common to clerics, among which are found the obligations imposed by canons 130 and 131.[251]

Finally, it may be pointed out that the matter of the junior clergy examinations and the clerical conferences has been treated in this place because the former obligation rests primarily on the shoulders of the local ordinaries, and only secondarily on the junior clergy,[252] and it seems that the obligation regarding the holding of clerical conferences is primarily the obligation of the local ordinaries and the rural deans.[253]

The second obligation of others in regard to ordinand members of Societies is the obligation of passing judgment on their fitness for the priestly state. The Instruction *Quantum Religiones,* which, as was seen above, is intended for Societies as well as for religious institutes,[254] deals with this problem in paragraph 12:

> As regards the ordination of religious, according to canonical legislation the major Superiors either give dimissorial letters to the ordaining Bishops (cc. 965 and 966, § 1), or at least provide the candidates for ordination with testimonial letters (c. 933, n. 5). By these testimonial letters the religious Superior not only attests that the persons in question are members of his religious family, but also certifies to the completion of their studies and to the fulfillment of other requirements of law (c. 995, § 1). Hence it follows that that same very grave obligation which rests upon Bishops, to train, approve, and select their own secular subjects who desire to receive sacred orders is incumbent in exactly the same way upon religious Superiors whose business it is to admit their own subjects to sacred orders. And although Bishops may according to law (c. 997, § 2) refuse to acquiesce in the testimonials

[251] Rothoff, *Sociétés,* p. 158.

[252] Coronata, *Institutiones,* I, 220.

[253] Cf. canon 131, § 1.

[254] Cf. pp. 58-59.

> of the Superiors, and may themselves examine the religious candidates for orders, yet they are not bound to do so. They may, before God and the Church, accept the favorable testimonials of Superiors and leave upon them the full responsibility regarding the due training and worthiness of the candidates (cc. 970, 995, § 2).[255]

From this paragraph it is evident that the consciences of superiors in Societies are fully burdened with the responsibility of admitting candidate members to Orders. They cannot claim that, since in matters of ordination Societies are governed by the laws regulating the ordination of secular clerics, the full responsibility lies on the shoulders of the local ordinaries who are the proper ordinaries for the ordination of the members, and on the shoulders of these ordinaries alone. It is true that the responsibility *does* lie on the shoulders of the proper ordinaries—the *full* responsibility. For canon 968, § 1, states that only he can be said to receive Orders licitly who is possessed of the qualities required by law in the judgment of his *own ordinary*. And canon 973, § 3, states that a bishop is to ordain *no one* without being morally certain of his canonical fitness. The ordaining bishop, however, is permitted to obtain moral certitude about the character of candidates in Societies by basing his judgments on the testimony rendered by the superiors of these candidates. It will be the bishop's duty to assure himself in some way of the soundness of judgment possessed by the superiors. If the bishop judges that he can trust the sound judgment of a particular superior of a house of studies in a Society, then the bishop will not have to make a personal test of the character of each candidate in that house.

In Societies subject to the Sacred Congregation for the Propagation of the Faith, it seems that admission to sacred Orders, as an act distinct from the issuing of dimissorial

[255] S. C. de Rel., instr. *Quantum Religiones*, 1 dec. 1931—*AAS*, XXIV (1932), 74-81, cf. pp. 78-79. The translation given above is taken from Bouscaren, *Digest*, I, 478-479.

letters, is always reserved to the superior general, who needs the consent of a majority of his council to act.[256]

In the Societies subject to the Sacred Congregation for Religious, there does not seem to be the same uniformity. The superior general with a majority consent of his council is alone competent to admit his subjects to sacred Orders in the Society of the Priests of Mercy[257] and in the Congregation of Jesus and Mary.[258] In the Congregation of the Most Precious Blood, the provincial superior, with the consent of his council, presents candidates for sacred Orders to the superior general, who by privilege has the right to issue dimissorial letters.[259]

The proper ordinary may not promote to Orders members of Societies unless, in his judgment, the members to be ordained are necessary or useful for the churches of his diocese.[260] This does not mean that the members will be expected to spend all their priestly lives laboring in the diocese of their proper ordinaries. For the requirement of necessity or usefulness applies equally to all the diocesan clergy, and certainly proper bishops are free to lend out other members of their diocesan clergy for service in other dioceses. It means simply that, if and when a member

[256] *Société des Missionnaires d'Afrique, Constitutions*, §§ 87, 122, pp. 30, 41; *The Society of African Missions, Constitutions and Directory*, §§ 63, 77, 115, pp. 15, 17, 25; *Constitutions of the Catholic Foreign Mission Society of America*, § 86, p. 16; *Constitutiones Societatis Sancti Columbani pro Missionibus apud Sinenses*, § 32, p. 11; *Costituzioni dell'Istituto delle Missioni Estere di Milano*, § 152, p. 37; *Constitutions of the Scarboro Foreign Mission Society*, §§ 135, 200, pp. 27, 37; Paventi, *Organización del Instituto Español*, p. 49.

[257] *Constitutions de la Société des Prêtres de la Miséricorde*, § 497, p. 135.

[258] *Constitutions de la Congrégation de Jésus et Marie*, §§ 208, 222, pp. 77, 83.

[259] *Regula et Constitutiones Congregationis Missionis a Pretioso Sanguine D. N. J. C.*, § 149, pp. 50-51.

[260] Canon 969, § 1.

should return to his diocese, he would be useful there.[261]

Finally, the prohibitions against forcing anyone to embrace the clerical state and against barring the canonically worthy apply both to the proper ordinaries and to major superiors of Societies in regard to members of Societies who are candidates for promotion to Orders.[262]

SECTION 2. REQUISITES IN THE ORDINANDS THEMSELVES

The Code lists eight requisites which must be verified in all candidates for Orders. The first requisite is the intention of advancing to the priesthood, and is treated in canon 973. The other seven requisites, as listed in canon 974, are: reception of Confirmation, moral character corresponding to the Order to be received, canonical age, due knowledge, reception of the lower Orders, observance of the prescribed intervals between Orders, and, if major Orders are in question, canonical title. Canons 975 to 982 treat further of the five last-mentioned requisites. All eight of these requisites must be verified in members of Societies in the same way in which they must be verified in other candidates for Orders among the secular clergy. It will be in order, however, to treat briefly of the intention of advancing to the priesthood, of due knowledge, and of the canonical title in their relation to members of Societies, and to indicate a ninth requirement which is binding on members of Societies in virtue of the Instruction *Quantum Religiones*.

Canon 973 states that First Tonsure and Orders are to

[261] It seems that even if a diocese were so well supplied with priests that members of Societies who might return there could never be considered necessary or useful, the bishop could still ordain the members with the intention of later excardinating them and having them incardinated in a diocese in which they would be useful. Cf. canon 969, § 2. It seems that the same bishop could also, with permission from another bishop in whose diocese the members would be useful, incardinate the members in the latter diocese by promoting them to First Tonsure for the service of that diocese. Cf. P. C. I., 24 iul. 1939—*AAS*, XXXI (1939), 321.

[262] Canon 971.

be conferred only on those who have the intention of ascending to the priesthood, and who give promise of becoming worthy priests. The Instruction *Quantum Religiones,* however, requires that members of Societies manifest the intention of ascending to the priesthood at a time that might come a number of years before promotion to First Tonsure. It requires this manifestation just before the candidate finishes his period of probation and becomes incorporated in the Society.[263]

Canon 976 treats in detail of the requirement of due knowledge. In this regard it is to be noted that although canon 972, § 2, allows, under certain conditions, that some aspirants to the priesthood can be permitted to live outside a seminary, nevertheless canon 976, § 3, demands that all candidates for the priesthood study Theology in schools set up for this purpose, and allows no exception whereby an aspirant may study Theology privately. Therefore, if a Society cannot afford to have its own house of studies, it must see to it that its scholastics attend classes in Theology in some seminary or university, although the same scholastics need not live in the seminary or on the campus of the university.

In the matter of the canonical title, the authors are unanimous in asserting that members of Societies must, by the common law, make use of the titles of secular clerics as contained in canons 979, 980 and 981, and may not use the title of poverty, which is reserved for regulars by canon 982, § 1, nor the titles of the common table or the congregation, which by canon 982, § 2, are reserved for religious with simple perpetual vows.[264] This applica-

[263] S. C. de Rel., instr. *Quantum Religiones,* 1 dec. 1931, n. 14—*AAS,* XXIV (1932), 74-81, cf. pp. 79-80.

[264] Bastien, *Directoire Canonique* (3. ed.), p. 345; Sipos, *Enchiridion Iuris Canonici,* p. 398; Stanton, *De Societatibus,* p. 137; Berutti, *Institutiones Iuris Canonici,* III, 370; Goyeneche, *Summa Principia,* p. 236; Claeys Bouuaert-Simenon, *Manuale,* I, 433; *Romani, Institutiones Juris Canonici,* I, 411; Cocchi, *Commentarium,* IV, 242; Naz, *Traité de droit canonique,* I, 713; Schaefer, *De Religiosis,* p. 994; Brys,

tion of canons 979, 980 and 981, and the exclusion of canon 982, § 1 and § 2, are made in virtue of canon 678, and not in virtue of canon 982, § 3. For the last-mentioned paragraph speaks of *"ceteri religiosi."* Members of Societies are not religious.[265] *"Ceteri religiosi"* in canon 982, § 3, refers to religious who belong to Religious Congregations in which perpetual vows are never pronounced.[266]

Members of Societies, then, may make use of the titles of benefice, patrimony or pension.[267] If none of these titles is available, the members may use the title of the service of the diocese, or, in places subject to the Sacred Congregation for the Propagation of the Faith, the title of the mission.[268] The use of these titles by members of Societies is regulated in the same way as their use by other secular clerics. Some remarks are in order, however, about the oath required by canon 981, § 1, for use of the titles either of the service of the diocese or of the mission.

In order to make use of the title of the service of the diocese or of the mission, an ordinand must take an oath to devote himself perpetually to the service of the diocese or to the mission. This oath implies more than the oath mentioned in canon 956 and required of one who has a domicile distinct from the place of origin. Whereas the latter is an oath to *remain*, the former is an oath to *serve*. Furthermore, the oath to remain, in canon 956, is only assertory,[269] whereas the oath to serve, in canon 981, § 1, is promissory.[270] Nevertheless, it seems that members of

Juris Canonici Compendium, I, 597; Ristuccia, *Societies,* pp. 204-205; Rothoff, *Sociétés,* pp. 173-174; Gil, "Studium," *CpRM,* XXVIII (1949), 22; Fanfani, *De Iure Religiosorum,* p. 714; Vermeersch-Creusen, *Epitome,* I, 631; De Carlo, *Jus Religiosorum,* p. 512; Abbo-Hannan, *The Sacred Canons,* I, 685.

265 Canon 673, § 1.

266 Cf. canon 488, n. 1. The writer has never been able to find an example of even one such clerical Religious Congregation.

267 Canon 979, § 1.

268 Canon 981, § 1.

269 Cf. *supra,* p. 110.

270 Coronata, *De Sacramentis,* II, 116; Beste, *Introductio,* p. 534.

Societies may take the oath to *serve* just as they seem to be capable of taking the oath to *remain.*[271] This contention of the writer seems to be justified by the following argument taken from the use of these titles by other secular clerics.

With regard to the use of the title of the service of the diocese, many diocesan clerics who are not members of Societies take the oath to serve their dioceses in order to use the title of the service of the diocese. And yet, some of these clerics are called upon by lawful authority to spend a great part of their priestly lives in the service of other dioceses. It seems, therefore, that when these clerics take the oath to serve their dioceses, all that is required of them is that they take an oath to serve their dioceses insofar as they are called upon so to serve by lawful authority. What, then, is there to prevent members of Societies from taking the same oath? In the case of members of Societies, lawful authority will have established that while they remain members they will be called upon to serve in the places designated by their superiors. Sometimes these places will be within their own dioceses; more often, perhaps, outside. Instead of deriving support from their own dioceses in virtue of their title of ordination, lawful authority will also have established that while they remain in their Societies, the Societies will be responsible for their support.

With regard to the use of the title of the mission, a similar argument could be formulated. Thus, members of Societies who are incardinated in vicariates and prefectures apostolic could take the oath of service mentioned in canon 981, § 1, even though they should foresee that they will be called upon by their superiors to serve in vicariates and prefectures apostolic other than the ones in which they are incardinated.

The foregoing seems to be a reasonable interpretation to place on the meaning of the oath of service to be taken in order to make use of the title of the service of the diocese

[271] Cf. *supra*, pp. 107-117.

or of the mission. For the purpose of the Church's law on the ordination title is, in the present discipline, primarily the guaranteeing of support for the clergy, and not the guaranteeing of laborers for one section of the vineyard. The purpose of guaranteeing service by oath, then, seems to be that of guaranteeing support to be derived as just compensation for this service. The purpose of the oath seems to be that of guaranteeing that no cleric in major Orders will be without support because he is without work. By the oath, therefore, it seems that a member of a Society simply promises that, should he ever cease getting support from his Society by reason of the fact that he should leave his Society, he would return to his diocese or mission and go to work there, and not become a burden on others, beg, engage in an occupation unbecoming to clerics, or become a problem to the Church in any way because of the lack of due support.

The oath of service taken by clerics who are incardinated in vicariates or prefectures apostolic in order that they may make use of the title of the mission is not to be confused with the oath by which members are incorporated in most missionary Societies. The latter oath is usually taken for three years at the end of the period of probation, and thereafter perpetually. This oath is usually an oath of obedience and of dedication to the work of the *missions* entrusted to the particular Societies.[272] The oath required for the use of the title of the mission as established in canon 981, § 1, on the other hand, is a promise of service in regard to a *particular mission,* that is, to a particular vicariate or prefecture apostolic. It is the oath taken by

[272] *Société des Missionnaires d'Afrique, Constitutions,* § 192, p. 61; *The Society of African Missions, Constitutions and Directory,* § 20, pp. 4-5; *Constitutions of the Catholic Foreign Mission Society of America,* § 14, pp. 2-3; *Constitutiones Societatis Sancti Columbani pro Missionibus apud Sinenses,* § 14, pp. 8-9; *Costituzioni dell'Istituto delle Missioni Estere de Milano,* p. 68; *Constitutions of the Scarboro Foreign Mission Society,* § 31, p. 12; Paventi, *Organización del Instituto Español,* pp. 23-26.

the native clergy in the mission fields when they wish to make use of the title of the mission.[273] The oath usually taken at the time of incorporation in a Society, then, is not sufficient to justify the use of the title of the mission according to the norm of canon 981, § 1. The members, in order to use this title, must take another oath to serve the particular mission in which they are incardinated. By taking this oath, they declare their intention, in the event that they should leave their Society, to repair to the mission in which they are incardinated and to serve that mission perpetually.

Canonical title is the last of eight requisites imposed by the Code on candidates for Orders. In addition to these eight requisites, there is a ninth imposed on members of Societies by the Instruction *Quantum Religiones.*

Members of Societies are not to be promoted to First Tonsure or to any other Order until after the completion of their period of probation.[274] Nor are members of Societies to be advanced to major Orders until after they have made their perpetual and definite choice, if that is provided for; if it is not provided for, the members are not to be advanced to major Orders before the expiration of three full years from their initial incorporation which followed their period of probation.[275] In the case of a man who joins a Society when he is already close to the priesthood, a problem is created by the fact that in virtue of the above-mentioned prescripts of the Instruction *Quantum Religiones* he would be obliged to wait three years before promotion to any major Order. The problem, when it occurs in a Society in which there is a perpetual bond of incorporation, is usually solved by the Holy See, not by dispensing with the prescripts of the Instruction, but by

[273] Coronata, *De Sacramentis*, II, 113-116; Paventi, *De Iuramento*, pp. 79-84, 111-112; Cappello, *De Sacramentis*, IV, 320-322.

[274] S. C. de Rel., instr., *Quantum Religiones*, 1 dec. 1931, n. 14—*AAS*, XXIV (1932), 74-81, cf. pp. 79-80.

[275] S. C. de Rel., instr. *Quantum Religiones*, 1 dec. 1931, n. 15—*AAS*, XXIV (1932), 74-81, cf. p. 80.

giving the member permission to become perpetually incorporated in the Society before the expiration of three full years from the time of his temporary incorporation.[276]

SECTION 3. IRREGULARITIES AND IMPEDIMENTS

The irregularities and impediments established by the Code are, in general, the same for all ordinands, whether religious or secular. The following notations, however, seem to be in order with regard to certain of these irregularities and impediments as they apply to members of Societies, with regard to the dispensation from irregularities and impediments in Societies, and with regard to one of the effects of irregularities and impediments which remains after a dispensation from the irregularities and impediments themselves has been granted.

If a member of a Society, before promotion to the subdiaconate, attempts marriage, even civil marriage, he certainly should not be considered fit for the reception of Orders. He would not, however, incur the irregularity of canon 985, n. 3, arising from the crime of attempting marriage while bound by simple vow, even though the bond by which he is incorporated in his Society be a private vow. For canon 985, n. 3, states that this irregularity arises when one is bound by religious vows; but members of Societies are never bound by the public vows of religion.[277]

In virtue of canon 987, n. 5, those who are bound by the civil law to ordinary military service are, before they have completed this service, simply impeded from the reception of Orders. In this connection it seems apropos to call to mind the following facts. In 1911, the Sacred Congregation for Religious issued the Decree *Inter reliquas,* which gave specific directives to religious institutes with regard to religious subject to compulsory military service. The ninth paragraph of this Decree declared that the prescripts

[276] Cf. S. C. Ep. et Reg., decr. *Auctis admodum,* 4 nov. 1892, § 2—*Fontes,* n. 2020; Many, *De Sacra Ordinatione,* pp. 384-385; Gil, "Studium," *CpRM,* XXVIII (1949), p. 29, nota (5).

[277] Cf. canon 673, § 1.

of the Decree were equally binding on ecclesiastical Societies which, though they had neither solemn nor simple vows, had simple promises binding the members to their respective Societies.[278] The year after the Code became binding, the same Sacred Congregation declared that the Decree *Inter reliquas* was still in effect. For although the Decree was by its nature temporary, providing for a mode of action to cope with civil laws which were contrary to Canon Law,[279] nevertheless, since the conditions which gave rise to the Decree still existed after the Code, the Decree continued to be binding. The Sacred Congregation on this occasion added further directives in this matter, supplementing the prescripts of the Decree.[280] Since the conditions which prompted the Decree *Inter reliquas* still exist today, the Decree itself must be considered as still binding.

With regard to the power of dispensing from certain irregularities as it is granted by canon 990, § 1, the ordinaries mentioned in that canon are to be understood ordinarily as the local ordinaries who are the proper ordinaries for the promotion to Orders of the members of Societies who are to receive the dispensation. If, however, a tonsured member of a Society is stationed outside the territory of the local ordinary who is his proper ordinary by reason of incardination, the power to dispense such a member is vested in the ordinary of the place where the member is stationed.[281]

Finally, if a member of a Society is dispensed from an irregularity or an impediment, it seems that he will not be barred by canon 991, § 3, from becoming a major superior in his Society. For canon 991, § 3, bars persons so

[278] S. C. de Rel., decr. *Inter reliquas*, 1 ian. 1911—*Fontes*, n. 4408.

[279] Cf. canons 614 and 680 collated with canon 121.

[280] S. C. de Rel., responsum, 15 iul. 1919—*AAS*, XI (1919), 321-323.

[281] Coronata, *De Sacramentis*, II, 209. Members of Societies seem to be subject to the ordinary jurisdiction of the bishop of the place where they are stationed by reason of the necessary domicile which they have in that place. Cf. *supra*, pp. 71-81.

dispensed from becoming major superiors in clerical exempt religious institutes. But Societies, by the common law, are not exempt.[282] Neither can Societies be included among religious institutes.[283]

Article 4. Preliminaries to Ordination in Societies

By preliminaries to ordination are meant those things which come immediately before ordination, as opposed to those remote preparations for the reception of Orders which extend over a period of years. These preliminaries are treated in canons 992 to 1001. These preliminaries may be summed up under five heads: the manifestation of the intention to receive Orders (canon 992), the gathering of the necessary documents and testimonials (canons 993 to 995), the examination of the ordinands (canons 996 and 997), the publication of the banns (canons 998 to 1000), and the spiritual retreat (canon 1001). To these preliminaries are to be added the profession of the Faith and the oath against Modernism.

Since the documents and testimonials which must be gathered for members of Societies include, as will be seen towards the end of the present Article, documents and testimonials which refer to the other preliminaries, it will be proper to treat of the gathering of the documents and testimonials last.

Canon 992 commands that all ordinands, at an opportune time before their ordination, manifest either personally or through others their intention to receive Orders. The manner in which this canon should be obeyed by members of Societies is outlined in detail in the Instruction *Quantum Religiones*. Candidates for membership in Societies, at the end of their period of probation and before taking the private vows, oath or promise by which they bind themselves to their Societies, shall make a petition in writing to their superiors, in which they shall expressly state their

[282] Cf. *supra*, p. 62.
[283] Canon 673, § 1.

vocation to the clerical state in their Societies, and at the same time announce their firm resolve to give themselves forever to service in the ranks of the clergy in their Societies. These petitions shall be kept in the archives of the Societies. In addition, the superiors themselves either in person or through some learned and prudent men who are qualified to win the confidence of the young men, shall ask them, so that the superiors may at last be sure that the young men are freely and consciously seeking Orders in their Societies.[284]

Before members of Societies are promoted to the subdiaconate, superiors shall require of them a declaration signed by the candidates in their own hand and sworn to before the superiors, attesting to their freedom, their knowledge of the obligations about to be embraced, especially that of chastity, their resolution to embrace these obligations, and their promise to live an edifying and useful life subject to ecclesiastical authority.[285]

The law regarding the examination on the Order to be received, and, in the case of those about to receive major Orders, on other tracts in Theology, is applicable to members of Societies in exactly the same way as it applies to other secular clerics.[286] This examination is to be regulated completely by the local ordinary who is the proper ordinary for the promotion of the members of Societies to Orders.[287] This local ordinary, however, is free to delegate superiors or professors in the Societies to conduct these examinations.[288]

All authors are in agreement that Societies are bound by canons 998, 999 and 1000, which regulate the publication

[284] S. C. de Rel., instr. *Quantum Religiones*, 1 dec. 1931, n. 14—*AAS*, XXIV (1932), 74-81, cf. pp. 79-80; Stanton, *De Societatibus*, p. 167; Coronata, *De Sacramentis*, II, 222-223.

[285] S. C. de Rel., instr. *Quantum Religiones*, 1 dec. 1931, n. 17—*AAS*, XXIV (1932), 74-81, cf. pp. 80-81.

[286] Cf. canon 678 collated with canons 996 and 997.

[287] Canon 997, § 1.

[288] Canon 996, § 3.

of the banns before the reception of major Orders.[289] According to canon 998, § 1, the banns are to be published in the parish church of the candidate. Since one's parish is determined by domicile or quasi-domicile,[290] and since members of Societies have a necessary domicile in the place in which is located the house to which they are attached,[291] it follows that the parish in which the banns are to be announced is the parish in which is located the house of the Society in which the ordinands are stationed.

If the proper ordinary of a member of a Society feels that publication of the banns in the parish in which is located the house to which the member is attached is insufficient, the proper ordinary is free to command that the banns be published in any of the parishes in which the member lived before his entrance into the Society, or in any parish in which is located a house of the Society in which the member was previously stationed.[292]

All ordinands are comprehended under canon 1001, which treats of the spiritual retreat to be made prior to the reception of Orders. The third paragraph of this canon, however, states that, whereas religious are to make this retreat in their own house or in another which might be designated by their superiors, seculars are to make the retreat in the seminary or in another pious or religious house designated by the bishop. Rothoff is of the opinion that this is a matter of internal government, and that therefore superiors in Societies have the right to indicate where their subjects are make their retreat.[293] Ristuccia, on the other hand, feels that it is the right of the bishop to indi-

[289] Bastien, *Directoire Canonique* (3. ed.), p. 345; Stanton, *De Societatibus*, p. 137; Berutti, *Institutiones Iuris Canonici*, III, 370; Naz, *Traité de droit canonique*, I, 713; Ristuccia, *Societies*, p. 198; Rothoff, *Sociétés*, pp. 178-179; Vermeersch-Creusen, *Epitome*, I, 631.

[290] Canon 94, § 1.

[291] Cf. *supra*, pp. 71-81.

[292] Canon 998, § 1.

[293] *Sociétés*, p. 147; cf. Stanton, *De Societatibus*, pp. 137-138, nota (92).

cate where the members of Societies who are candidates for the reception of Orders are to make their retreat.[294] It seems that the latter view is the correct one. For, although the annual retreat made in Societies may be considered a matter of internal government, since it is one of the obligations of religious which have been imposed on members of Societies,[295] nevertheless the obligation of members of Societies to make a retreat before the reception of Orders rises only from the law of ordination,[296] in which law members of Societies are equivalated to other secular clerics.[297]

Before their promotion to the subdiaconate, members of Societies are required to make a profession of the Faith[298] and to take the formulated oath against Modernism.[299]

With regard to the documents and testimonials mentioned in canons 993, 994 and 995, Societies, by the common law, are in no way affected by canon 995, which treats of the dimissorial letters given by some religious superiors. Societies are bound rather by the prescripts of canons 993 and 994, which deal with the testimonials required in the case of those who become ordained in accord with the law for the ordination of secular clerics.[300] Thus, ordinand members of Societies are required to bring testimony of their latest ordination, or, if there be question of promotion to First Tonsure, of their Baptism and Confirma-

[294] *Societies*, p. 199.

[295] Cf. canon 679, § 1, collated with canon 595, § 1, n. 1.

[296] Canon 1001.

[297] Canon 678.

[298] Canon 1406, § 1, n. 7.

[299] Pius X, motu propr. *Sacrorum antistitum*, 1 sept. 1910—*AAS*, II (1910), 669; S. C. S. Off., decr., 22 mart. 1918—*AAS*, X (1918), 136.

[300] Bastien, *Directoire Canonique* (3. ed.), p. 345; Goyeneche, *Summa Principia*, p. 236; Romani, *Institutiones Juris Canonici*, I, 411; Paventi, *De Iuramento*, p. 96; Schaefer, *De Religiosis*, pp. 993-994; Ristuccia, *Societies*, p. 199; Vermeersch-Creusen, *Epitome*, I, 631.

tion;[301] testimony of the completion of the studies required for the Order which they are about to receive;[302] testimony of their good morals from the rector of the seminary, or from the priest to whose care they were entrusted if they were permitted to live outside the seminary;[303] and testimonial letters from the ordinaries of the places in which they spent enough time to contract a canonical impediment.[304]

The fifth number of canon 993 requires that those ordinands who are affiliated with a religious institute bring testimonials from their major superiors. Since only those who are affiliated with religious institutes are mentioned, some authors claim that members of Societies are not included in this number.[305] Canon 993, n. 5, however, is applied to members of Societies in virtue of the Instruction *Quantum Religiones*.[306] Thus, ordinand members of Societies must bring with them testimonials from their major superiors.[307]

The Instruction *Quantum Religiones* states that in their testimonials major superiors not only attest that the ordinands are their subjects, but also certify to the completion of their studies and to the fulfillment of the other requirements of law.[308] The requirements of law regarding the fulfillment of which the major superiors are to give testimony are the following: the absence of all the impediments and irregularities listed in canons 984, 985 and 987; the positive requisites mentioned in canon 973 to 981; the

301 Canon 993, n. 1.

302 Canon 993, n. 2; cf. canon 976.

303 Canon 993, n. 3.

304 Canon 993, n. 4; cf. canon 994.

305 Oesterle, "Weihekandidaten aus einer Diözesan-Priestergenossenschaft," *ThPrQs*, LXXXV (1932), 570; Quinn, *Documents Required for the Reception of Orders*, p. 153.

306 S. C. de Rel., instr. *Quantum Religiones*, 1 dec. 1931, n. 12—*AAS*, XXIV (1932), 74-81, cf. pp. 78-79.

307 Ristuccia, *Societies*, p. 197; Rothoff, *Sociétés*, p. 177.

308 S. C. de Rel., instr. *Quantum Religiones*, 1 dec. 1931, n. 12—*AAS*, XXIV (1932), 74-81, cf. pp. 78-79.

status of the members within the Societies with regard to temporary or perpetual incorporation; the intention of receiving the Order in question (unless the proper ordinaries should choose to inquire about this intention personally according to the norm of canon 992); the examinations to be given before ordination according to the norm of canons 996 and 997 (unless the proper ordinaries should choose to conduct these examinations personally); the publication of the banns as required by canons 998, 999 and 1000; the spiritual retreat as mentioned in canon 1001; the profession of the Faith as mentioned in canon 1406, § 1, n. 7, and the oath against Modernism as prescribed by Pope Pius X (whenever these are taken beforehand before a delegate of the proper ordinaries); and the prescriptions of the Instruction *Quantum Religiones*.[309]

Canon 993 merely states that the ordinands must *bring* the testimonial letters mentioned in that canon. It does not state explicitly *to whom* they must bring these testimonials. It seems, however, that the testimonials must be brought to that local ordinary who has the authority to promote to Orders. It is not sufficient that major superiors in Societies simply collect the testimonials and documents mentioned in canon 993, nn. 1, 2, 3, 4, retain them in their own archives, and forward to the proper ordinaries only their own testimonials, namely, the ones required by canon 993, n. 5, in conjunction with the Instruction *Quantum Religiones*. The reason why the last-mentioned testimonials alone are insufficient is that the proper ordinaries are the final and absolute judges of the worthiness of ordinand members of Societies.[310] They should, therefore,

[309] Stanton, *De Societatibus*, p. 137; Gallagher, *The Examination of the Qualities of the Ordinand*, The Catholic University of America Canon Law Studies, n. 195 (Washington, D.C.: The Catholic University of America Press, 1944), pp. 104-109; Coronata, *De Sacramentis*, II, 230; Quinn, *Documents Required for the Reception of Orders*, pp. 154-155.

[310] Canons 968, § 1, and 973, § 3; Gallagher, *The Examinations of the Qualities of the Ordinand*, p. 101.

have on hand all the documents necessary for them to pass final judgment. Confirmatory of this contention is the fact that they are forbidden to issue dimissorial letters until they have at hand all the testimonials demanded by canons 993 to 1000.[311]

Proper ordinaries can justly expect that the major superiors of Societies will take upon themselves a great part of the burden of the initial gathering of the testimonials required by canon 993, nn. 1, 2, 3, 4. As a matter of fact, at the time when members of Societies begin to prepare for the reception of Orders, their major superiors will have had some of these testimonials and documents on hand for quite some time. For the Constitutions of most Societies demand that certain of these testimonials be at hand when candidates apply for admission to the Societies.[312] And even if the Constitutions of a particular Society did not make this demand, it seems that the testimonials and documents should be required of the candidates just the same by reason of the fact that the situation of applicants to clerical Societies is analogous to the situation of applicants to a religious institute or to a diocesan seminary. Testimonials and documents are required of candidates for admission into religious institutes by canons 544 and 545, and of candidates for admission into a diocesan seminary by canon 1363. Surely the Church is no less solicitous about candidates for admission into clerical Societies.[313]

All the documents and testimonials collected in fulfillmen of the prescripts of canon 993 are to be kept in the

[311] Canon 960, § 1; Gallagher, *The Examination of the Qualities of the Ordinand,* p. 101.

[312] *Constitutions of the Society of Missionary Priests of Saint Paul the Apostle,* § 14, p. 14; *Constitutions of the Society of Saint Joseph of the Sacred Heart,* §§ 24-25, pp. 17-18; *The Society of African Missions, Constitutions and Directory,* § 12, p. 3; *Constitutions of the Catholic Foreign Mission Society of America,* §§ 140-141, pp. 24-25; *Costituzioni dell'Istituto delle Missioni Estere de Milano,* § 122, p. 31; *Constitutions of the Scarboro Foreign Mission Society,* § 18, p. 10; etc., etc.

[313] Waters, *Probation in Societies.* pp. 89-91.

curial archives of the proper ordinaries to whom they are presented.[314]

Article 5. Rites and Ceremonies, Time and Place, Annotation and Proof of Ordination in Societies

The rites and ceremonies of sacred ordination are the same for the ordination of members of Societies as they are for the ordination of any other cleric. A word should be said, however, with regard to precedence and with regard to the promise of obedience made in the ceremony for the ordination of a priest.

Experience teaches that members of Societies will often be ordained together with other members of the secular clergy and with religious. On these occasions the laws of precedence as established in the Code are to be followed.[315] In this connection, however, it is to be noted that members of Societies are counted among the secular clergy. Thus, in the ordination ceremony they precede all religious, even regulars, except when the ceremony is held in a church or oratory belonging to some religious institute. In this case the religious of this institute precede all the secular clergy.[316] The contrary practice, which merely as a matter of fact is observed in Rome, is explained perhaps by the fact that nowhere is there a complete list of Societies; and since Societies are listed in the *Annuario Pontificio* right along with Religious Congregations whose members profess simple public vows, no attention is paid to

[314] Coronata, *De Sacramentis*, II, 226; Cappello, *De Sacramentis*, IV, 396; cf. canon 1010, § 1.

[315] Canons 106 and 491.

[316] S. R. C., *Imolen.*, 19 aug. 1719, ad 1—*Decreta Authentica Congregationis Sacrorum Rituum* (5 vols. et 2 Appendices, Romae: Typis Polyglottis Vaticanis, 1898-1927), n. 2265; S.R.C., *Mechoacana*, 21 ian. 1769, ad 3—*Decreta Authentica Congregationis Sacrorum Rituum*, n. 2485; Larraona, "Commentarium Codicis: Can. 491," *CpR*, IV (1923), 172-173, 210-218, 273-280, cf. pp. 273-274; Stanton, *De Societatibus*, p. 98; Coronata, *Institutiones*, I, p. 619, nota 2; Cocchi, *Commentarium*, IV, 19; Schaefer, *De Religiosis*, p. 104; Ristuccia, *Societies*, pp. 67-69.

the right of precedence enjoyed by Societies.[317] Among various clerical Societies, Societies of pontifical approval precede Societies of diocesan approval. Within each of these groups, that Society precedes which is in undisputed quasi-possession of precedence. If there is no certainty about the right of quasi-possession, that Society precedes which first had a house founded in the place where the Ordination takes place.[318]

At the end of the ceremony for the ordination of priests, each newly-ordained priest places his hands in the hands of the ordaining bishop and makes a promise of obedience. The Roman Pontifical states that, if the bishop is the proper ordinary of the ordained, he is to ask: *Promittis mihi, et Successoribus meis reverentiam, et obedientiam?* The ordained is to answer: *Promitto.* If the bishop is not the proper ordinary of the ordained, he is to say to secular priests: *Promittis Pontifici Ordinario tuo pro tempore existenti reverentiam, et obedientiam?* and to regulars: *Promittis Praelato Ordinario tuo pro tempore existenti reverentiam, et obedientiam?*[319] Nabucho states that the word *"praelato"* is to be substituted for the word *"pontifici"* also in the case of a secular cleric who is being ordained by a bishop not his proper ordinary upon the issuance of dimissorial letters from his proper ordinary who does not have episcopal consecration.[320]

Since clerical members of Societies are counted among the members of the secular clergy, and since their major superiors are not, by the common law, ordinaries, it seems clear that the one to whom they are to promise reverence and obedience is, by the common law, the local ordinary in

[317] Cf. *Annuario Pontificio*, pp. 765-793; Stanton, *De Societatibus*, p. 99, nota (27).

[318] Canon 106, n. 5; Schaefer, *De Religiosis*, p. 105.

[319] *Pontificale Romanum* (Summorum Pontificum jssu editum, et a Benedicto XIV. Pont. Max. recognitum et castigatum, 3 partes, Mechliniae, 1873), tit. *De ordinatione presbyteri.*

[320] *Pontificalis Romani Expositio Juridico-Practica* (3 tomi, Petropoli, Brasilia: Sumptibus Editôra Vozes Ltda., 1945), I, 125.

whose territory they are incardinated. Thus, if they are ordained by their proper ordinary, the latter will say: *Promittis mihi...?* If they are ordained upon the issuance of dimissorial letters from their proper ordinary and this proper ordinary has episcopal consecration, the ordaining bishop will say: *Promittis Pontifici Ordinario tuo...?* And if the members of Societies are ordained upon issuance of dimissorial letters from their proper ordinary and this proper ordinary lacks episcopal consecration, the ordaining bishop will say: *Promittis Praelato Ordinario tuo...?* In the last case, the word *"praelato"* will refer not to the major superior, but to the proper ordinary.

From this promise there arises on the part of priests a special obligation of obedience and reverence over and above the obligation common to all secular clerics of obeying and revering their proper ordinaries.[321]

The law governing the time and place of sacred ordination is the same for the ordination of members of Societies as it is for the ordination of any other clerics. Special care should be taken, however, for the observance of the following relevant prescripts of law when members of Societies are ordained upon the issuance of dimissorial letters from their proper ordinaries, or are ordained in their own churches or oratories.

When members of Societies receive from their proper ordinaries dimissorial letters which can be presented to any bishop, the superiors in the Societies sometimes invite an outside bishop to come and ordain the members in churches or oratories belonging to the Societies. It should be remembered on these occasions that the visiting bishop needs permission from the ordinary of the place in which the ordinations are held before he can confer Orders when the use of pontificals is involved.[322] It should be noted in this connection that First Tonsure and the minor Orders may be conferred with or without the use of pontificals,[323]

[321] Cf. canon 127; Coronata, *Institutiones*, I, p. 218, nota 1.

[322] Canon 1008.

[323] Coronata, *De Sacramentis*, II, 308.

whereas the major Orders may not be conferred without the use of pontificals.

First Tonsure may be conferred at any time in any church or oratory belonging to a Society; and minor Orders may be conferred in any church or oratory belonging to a Society on any Sunday or feast day which is a double.[324]

The place where major Orders may be conferred depends on whether or not the ordinations are general or particular. According to the common teaching of the authors, general ordinations are those which take place on any one of the six Saturdays enumerated in canon 1006, § 2, namely, the four Ember Saturdays, the Saturday before Passion Sunday, and Holy Saturday; particular ordinations are those which take place on any other day.[325] It seems, however, that ordinations held on other days are also to be termed general if many candidates are ordained and many Orders are conferred.[326] General ordinations are to be held publicly in the cathedral church; and if the ordinations are held in another place of the diocese, the most prominent church should, in so far as possible, be chosen for the purpose, and the clergy of that place shall attend. The bishop, however, is not forbidden to have particular ordinations for any just reason in other churches—even in the chapel of the bishop's residence, of the seminary, or of a religious house.[327] Thus, major Orders can be conferred in churches belonging to Societies, or even in the principal oratory of a house of a Society,[328] unless the ordination be held

[324] Canons 1006, § 4, and 1009, § 3.

[325] Vermeersch-Creusen, *Epitome*, II, 186; Beste, *Introductio*, p. 547; Ramstein, *A Manual of Canon Law*, p. 441; Bouscaren-Ellis, *Canon Law*, p. 449; Abbo-Hannan, *The Sacred Canons*, II, 158.

[326] Coronata, *De Sacramentis*, II, 309; Cappello, *De Sacramentis*, IV, 420.

[327] Canon 1009, §§ 1, 2.

[328] Canon 1009, § 2 states: *Non prohibetur autem Episcopus, iusta suadente causa, ordinationes particulares habere in aliis etiam ecclesiis itemque in oratorio domus episcopalis aut Seminarii aut religiosae domus.* But the listing of these three distinct oratories in which the bishop may hold ordinations should not be taken, so it appears from

on one of the six Saturdays mentioned in canon 1006, § 2, and at the same time many Orders be conferred on many candidates. If a Society should desire that many Orders be conferred on many of its members on one of the six Saturdays mentioned above and in one of its own churches or oratories, it seems that a notable church or oratory of the Society should be chosen and the local clergy invited.

With regard to the annotation of the ordinations of members of Societies, it should be noted that whenever members are ordained in territories outside of the ones in which they are incardinated, annotations of their ordinations should be made in both the Curia of the place where the ordinations took place and in the Curia of the place in which they are incardinated.[329] Finally, it is the obligation of the proper ordinary for promotion to Orders, and not the obligation of the major superior of the ordained members of Societies, nor the obligation of a prelate who may have ordained upon the issuance of dimissorial letters from the proper ordinary, to see to it that notice of the conferral of the subdiaconate be sent to the pastor of the church of baptism for annotation in the baptismal register.[330]

the immediate context, as an all-inclusive listing. And thus, the principal oratory, public or semi-public, of a house of a Society may likewise be regarded as offering a lawful place in which to hold an ordination to major Orders.

[329] Canon 1010, §§ 1, 2.

[330] Canon 1011; Cappello, *De Sacramentis,* IV, 425; Coronata, *De Sacramentis,* II, 315.

CHAPTER IV

SINGULAR LAW FOR THE ORDINATION OF MEMBERS OF SOCIETIES

ARTICLE 1. THE PRIVILEGE OF GRANTING DIMISSORIAL LETTERS

SECTION 1. HISTORY OF THE LAW REGARDING THE RIGHT TO ORDAIN REGULARS

In the year 451, the Council of Chalcedon gave expression to what had been the fundamental juridical principle regarding the relations between monks and bishops since the foundation of monasticism in the middle of the third century. During these two hundred years, the ordination of monks—a rare occurrence before the middle of the fourth century—was completely in the hands of the local bishop. From the middle of the fifth century, however, ecclesiastical legislation began to require that local bishops obtain an abbot's consent before ordaining one of his monks. From the sixth century, it is necessary to distinguish the law regulating the ordination of monks as this law existed in continental Europe from the same law as it existed in Africa and in the British Isles. In Europe, during the Merovingian Era, many monasteries received charters of episcopal emancipation, about half of which allowed the monks to ask whom they would to ordain them. These privileges ceased during the Carolingian Era. During both the Merovingian Era and the Carolingian Era very few monasteries received papal exemption. This was the situation in Europe. The situation in Africa and in the British Isles was somewhat different. In Africa, monastic exemptions, even in the matter of ordination, were not unknown. The Council of Carthage of 536, however, reestablished the common law whereby monks had to be ordained by the local bishop, who, in turn, needed the permission of the abbot. In the British Isles, the organization of the Church was different from that in other parts of the

Western Church. The abbot was usually either a bishop, or at least exercised the authority of a bishop. Under this regime the ordination of monks was completely under the control of the abbot. This brief summary of the history of the ancient law regulating the ordination of monks takes one up to the middle of the ninth century.[1]

In the year 628, Pope Honorius I (625-638) granted complete papal exemption to the Columban Monastery at Bobbio.[2] The letter in which Honorius I granted this exemption from the jurisdiction of the local bishop did not mention *iura pontificalia.* McLaughlin thinks that *iura pontificalia* would have been mentioned if the bishop retained them.[3] Thus it seems that Bobbio may well have been the first monastery to enjoy, in virtue of a papal exemption, the privilege of asking any bishop to ordain its monks.

About eight instances of papal exemptions similar to that granted to Bobbio and prior to the time of Cluny are given by Kurtscheid (1877-1941),[4] McLaughlin,[5] and Schmitz.[6] But such grants were not numerous enough to

[1] These are the conclusions of Lafontaine in his work entitled *L'Évêque d'Ordination des Religieux des débuts du monachisme à la mort de Louis le Pieux (840)*, Universitas Catholica Ottaviensis, Dissertationes, Series canonica, Tomus 22 (Ottawa: Les Éditions de l'Université d'Ottawa, 1951), pp. 235-237.

Cf. MacLaughlin, *Le Très Ancien Droit Monastique de l'Occident*, Archives de la France Monastique, Vol. XXXVIII (Vienne: Abbaye Saint-Martin—Paris: A. Picard, 1935), pp. 111-128, 162-199.

[2] Honorius I, ep. *Si semper sunt concedenda*, 11 iun. 628—*Bull. Rom. Taur.*, I, 178; Jaffé, *Regesta Pontificum Romanorum ab condita Ecclesia ad annum post Christum natum MCXCVIII* (2. ed. correctam et auctam auspiciis Gulielmi Wattenbach, curaverunt S. Loewenfeld, F. Kaltenbrunner, P. Ewald, 2 vols., Lipsiae, 1885-1888), n. 2017 (hereafter cited JL for documents from 882 to 1198).

[3] *Le Très Ancien Droit Monastique de l'Occident*, pp. 188-189.

[4] *Historia Iuris Canonici, Historica Institutorum ab Ecclesiae Fundatione usque ad Gratianum* (reimpressio, Romae: Officium Libri Catholici, 1951), p. 318.

[5] *Le Très Ancien Droit Monastique de l'Occident*, pp. 186-199.

[6] *Histoire de l'ordre de Saint Benoît* (7 tomes, Tom. I, *Origines, Diffusion et Constitution jusqu'a XII° Siècle*, Maredsous: Les éditions de Maredsous, 1942), I, 312-313.

constitute anything more than a precedent.

That local bishops at the end of the Carolingian Era still retained by the common law the power to ordain the monks within their dioceses is attested to by canon 21 of the Canons of Abbo.[7] These canons were compiled between the years 988 and 996, and had as one of their aims the defense of monasticism.[8] It seems that if the common law had been any more liberal at that time, the fact would have been mentioned by Abbo.

Papal exemption grew into a common practice in the tenth, eleventh and twelfth centuries, following the development of the Monastic Reform, the Gregorian Reform, and the Roman Curia. The trend began with the tenth century reformations within monasticism. A great part of the decline of monastic discipline had been due to lay investiture practiced with regard to the abbeys. To remedy this abuse, reform-minded founders gave the proprietary rights of the abbeys which they founded to Saint Peter, to be administered by the popes. Thus the *ius abbatiae* passed to Rome, or to whomever the popes might delegate, and worthy men could be installed as abbots. The popes also collected an annual tax from such abbeys. In recognition to their efforts at reform, as a guarantee that these efforts be not interfered with, and in appreciation for the tax received annually, the popes granted these monasteries complete papal exemption. This was called the *libertas Romana*.[9]

The greatest of these early reform movements was that of Cluny. It began in the year 910. Before many years

[7] *Canones Domni Abbonis Abbatis et Regis Hugonis, et Roberti Filii ejus Francorum Regis*, canon XXI—Migne, *Patrologiae Cursus Completus, Series Latina* (221 vols., Paris, Vols. I-CCXVII, 1844-1855, et 4 indices: Vol. CCXVIII, 1887; Vol. CCXIX, 1879; Vol. CCXX, 1863; Vol. CCXXI, 1864), CXXXIX, 487 (hereafter cited as *MPL*).

[8] Van Hove, *Commentarium*, I, 238-239.

[9] Dumas, *Les églises monastiques*, in Fliche-Martin, *Histoire de l'Église*, Vol. VII, *L'Église au pouvoir des laïques* (Paris: Bloud & Gay, 1948), Livre III, pp. 320-332.

a great number of monasteries had joined this movement and had subjected themselves to Cluny. In the year 998 or 999, Pope Gregory V (996-999) granted Cluny complete papal exemption. Among other privileges, the Abbot of Cluny could have his monks ordained to any Order by any bishop in any place, and all bishops were forbidden to ordain at Cluny unless they had been invited to do so by the Abbot.[10]

The common law, however, remained the same during the period of the Monastic Reform and in the period prior to the Gregorian Reform. In a Council held at Anse in the year 1025, the bishop in whose diocese Cluny was located objected to the fact that an outside bishop accepted Cluny's invitation to ordain some monks. The invitation was made in virtue of the papal privilege granted in the letter of exemption of Pope Gregory V in 998 or 999. The Council decided that the act was against the legislation enacted in the General Council of Chalcedon (451).[11] Although the Council was wrong in not recognizing the legitimate exercise of papal power, it nevertheless bore witness to the common law of the time.

During the eleventh and twelfth centuries, monastic privileges with regard to ordination became more frequent, but did not yet become universal. In a study of eighty-seven letters of exemption sent by the popes to the Cluniacs, Camaldolese, Carthusians, Vallombrosians and Cistercians between the years 998 and 1177, the present writer has found the following facts concerning the privileges therein granted regarding the ordination of monks. Of the eighty-seven letters examined, 15 were sent to the Cluniacs, 23 to the Camaldolese, 12 to the Carthusians, 8 to the Vallombrosians, and 29 to the Cistercians. Those sent to the Carthusians and Cistericians contained no ordination privileges. Of the remaining 46 letters, 19 contained ordination

[10] Gregorius V, ep. *Desiderium, quod religiosorum,* 998 vel 999—*MPL,* CXXXVII, 935; JL, n. 3896.

[11] Mansi, XIX, 423-424.

privileges. Of these, 7 were sent to the Cluniacs, 8 to the Camaldolese, and 4 to the Vallombrosians. Thirteen of the nineteen privileges gave the monks unqualified permission to seek ordination from any Catholic bishop in the favor of and in communion with the Apostolic See. The other six granted such permission only if the local bishop did not enjoy the favor and communion of the Holy See, or if he required a simoniacal price for the ordinations.

The first privilege was the one granted to Cluny in 998 or 999.[12] The next nine privileges were granted between the years 1090 and 1120. Some of these were granted to particular monasteries; others were granted to all the monasteries of a particular monastic congregation; still others were merely confirmations by one pope of privileges which had been granted by others, his predecessors.[13]

In the year 1123 the I General Council of the Lateran was held. In this Council the common law for the ordination of monks was for the first time officially promulgated as a general written law of the Church. In canon 17 the Council decreed that monks were to receive Orders from the bishops in whose dioceses the houses to which they belonged were located.[14]

None of the examined papal letters of exemption dating

[12] Gregorius V, ep. *Desiderium, quod religiosorum,* 998 vel 999—*MPL,* CXXXVII, 935; JL, n. 3896.

[13] Urbanus II, ep. *Cum universis,* 6 apr. 1090—*MPL,* CLI, 322, JL, n. 5433; ep. *Cum omnium fidelium,* 9 ian. 1097—Marrier et Quercetanus, *Bibliotheca Cluniacensis* (Matiscone, 1915), cols. 520-521, JL, n. 5676; Paschalis II, ep. *Officii nostri nos,* 29 maii 1102— Pflugk-Harttung, *Acta Pontificum Romanorum Inedita* (3 vols., Vol. I, Tübingen, 1881; Vol. II, Stuttgart, 1884; Vol. III, Stuttgart, 1886), I, 74, JL, n. 5920; ep. *Quia documentis,* nov. 1102—*MPL,* CLXIII, 103, JL, n. 5924; ep. *Justis votis,* 20 mart. 1105—Pflugk-Harttung, *Acta Pontificum Romanorum Inedita,* II, 185, JL, n. 6012; ep. *Ad hoc nos,* 23 mart. 1105—*MPL,* CLXIII, 153, JL, n. 6014; ep. *Gratias deo,* 4 nov. 1113—*MPL,* CLXIII, 331, JL, n. 6357; ep. *Desiderium, quod,* 8 febr. 1115—Pflugk-Harttung, *Acta Pontificum Romanorum Inedita,* II, 209, JL, n. 6447; Callixtus II, ep. *Religionis monasticae,* 22 febr. 1120—*MPL,* CLXIII, 1165, JL, n. 6821.

[14] Mansi, XXI, 285.

from between the I General Council of the Lateran in the year 1123 and the year 1146 contains any explicit mention of privileges with regard to the ordination of monks. After this period of silence, however, explicit mention of such privileges again begins to appear, and nine such are found between the years 1147 and 1177.[15]

During the twelfth century practically all the monasteries of the Cluniacs, Camaldolese, Carthusians, Vallombrosians and Cistercians received some degree of papal exemption.[16] When new religious institutes such as the Canons Regular, the Mendicants and the Clerks Regular came into existence, they, too, soon received papal exemption. And by the time of the Council of Trent (1545-1563) practically every religious institute approved by the Holy See according to the prescripts of the IV General Council of the Lateran (1215) and the II General Council of Lyons (1274)[17] possessed papal exemption.[18] As time went on,

[15] Eugenius III, ep. *Religiosis desideriis*, 6 febr. 1147—*MPL*, CLXXX, 1189, JL, n. 9000; ep. *Cognoscentes, quod servos*, 3 nov. 1147—*MPL*, CLXXX, 1295, JL, n. 9156; Anastasius IV, ep. *Religiosis desideriis*, 16 iun. 1153—*MPL*, CLXXX, 1605, JL, n. 9731; Hadrianus IV, ep. *Officii nostri*, 14 mart. 1155—*MPL*, CLXXXVIII, 1397, JL, n. 10015; ep. *Officii nostri*, 4 oct. 1155—*MPL*, CLXXXVIII, 1437, JL, n. 10092; Alexander III, ep. *Religiosam vitam*, 5 iun. 1163—*MPL*, CC, 229, JL, n. 10875; ep. *Officii nostri nos*, 17 mart. 1176—*MPL*, CC. 1066, JL, n. 12688; ep. *Desiderium quod ad*, 20 apr. 1176—*MPL*, CC, 1068, JL, n. 12695; ep. *Quoties illud a*, 9 febr. 1177—*MPL*, CC, 1097, JL, n. 12778.

[16] Schreiber, *Kurie und Kloster im 12. Jahrhundert*, Kirchenrechtliche Abhandlungen herausgegeben von Dr. Ulrich Stutz, 65-68 Heft. (Stuttgart, 1910); Hüfner, "Das Rechtsinstitut der klösterlichen exemtion in der abendländischen Kirche," *Archiv für katholisches Kirchenrecht* (Innsbruck, 1857-1861; Mainz, 1862-), LXXXVI (1906), 302-318, 629-651; LXXXVII (1907), 71-86, 270-284, 462-479, 599-636; cf. LXXXVII (1907), 71-86; Kurtscheid, *Historia Iuris Canonici, Historia Institutorum ab Ecclesiae Fundatione usque ad Gratianum*, p. 319.

[17] Cf. *supra*, pp. 18-19.

[18] Hüfner, "Das Rechtsinstitut der klösterlichen Exemtion in der abendländischen Kirche," *Archiv für katholisches Kirchenrecht*, LXXXVII (1907), 270-284; Kurtscheid, *Historia Iuris Canonici*,

more and more of these papal exemptions began to include the privilege whereby the monks could be presented for ordination to any bishop in communion with the Apostolic See. This derogation from the common law became so frequent that just prior to the Council of Trent practically every institute of regulars enjoyed the privilege of having its members ordained by any bishop.[19]

The first noteworthy attempt to curtail the privileges of regulars came in the year 1516 during the V General Council of the Lateran. During this Council, Pope Leo X (1513-1521) by means of a Constitution read in a public session restricted the privileges of regulars in many details, and specifically in regard to the conferral of Orders. Regulars were forbidden to ask any bishop to ordain them except the local bishop, unless the local bishop, though he had been respectfully asked to ordain, refused without a cause, or unless the local bishop was absent.[20] But in spite of this effort of Pope Leo X, regulars continued to enjoy extensive privileges, right up until the time of the Council of Trent.

The Council of Trent restricted in many details the privilege of exemption which was enjoyed by regulars at that time.[21] After the Council had ended, it was highly

Historia Institutorum ab Ecclesiae Fundatione usque ad Gratianum, pp. 319-320; Melo, *De Exemptione Regularium,* The Catholic University of America Canon Law Studies, n. 12 (Washington, D.C., 1921), pp. 15-22; Wernz-Vidal, *Ius Canonicum,* III, 422; Schaefer, *De Religiosis,* p. 757.

[19] Kurtscheid, *Historia Iuris Canonici, Historia Institutorum ab Ecclesiae Fundatione usque ad Gratianum,* p. 320; Wernz-Vidal, *Ius Canonicum,* Tom. IV, Vol. I, p. 226; Many, *De Sacrae Ordinatione,* pp. 378-379; cf. Benedictus XIV, const. *Impositi Nobis,* 27 febr. 1747, § 2—*Fontes,* n. 376.

[20] Leo X, const. *Dum, intra mentis arcana,* 19 dec. 1516, § 11—*Bull. Rom. Taur.,* V, 685-689, cf. p. 687; Mansi, XXXII, 970-974, cf. col. 972.

[21] Conc. Trident., sess. XXIV, *de ref.,* c. 11; sess. XXV, *de regularibus,* cc. 5, 8, 9, 12, 13, 14, 17, 22; cf. Melo, *De Exemptione Regularium,* pp. 22-24; Wernz-Vidal, *Ius Canonicum,* III, 422; Schaefer, *De Religiosis,* p. 757.

controverted whether or not the Council had intended to revoke the privileges whereby regular superiors could send their subjects to any bishop for ordination.[22] In 1567, just four years after the Council had closed, Pope Pius V (1566-1572) declared that these privileges had not been revoked by the Council.[23] But only six years later, in 1573, Pope Gregory XIII (1572-1585) reversed the decision of Pope Pius V and declared that regulars were held, in the matter of the proper bishop for ordination, to the decrees of the Council of Trent.[24] In the same year Pope Gregory XIII ratified a decree of the Sacred Congregation of the Council whereby certain Carthusians were required to obtain the express permission of the local bishop before sending their members to be ordained by an outside bishop.[25]

Controversies again arose between bishops and regulars. Pope Sixtus V (1585-1590), therefore, in January of 1586, after consulting the Sacred Congregation of the Council, settled the dispute. He declared that superiors of regulars had the right to issue dimissorial letters for the ordination of their subjects, but they had to send their subjects to the local ordinary for ordination, unless the local ordinary was absent or was not going to ordain at the time; and then the superiors could send their subjects to any bishop, provided that the bishop to whom the subjects were sent examined them in doctrinal matters.[26]

[22] Cf. Conc. Trident., sess. VII, *de ref.*, c. 11; sess. XXIII, *de ref.*, c. 8.

[23] Pius V, const. *Etsi Mendicantium,* 16 maii 1567, § 2, 7°—*Bull. Rom. Taur.*, VII, 578.

[24] Gregorius XIII, const. *In tanta,* 1 mart. 1573—*Bull. Rom. Taur.*, VIII, 39-41.

[25] Pallottini, *Collectio omnium conclusionum et resolutionum quae in causis propositis apud Sacram Congregationem Cardinalium S. Concilii Tridentini Interpretum prodierunt ab eius institutione anno MDLXIV ad annum MDCCCLX, distinctis titulis alphabetico ordine per materias digesta* (17 vols., Romae, 1868-1893), XVI, 73 (hereafter cited as Pallottini); cf. Benedictus XIV, const. *Impositi Nobis,* 27 febr. 1747, § 3—*Fontes,* n. 376.

[26] Pallottini, XVI, 73; cf. Benedictus XIV, const. *Impositi Nobis,*

In 1589 the Sacred Congregation of the Council again declared that superiors of regulars could grant dimissorial letters for the ordination of their subjects. The superiors had to send these letters to the local bishop. But if the local bishop was away, the superiors could send the letters to any bishop, provided that the bishop examined the subjects on matters of doctrine.[27] The same Sacred Congregation handed down the same decision again in 1595.[28]

In 1596 the Sacred Congregation of the Council settled a case involving certain regulars in the Archdiocese of Seville. In its degree, the Sacred Congregation iterated the contents of the decree of 1586, but forbade the regulars deliberately to put off the issuance of dimissorial letters until a time when the Archbishop was going to be away or was not going to have ordinations. It also commanded that when the regular superiors did present dimissorial letters to an outside bishop, they state the cause of the Archbishop's absence or why he was not going to have ordinations.[29] Two months later, the Sacred Congregation, by command of Pope Clement VIII (1592-1605), iterated as universal law the decree handed down in the Seville case. Since this universal law was often cited in indults granted to Secular Congregations before the Code, it is quoted here:

> Congregatio Concilii censuit, Superiores Regulares posse suo subdito itidem Regulari qui praeditus qualitatibus requisitis Ordines suscipere voluerit, Literas dimissorias concedere, ad Episcopum tamen Dioecesanum, nempe illius Monasterii, in cuius familia ab iis, ad quos pertinet,

27 febr. 1747, § 4—*Fontes*, n. 376.

Benedict XIV did not offer any date for this declaration of Sixtus V. The date given in Pallottini, 1580, is an evident mistake, because Sixtus V reigned from 1585 to 1590. The writer arrived at the date 1586 by placing the *Liber Decretorum* reference given by Pallottini and Benedict XIV (IV, 108) in its proper chronological position in the *Fontes* of Gasparri, cf. nn. 2150-2154.

[27] S. C. C., *Hispaniarum*, mense sept. 1589—*Fontes*, n. 2216.

[28] S. C. C., *Catanien.*, 26 ian. 1595—*Fontes*, n. 2280.

[29] S. C. C., *Hispalen.*, 11 ian. 1596—Pallottini, XVI, 73.

Regularis positus fuerit, et, si Dioecesanus abfuerit, vel non esset habiturus Ordinationes, ad quemcumque alium Episcopum, dum tamen ab eo Episcopo, qui Ordines contulerit, examinetur quoad doctrinam, et dum ipsi Regulares non distulerint de industria concessionem dimissoriarum in id tempus, quo Episcopus Dioecesanus vel abfuturus, vel nullas esset habiturus Ordinationes. Verum, cum a Superioribus Regularibus, Episcopo Dioescesano absente, vel Ordinationes non habente, Literae Dimissoriae dabuntur, in eis utique huiusmodi causam absentiae Diocesani Episcopi, vel Ordinationum ab eo non habendarum, exprimendam esse. Quod qui non fecerint, officii, et dignitatis, seu administrationis, ac vocis activae, et passivae privationis, ac alias arbitrio eiusdem Sanctissimi Domini Nostri Papae reservatas poenas incurrant.[30]

The only exceptions mentioned in this decree of 1596 were the cases in which the local bishop was away or was not going to hold ordinations. To these two exceptions, the Sacred Congregation of the Council in 1600 added a third, namely, the case in which the diocese was vacated.[31] The Sacred Congregation iterated this third exception in a decree in 1619.[32]

In 1654 the Sacred Congregation of the Council declared that regulars desiring promotion to Orders were not held to the presenting of dimissorial letters from the bishops of their place of origin. If they observed the decree issued by order of Pope Clement VIII in 1596, that sufficed.[33] This ruling was repeated in another decree dated March 17, 1674.[34]

In the beginning of the eighteenth century two doubts arose with regard to privileges granted to regulars whereby they could be ordained by any bishop. It was doubted

[30] S. C. C., decr., 15 mart. 1596—*Fontes*, n. 2294.

[31] S. C. C., *Nullius*, 22 sept. 1600—*Fontes*, n. 2334.

[32] S. C. C., decr., 24 aug. 1619—*Fontes*, n. 2418.

[33] S. C. C., *Senonen.*, 28 febr. 1654, ad 9—*Fontes*, n. 2734.

[34] Pallottini, XVI, 74; cf. Benedictus XIV, const. *Impositi Nobis*, 27 febr. 1747, § 7—*Fontes*, n. 376.

first whether it was sufficient that such privileges were granted after the Council of Trent, or whether they had to be dated after the decree that was issued by the Sacred Congregation of the Council under date of March 15, 1596, and approved by Pope Clement VIII. Secondly, it was doubted whether it was sufficient that such privileges were derived by way of interparticipation with others in them, or whether they had to be granted directly. The doubts were resolved by a particular congregation of cardinals appointed by Pope Innocent XIII (1721-1724) in 1723 to study the problem. It was resolved that such privileges were valid provided that they were granted after the Council of Trent, and provided that they were granted by direct concession, and not by way simply of interparticipation. In the same year Pope Innocent XIII iterated this decision in a Constitution written for the Church in Spain.[35] In the following year Pope Benedict XIII (1724-1730) confirmed the Constitution of Pope Innocent XIII with the Constitution *In supremo.* The pertinent part of this Constitution was sometimes cited in ordination indults granted to Secular Congregations, and is therefore given here.

> Quoties vero Regulares ad Ordines erunt promovendi, servetur omnino Decretum Congregationis Cardinalium Concilii Tridentini Interpretum a piae mem. Clemente Papa VIII Praedecessore etiam nostro confirmatum die 15 martii 1596, quo sancitur non ad alium, quam ad Episcopum Dioecesanum literas dimissorias pro eorumdem Ordinum susceptione a suis Superioribus esse dirigendas, praeterquam in casu quo Dioecesanus a Dioecesi abesset, vel Ordinationes non esset habiturus; quo etiam casu in literis dimissoriis ad alium Episcopum dirigendis expressa fieri debeat mentio, vel de praedicta Episcopi Dioecesani absentia, vel de illa alia causa, videlicet, quod Ordinationes non sit habiturus: exceptis tamen quoad praedicta Regularibus illis, quibus per speciale privilegium a Sede Apostolica post Concilium Tri-

[35] Innocentius XIII, const. *Apostolici ministerii,* 23 maii 1723—*Fontes,* n. 280.

> dentinum fuerit concessum, ut a quolibet Catholico Antistite Ordines suscipere possint, super quo indulto nihil per praesentes innovare intendimus.[36]

Finally, in the year 1747, Pope Benedict XIV (1740-1758) in his famous Constitution *Impositi Nobis,* not only confirmed the law for the ordination of regulars as established by Popes Gregory XIII, Sixtus V and Clement VIII, but also confirmed the Constitution *Apostolici ministerii,* which Innocent XIII had sent to the Spanish Church, and extended the same to the universal Church.[37]

In the year 1857, the Sacred Congregation for the State of Regulars, by command of Pope Pius IX, required three years of temporary profession before solemn profession.[38] In the following year, the same Sacred Congregation declared that regular superiors could grant dimissorial letters to those in temporary profession only for promotion to First Tonsure and to minor Orders.[39]

The law for the ordination of regulars as it stood in 1858 has been incorporated into the Code, and has remained essentially the same to the present day.[40]

SECTION 2. THE PRIVILEGE OF GRANTING DIMISSORIAL LETTERS IN SECULAR CONGREGATIONS BEFORE THE CODE

Before the Code, superiors in Secular Congregations did not, by the common law, have the power to grant dimissorial letters for the ordination of their subjects. By the common law, Secular Congregations had to follow the law for the ordination of secular clerics.[41] As a matter of fact, however, many Secular Congregations possessed the privi-

[36] Benedictus XIII, const. *In supremo,* 23 sept. 1724, § 14—*Fontes,* n. 283.

[37] Benedictus XIV, const. *Impositi Nobis,* 27 febr. 1747, § 11—*Fontes,* n. 376; cf. Many, *De Sacra Ordinatione,* p. 381, nota 2.

[38] S. C. super Statu Reg., litt. encycl. *Neminem latet,* 19 mart. 1857 —*Fontes,* n. 4381.

[39] S. C. super Statu Reg., declar., 12 iun. 1858, § VII—*Fontes,* n. 4383.

[40] Cf. canons 615; 964, nn. 2, 3; 965; 966; 967.

[41] Cf. *supra,* pp. 25-26.

lege whereby superiors could grant dimissorial letters for the ordination of their subjects.

The privilege of granting dimissorial letters was possessed by Secular Congregations before the Code in either one of two ways. First, those Secular Congregations which had the privilege of exemption had the privilege of granting dimissorial letters in virtue of the privilege of exemption. Secondly, many of the Secular Congregations which did not have the privilege of exemption possessed the faculty of granting dimissorial letters in virtue of particular indults. One may well discuss these two cases separately, beginning with those Secular Congregations which possessed the privilege of exemption.

Although practically every institute of regulars in existence from the late Middle Ages to the advent of the Code was exempt, yet, it cannot be said that all regulars were exempt during that period by the common law, the manner in which they are exempt today.[42] It can be said, however, that from the year 1586 all regulars were, by the common law, exempt from the authority of the local ordinaries at least to this extent, that they could be promoted to Orders upon the issuance of dimissorial letters from their superiors.[43] It seems, therefore, that from the year 1586 any institute that enjoyed the privilege of total exemption from the local ordinaries *a fortiori* enjoyed the privilege of granting dimissorial letters as a particular privilege contained in the general privilege of exemption. If, therefore, a Secular Congregation before the Code obtained the privilege of total exemption, implicitly included in this general privilege seemed to be the privilege of granting dimissorial letters. Such, as a matter of fact, was the case, as is seen in a series of enactments of the Holy See concerning the Congregation of the Mission.

In the year 1632, Pope Urban VIII (1623-1644) granted

[42] Melo, *De Exemptione Regularium*, p. 24; Wernz-Vidal, *Ius Canonicum*, III, 421; cf. canon 615.

[43] Cf. *supra*, p. 160.

the Congregation of the Mission complete exemption from the local ordinaries in all save what pertained to the missions.[44] This privilege was confirmed by Pope Alexander VII (1655-1667) in the year 1655.[45] In virtue of this exemption, in the granting of which nothing was said about the issuance of dimissorial letters, the superiors of the Congregation of the Mission used to issue dimissorial letters for the ordination of their subjects. In the year 1657, however, when Martius Cardinal Ginettus was Alexander VII's Vicar General *in Urbe* in spiritual matters, a difficulty about this point was proposed to the Cardinal by his auditor. The Cardinal committed the problem to a particular congregation for solution. The decision as then rendered approved the practice of the Congregation of the Mission. Since this decision was not well known in France, however, some French bishops at the beginning of the eighteenth century refused to recognize the right of the Congregation of the Mission to issue dimissorial letters for the ordination of its members. Because of this refusal, the Superior General of the Congregation of the Mission, John Bonnet (1711-1735), petitioned a declaration in this matter from Pope Benedict XIII. Whereupon Pope Benedict XIII, in the year 1725, declared that the Congregation of the Mission had obtained the privilege of granting dimissorial letters to its members in virtue of the privilege of exemption granted to it by Pope Urban VIII in 1632 and ratified by Pope Alexander VII in 1655, and that it still retained this privilege.[46] Just nineteen years after this declaration of Pope Benedict XIII, Pope Benedict XIV, in the year 1744, again declared that the Congregation of the Mission enjoyed the privilege of granting dimissorial letters to its members in virtue of the privilege of exemp-

[44] Urbanus VIII, bulla *Salvatoris Nostri*, 12 ian. 1632—*Acta Ap. in gratiam C. M.*, pp. 3-9.

[45] Alexander VII, bulla *Ex commissa Nobis*, 22 sept. 1655—*Acta Ap. in gratiam C. M.*, pp. 16-18; *Bull. Rom. Taur.*, XVI, 67-69.

[46] Benedictus XIII, brevis *Exponi Nobis*, 17 sept. 1725—*Acta Ap. in gratiam C. M.*, pp. 89-90; *Bull. Rom. Taur.*, XXII, 267-268.

tion granted to it by Pope Urban VIII in 1632 and ratified by Pope Alexander VII in 1655.[47]

In addition to the Congregation of the Mission, there were other Secular Congregations which enjoyed the privilege of exemption before the Code, e.g., the Congregation of the Passion,[48] the Congregation of the Most Holy Redeemer,[49] the Pious Workmen,[50] the Institute of Charity,[51]

[47] Benedictus XIV, brevis *Aequa apostolica,* 5 apr. 1744—*Acta Ap. in gratiam C. M.*, pp. 144-151, cf. p. 147; Honorante, *Praxis,* pp. 127-130.

[48] Clemens XIV, const. *Supremi apostolatus,* 16 dec. 1769, § 11—*Bullarii Romani Continuatio Summorum Pontificum Benedicti XIV, Clementis XIII, Clementis XIV, Pii VI, Pii VII, Leonis XII et Pii VIII* (14 vols., Prati, 1840-1856), VII, 73-79, cf. p. 78 (hereafter cited as *Bull. Rom. Cont.*).

[49] Pius VI, brevis *Sacrosanctum apostolatus,* 21 aug. 1789—*Bull. Rom. Cont.*, X, 2111-2113; Pius VII, brevis *Qui sicut boni Christi milites,* 9 ian. 1807—*Bull. Rom. Cont.*, XI, 887-888; S. C. Ep. et Reg., *Congregationis Presbyterorum Saecularium,* 16 sept. 1864—*Fontes,* n. 1993.

[50] Pius VI, const. *Inter multiplices,* 14 dec. 1792, § 3—*Bull. Rom. Cont.*, X, 2569-2570.

The Pious Workmen were founded by Venerable Charles Caraffa in Naples in 1600. The members did not pronounce any vows, but followed a severe rule. The institute was approved in 1606. Cf. *Annuario,* p. 766; Holstenius, *Codex regularum,* VI, 512-529; Helyot, *Ordres,* III, 102-110; Heimbucher, *Die Orden,* II, 573-574; Currier, *Orders,* pp. 615-616; Kapsner, *Orders,* p. 207.

On June 28, 1943, the Pious Workmen were united to the Rural Catechists to form an institute known today as the Pious Workmen Rural Catechists. Cf. *Annuario,* p. 766. The writer has learned by private communication that the Rural Catechists were founded in the Diocese of Cosenza in 1928 by Reverend Caietano Mauro, and that the Pious Workmen Rural Catechists constitute a Religious Congregation with simple public vows.

[51] Gregorius XVI, bulla *In sublimi militantis Ecclesiae solio,* 20 sept. 1839—*Acta Gregorii Papae XVI* (cura ac studio Antonii Mariae Bernasconi, 4 vols., Romae, 1901-1904), II, 361-373.

The Institute of Charity, also known as the Rosminians, was founded by Anthony Rosmini (1797-1855) in 1828 at Monte Calvario near Domodossola. The members of the Institute take the simple public vows of religion. The Constitutions of the Institute are contained in, and were approved by, the Bull of Gregory XVI cited in this foot-

and the Society of the Catholic Apostolate.[52] In virtue of their exemption, these Secular Congregations, too, enjoyed the privilege of issuing dimissorial letters for the ordination of their members.

Although the privilege of exemption included the privilege of issuing dimissorial letters, it did not include the privilege of sending the ordinands to any bishop for the conferral of Orders.[53] Thus, the exempt Secular Congregations were obliged to use their privilege of granting dimissorial letters in accord with the prescripts enacted by Pope Clement VIII in 1596[54] and by Pope Benedict XIII in 1724,[55] unless they enjoyed, over and above the general privilege of exemption, the special privilege of sending ordinands to any bishop for the conferral of Orders.

In addition to the exempt Secular Congregations, a number of non-exempt Secular Congregations also possessed the privilege of issuing dimissorial letters before the Code. These non-exempt Secular Congregations, however, obtained this privilege in a way different from that in which the exempt Secular Congregations obtained it. The non-exempt Secular Congregations obtained the privilege by indult. The indults by which this privilege was granted usually commanded that the dimissorial letters be granted in accord with the prescriptions either of the decree of Pope Clement VIII dated March 15, 1596[56] or of the Constitution *In*

note. Cf. *Annuario*, p. 771; Heimbucher, *Die Orden*, II, 634-635; Currier, *Orders*, p. 514; Kapsner, *Orders*, p. 132.

[52] Pius IX, 2 sept. 1847; S. C. Ep. et Reg., 10 maii 1904; 20 dec. 1905. The writer could not find the texts of these documents. But all three are reported both in the *Promptuarium Facultatum Piae Societatis Missionum iussu Sexti Capituli Generalis Editum*, pp. 8-9; and in *CpR*, I (1920), 144.

[53] Cf. *supra*, pp. 159-162.

[54] Cf. *supra*, pp. 161-162.

[55] Cf. *supra*, pp. 163-164.

[56] Cf. *supra*, pp. 161-162. It was to this decree that indults granted after the year 1894 usually referred. Cf. Many, *De Sacra Ordinatione*, p. 412.

supremo of Pope Benedict XIII, dated December 23, 1724.[57] The indults were usually limited either in the duration of the time for which they could be used or in the number of cases wherein they could be applied; but they were readily renewed. The indults sometimes required that the ordinands have letters of excardination from the dioceses of their place of origin before they could be granted dimissorial letters by their superiors.[58] The indults usually provided that, if a member was promoted to Orders in virtue of dimissorial letters from his superior and then left the institute, he would remain suspended until he found a benevolent bishop willing to receive him. The indults were granted by the Sacred Congregation for the Propagation of the Faith in the case of Secular Congregations engaged exclusively in the work of the foreign missions. Other Secular Congregations obtained the indults from the Sacred Congregation of Bishops and Regulars before the Constitution *Sapienti Consilio* of Pius X, dated June 29, 1908;[59] and after this Constitution, from the Sacred Congregation for Religious. These facts appear in indults such as those granted to the Society of the Priests of Mercy,[60] the Congregation of Jesus and Mary,[61] the Congregation of the Oratory of Jesus and of Mary Immaculate,[62] the Missionaries of Africa,[63] and the Society of Saint Joseph of the Sacred Heart.[64]

As seen in the preceding paragraph, each non-exempt

[57] Cf. *supra*, pp. 163-164.

[58] It is to be noted in this connection that the excardination of laymen was an actual practice from the second half of the nineteenth century to the advent of the Code. Cf. *supra*, pp. 51-53.

[59] *Fontes*, n. 682.

[60] S. C. Ep. et Reg., *Lugdun.*, 21 sept. 1838—Bizzarri, *Collectanea*, p. 708; *ASS*, I (1865), 364; *Anal. J. P.*, XIII (1874), 547.

[61] S. C. Ep. et Reg., 19 febr. 1864—Stanton, *De Societatibus*, pp. 139-140.

[62] S. C. Ep. et Reg., 22 mart. 1864—*Anal. J. P.*, VII (1864), 763.

[63] S. C. de Prop. Fide, 31 iul. 1899—Paventi, *De iuramento*, pp. 107-108.

[64] S. C. de Rel., 23 febr. 1910—from private communication.

Secular Congregation which by indult enjoyed the privilege of granting dimissorial letters was obliged, in the use of this privilege, to follow the particular prescriptions contained in the indult. Exempt Secular Congregations, on the other hand, were obliged to follow the laws regulating the granting of dimissorial letters in institutes of regulars, as seen above.[65] To these restrictions, others were added in the year 1892, which affected all Secular Congregations, exempt or non-exempt, in which simple vows were pronounced. For in that year the Sacred Congregation of Bishops and Regulars, by command of Pope Leo XIII, issued a decree forbidding superiors of Secular Congregations to give dimissorial letters for promotion to major Orders under the title of the common table or the mission unless those to whom such dimissorial letters were issued had first been perpetually aggregated to their institutes by perpetual profession, or, in the case of those institutes in which perpetual profession was deferred longer than three years, had remained at least three years in temporary profession.[66] The purpose of this decree was the avoidance of the inconvenience that arose from the frequent egress from Secular Congregations of men in major Orders.[67]

De Langogne, in a commentary he wrote on this decree in 1893, stated that the decree in no way applied to Secular Congregations in which there was no profession of vows.[68] It seems that this conclusion was justified, not only because of the wording of the decree, which mentions institutes of simple vows, but also because a number of the Secular Congregations in which there was no profession of vows were subject not to the Sacred Congregation of Bishops and Regulars, whence the decree emanated,

[65] Cf. *supra*, p. 168.

[66] S. C. Ep. et Reg., decl. *Auctis admodum*, 4 nov. 1892, § 1—*Fontes*, n. 2020.

[67] Cf. *supra*, pp. 49-50.

[68] "Sur le Décret 'Auctis admodum,'" *Le Canoniste Contemporain*, XVI (1893), p. 87, note (1).

but to the Sacred Congregation for the Propagation of the Faith.[69] It seems, however, that the decree did apply to those Secular Congregations whose members take vows that today are called private. For although the decree used the term "simple vows," nevertheless in the year 1892 that term, for most of the canonists, referred to all vows which were not solemn.[70]

In the year 1895, the Sacred Congregation of Bishops and Regulars declared that, for the ordination of members of institutes in which only simple vows were pronounced, testimonial letters from the ordinaries of those dioceses in which the members had lived long enough to contract a canonical impediment were not required; the dimissorial letters of the superiors general sufficed.[71]

In the year 1899, the Sacred Congregation of Bishops and Regulars settled a doubt which arose in certain institutes in which only simple vows were pronounced and which enjoyed by indult the privilege of issuing dimissorial letters. The dimissorial letters had to be sent to the ordinaries of the place in which was located the house to which the ordinands were assigned. In some institutes, however, the students were sent to a seminary after their profession without being attached to any house of the institute. The Sacred Congregation decided that in this case the dimissorial letters could be sent to the ordinary of the place in which the seminary was located, provided that the students had spent a year in that place.[72]

SECTION 3. THE PRIVILEGE OF GRANTING DIMISSORIAL LETTERS IN SOCIETIES AFTER THE CODE

Under the law of the Code, exempt Societies enjoy the

[69] Cf. *supra*, pp. 5-8.

[70] Cf. *supra*, pp. 16-17.

[71] S. C. Ep. et Reg., 1 mart. 1895—Vermeersch, *De Religiosis Institutis et Personis Tractatus Canonico-Moralis* (2 vols., Vol. II, *Supplementa et Monumenta*, 4. ed., Brugis, 1909), II, 517.

[72] S. C. Ep. et Reg., decr. 7 iun. 1899—*ASS*, XXXVII (1904-1905), 240-241.

privilege of granting dimissorial letters in virtue of their exemption just as they did before the Code. In the exercise of this privilege, therefore, they are bound by the laws which regulate exempt religious institutes in the granting of dimissorial letters.[73] These laws are found in canons 964, nn. 3, 4; 965; 966; 967. These canons are a restatement, for the most part, of the pre-Code law regulating the issuance of dimissorial letters both by regulars and by superiors of Secular Congregations possessing the privilege of issuing dimissorial letters either in virtue of exemption or in virtue of indults.[74] This, then, is the law which regulates exempt Societies after the Code in the use of their privilege of granting dimissorial letters.

The only exempt Societies which have been in existence since the Code, however, have been the Congregation of the Mission, the Pious Workmen, and the Society of the Catholic Apostolate; and today only the Congregation of the Mission and the Society of the Catholic Apostolate remain.[75] The authors are in agreement in stating that today, under the law of the Code, the privilege of exemption in Societies automatically carries with it the privilege of issuing dimissorial letters.[76] Thus, the Constitutions of the Society of the Catholic Apostolate state: "It is the office of the Major Superior to grant dimissorial letters."[77] And the Directory of the same Society states: *Alumni professi Societatis possunt ordinari a proprio Superiore maiore, si necessariam potestatem habeat; ab alio autem nemine*

[73] Stanton, *De Societatibus*, pp. 138-139; Berutti, *Institutiones Iuris Canonici*, III, 370-371; Goyeneche, *Summa Principia*, pp. 236-237; Romani, *Institutiones Juris Canonici*, I, 411; Schaefer, *De Religiosis*, p. 994; Ristuccia, *Societies*, pp. 198-199; Rothoff, *Sociétés*, pp. 175-178; Vermeersch-Creusen, *Epitome*, I, 631.

[74] Cf. *supra*, pp. 153-171.

[75] Cf. *supra*, pp. 165-168.

[76] Berutti, *Institutiones Iuris Canonici*, III, 370-371; Romani, *Institutiones Juris Canonici*, I, 411; Cappello, *Summa*, II, 100; Cocchi, *Commentarium*, IV, 242; Regatillo, *Institutiones*, I, 438; Rothoff, *Sociétés*, p. 176.

[77] *Constitutions of the Pious Society of the Missions*, § 172, p. 43.

licite ordinantur sine litteris dimissoriis eiusdem Superioris maioris.[78]

The majority of Societies in existence today are non-exempt. Members of these non-exempt Societies are obliged, by the common law, to follow the laws regulating the ordination of secular clerics,[79] just as they were before the Code.[80] In practice, however, bishops often refused absolutely to promote to Orders members of Societies, lest, without any utility to their own dioceses, they should expose themselves to the danger of having to accept these men as their own incardinated clerics in the case of their egress from their Societies. If the bishops did not refuse absolutely to ordain the members, they consented with more and more difficulty as time went on, often imposing conditions which were contrary to the concept of incardination, e.g., if the ordinands should leave the Societies, the bishops would not be reponsible for them.[81]

Cognizant of this difficulty, and unwilling to bring pressure to bear upon the bishops, the Sacred Congregation for the Propagation of the Faith and the Sacred Congregation for Religious adopted practices calculated to overcome the difficulty. Before the year 1947, the practice of the one differed slightly from the practice of the other. Both Sacred Congregations, however, found justification for their procedures in the last clause of canon 678: *salvis peculiaribus praescriptionibus a Sancta Sede datis.*

Before the year 1947, the Sacred Congregation for the Propagation of the Faith proceeded along these lines. First, it granted to missionary Societies an indult whereby the superiors could present their subjects for ordination upon the issuance simply of testimonial letters, dispensing from the law regarding dimissorial letters.[82] Gil states that the Sacred Congregation, in granting this indult, depended upon

[78] *Directorium Piae Societatis Missionum,* § 410.

[79] Canon 678.

[80] Cf. *supra,* 25-56.

[81] Gil, "Studium," *CpRM,* XXVIII (1949), 22-23.

[82] Stanghetti, *Prassi,* pp. 41-42; Paventi, *De Iuramento,* p. 103;

Pope Urban VIII's Brief *Ad uberes,* May 18, 1638, which granted to certain seminaries and colleges the privilege of ordaining their students apart from the issuance of dimissorial letters,[83] and which was confirmed by the Sacred Consistorial Congregation on November 6, 1920.[84] Be that as it may, on March 29, 1944, the Superior General of the Foreign Mission Society of the Province of Quebec wrote a letter to the Sacred Congregation for the Propagation of the Faith, asking if the privilege of presenting members of the Society for Orders apart from the use of dimissorial letters and with the employment simply of testimonial letters, as granted by the Sacred Congregation on January 27, 1944,[85] had any relation to Pope Urban VIII's Brief *Ad uberes,* dated May 18, 1638.[86] On June 15, 1944, the

Gil, "Studium," *CpRM,* XXVIII (1949), 23. The following Societies received such an indult:

the Paris Foreign Mission Society—Paventi, *De Iuramento,* pp. 110-111;

the Society of Missionaries to Africa—for this indult, cf. Rothoff, *Sociétés,* p. 179;

the Society of Missionaries of Saint Joseph of Mill Hill—Litterae S. C. de Prop. Fide, 7 iun. 1927—from private communication;

the Society of Maryknoll for Foreign Missions—Litterae S. C. de Prop. Fide, 12 iun. 1923, Prot. n. 1523/23—from private communication;

the Society of Saint Columban for the Foreign Missions in China—from private communication;

the Foreign Mission Society of the Province of Quebec—Litterae S. C. de Prop. Fide, 27 ian. 1944, Prot. n. 148/44—from private communication;

the Foreign Mission Society of Bethlehem in Switzerland—Litterae S. C. de Prop. Fide, 1941, Prot. n. 2048/41—from private communication.

[83] *Iuris Pontificii De Propaganda Fide* (2 partes, cura ac studio Raphaelis de Martinis, Pars I, 7 vols. in 8, Romae, 1888-1897; Pars II, 1 vol., Romae, 1909), Pars I, Vol. I, pp. 173-174 (hereafter cited as *Iuris Pont. de Prop. Fide*).

[84] *AAS,* XIII (1921), 259; cf. Gil, "Studium," *CpRM,* XXVIII (1949), 23.

[85] Prot. n. 148/44—from private communication.

[86] The writer received a transcript of this letter of the Superior General by private communication.

Sacred Congregation sent the following response.

> Prot. N. 867/44
> Reverendissime Domine,
>
> Dubia, quae obtulisti ad hanc S. Congregationem circa rescriptum concessum 27 Januarii v. a., rite perpendi et quae sequuntur Tibi, Rev.me Domine, respondeo.
>
> Rescriptum loquitur de facultate concedendi alumnis litteras testimoniales, quia litterae dimissoriales potius dantur ab Ordinariis. Sed testimoniales litterae id genus eumdem prorsus sortiuntur in praxi effectum ac litterae dimissoriales, unde Tui alumni accedere possunt ad sacros ordines litteris tantum testimonialibus muniti.
>
> Quoad dubia circa Breve *"Ad uberes"* Urbani VIII tibi significo illud breve nullam relationem habere cum facultate contenta in rescripto supra citato.[87]

The Sacred Congregation for the Propagation of the Faith solved the problems connected with canonical incorporation (*adscriptio*) either by having the following provisions incorporated into the Constitutions of Missionary Societies, or by incorporating these provisions into the law of these Societies by way of indult. The perpetual bond of incorporation in the Society—be it by reason of a private vow, an oath, or a promise—has the effect of canonical affiliation with the Society according to the norm of canon 111, § 1. The perpetual bond also has the effect, in the case of a man who has entered the Society as a cleric already incardinated in some diocese, of excardination according to the norms of canons 115 and 585. In the case of egress from the Society, a member remains suspended according to the norm of canon 641 until he finds a benevolent bishop willing to receive him.[88]

With regard to these provisions as found in Constitutions of these Societies, Paventi quotes the following from the Constitutions of the Pontifical Institute of the Holy Apos-

[87] From private communication.

[88] Gil, "Studium," *CpRM*, XXVIII (1949), 24; Stanghetti, *Prassi*, pp. 38-41.

tles Peter and Paul and of Saints Ambrose and Charles: *"Il giuramento perpetuo ha lo stesso valore della professione religiosa (can. 115, 585), di modo che, per esso, il nuovo membro è escardinato dalla propria diocesi ed incardinato all'Istituto."*[89] The Constitutions of this Society have been the model for the Constitutions of all recent Missionary Societies.[90] Thus, a number of Missionary Societies have incorporated such a provision into their new or revised Constitutions.[91]

With regard to these provisions as found in particular indults, such a procedure has been followed in the case of the Society of Saint Columban for the Missions in China,[92] the Foreign Missionary Society of the Province of Quebec,[93] and the Society of Maryknoll for Foreign Missions.[94]

Before the year 1947, this practice of the Sacred Congregation for the Propagation of the Faith was slightly different from that of the Sacred Congregation for Religious. The Sacred Congregation for Religious felt that the dispensation from dimissorial letters ran counter to the fundamental principle of the law for ordination as enacted in canon 955, § 1: *Unusquisque a proprio Episcopo ordinetur aut cum legitimis eiusdem litteris dimissoriis.* This Sacred Congregation, therefore, granted to all the Societies petitioning them the temporary faculties to issue dimissorial letters. The Sacred Congregation also granted these Societies the faculty of enrolling their members ac-

[89] *De Iuramento,* p. 93.

[90] Paventi, *De Iuramento,* p. 88, nota 6.

[91] Cf. *The Society of African Missions, Constitutions and Directory,* n. 22, p. 5; *Constitutions of the Scarboro Foreign Mission Society,* n. 36, p. 13; *Organización del Instituto Español,* p. 25; Paventi, *De Iuramento,* p. 93, nota 10.

[92] The source of this information is private communication.

[93] The writer has learned from private communication that this disposition was made by the Sacred Congregation for the Propagation of the Faith in 1938.

[94] Litterae S. C. de Prop. Fide, 12 iun. 1923, Prot, n. 1523/23—from private communication.

cording to the norm of canon 111, § 1, either at the time of perpetual incorporation, or, in cases wherein there was no perpetual incorporation, after a specified period of temporary incorporation, e.g., after three or six years. This enrollment had the effect of excardination according to the norms of canons 115 and 585 in the case of a member who came to the Society as a cleric already incardinated in some diocese. Thus, those who left the Society in sacred Orders remained suspended, according to the norm of canon 641, until they found a benevolent bishop willing to receive them. For some time now, the Sacred Congregation has been inserting these provisions in revised Constitutions of Societies subject to it.[95] As will be seen in the next paragraph, the Sacred Congregation for Religious continued to act in the same way even after the year 1947. Thus, examples of the above-mentioned dispositions made by the Sacred Congregation for Religious between the time when the Code went into effect and the present time, either by means of particular indult or by means of incorporation in newly-approved Constitutions, can be found in regard to the Institute of the Oratory of Saint Philip Neri,[96] the Congregation of the Most Precious Blood,[97] the Con-

[95] Gil, "Studium," *CpRM*, XXVIII (1949), 24-25.

[96] The following information, taken from the Constitutions of the Institute of the Oratory, was obtained by private communication. Superiors can grant dimissorial letters to subjects in their three-year period of temporary aggregation for First Tonsure and minor Orders. If these subjects leave the Institute, they are automatically reduced to the lay state, unless they shall have found a benevolent bishop willing to receive them. Superiors can grant dimissorial letters for promotion to major Orders to those members who are perpetually aggregated. A member in major Orders cannot leave the Institute before he has found a benevolent bishop willing to receive him. If he should leave before finding a benevolent bishop, he remains suspended.

[97] It has been learned by private communication that around the year 1921, the Moderator General of this Society obtained an indult to grant dimissorial letters to members of the Italian Province only; and that around the year 1932 or 1933 the Moderator General obtained an indult to grant dimissorial letters in a hundred cases. The

gregation of Jesus and Mary,[98] and the Society of Missionary Priests of Saint Paul the Apostle.[99]

During the year 1944, or at some time previous to that date, the Sacred Congregation for the Propagation of the Faith and the Sacred Congregation for Religious began to be concerned about the discrepancy which existed at the time between the former's practice of granting indults for the presenting of members of Societies for the reception of Orders with the use simply of testimonial letters, dispensing from the law regarding dimissorial letters, and the latter's practice of granting indults to Societies whereby the superiors could issue dimissorial letters. On October 4, 1944, therefore, the Sacred Congregation for the Propagation of the Faith asked Pope Pius XII for per-

latter indult was not limited to the Italian Province, and could be renewed.

The Constitutions of this Society, approved *ad septennium* on May 24, 1946, contain the following provisions: § 141. Per aggregationem perpetuam sodalis ipso jure amittit propriam, quam ante habebat dioecesim. § 149. Debitis cum informationibus, Superior provincialis, de consensu sui Consilii, alumnos temporaliter aggregatos ad primam tonsuram et ad ordines minores, alumnos vero perpetuo aggregatos ad ordines majores, praesentat Moderatori generali, cui jus est litteras dimissorias concedere.—*Regula et Constitutiones Congregationis Missionis a Pretioso Sanguine D. N. J. C.*, pp. 49-51.

[98] This Society obtained from the Sacred Congregation for Religious, at some time before March 15, 1932, the indult of issuing dimissorial letters. On the latter date the indult was renewed. Cf. Stanton, *De Societatibus*, p. 140. It was learned by private communication that the privilege was granted again by indult *ad quinquennium* on March 20, 1945. It was also learned that the Sacred Congregation, on March 4, 1948, added the following sentence to the indult: Quod si praefati Alumni ad Sacros Ordines promoti a pia Congregatione quacumque ex causa discedant, suspensi maneant ab Ordinum exercitio, nec ad Superiores Ordines, si nondum Presbyteratum assecuti fuerint, promoveri possint, donec canonico titulo Sacrae Ordinationis provideantur.

[99] On September 12, 1941, the Sacred Congregation for Religious granted to this Society an indult whereby the Superior General could, for a term of five years, grant dimissorial letters. Prot. n. 5164/41. This indult was renewed on May 16, 1951, for five years.—*The Register of the Paulist Fathers*, p. 25.

mission for both Sacred Congregations to present a joint interrogation to the Code Commission, asking who had the right to grant dimissorial letters for the ordination of members of Societies. Subsequently the Sacred Congregation for Religious gave the Sacred Congregation for the Propagation of the Faith detailed information about its practice in the matter. On June 12, 1946, the Sacred Congregation for the Propagation of the Faith communicated to the Code Commission both its own practice and the practice of the Sacred Congregation for Religious. The Code Commission discussed the matter in plenary session on May 29, 1947. A consultation with Pope Pius XII followed on June 18, 1947. In another plenary session of the Code Commission held on June 26, 1947, it was decided that the interrogation should be answered as follows. The right to grant dimissorial letters for the ordination of members of Societies pertains to the ordinary of the place according to the norm of canon 678. But since the exercise of this right involves great difficulty, the Code Commission submitted the following recommendations. The faculty in question should be granted to the major superiors of Societies, and this faculty of granting dimissorial letters should be regulated according to the norm of the canons regulating the granting of dimissorial letters in religious institutes.[100] This procedure is preferred to that whereby major superiors are authorized to present their subjects for ordination upon the issuance simply of testimonial letters and with a dispensation from the law which requires dimissorial letters. The members should be affiliated with their Societies according to the norm of canon 111, § 1. The loss of their diocese is to take place at the time of perpetual incorporation, or, in the case in which there is no perpetual incorporation, after three or six years of temporary incorporation, to be determined by the Constitutions. In the case of egress from the Society, a member would remain suspended according to the norm of canon 641 until he

[100] Cf. canons 964, nn. 2, 3; 965; 966; 967.

find a benevolent bishop willing to receive him. All these recommendations were made as being in harmony with the provision made for such indults in the last clause of canon 678: *salvis peculiaribus praescriptionibus a Sancta Sede datis.* Finally, the Code Commission was of the opinion that the faculties granted in Urban VIII's Brief *Ad uberes,* dated May 18, 1638,[101] were applicable not to members of missionary Societies of the Common Life, but only to students of seminaries and colleges subject to the Sacred Congregation for the Propagation of the Faith. These findings and recommendations of the Code Commission were approved on July 16, 1947, by Pope Pius XII, who ordered that the said findings and recommendations be communicated to the Sacred Congregation for the Propagation of the Faith and to the Sacred Congregation for Religious by way of the Sacred Congregation for Extraordinary Ecclesiastical Affairs. Whereupon the Very Reverend Acacius Coussa, Secretary of the Code Commission, communicated a summary of the whole matter to the Sacred Congregation for Extraordinary Ecclesiastical Affairs by letter under date of July 24, 1947.[102]

Since 1947, the Sacred Congregation for the Propagation of the Faith has ceased to give indults dispensing from the issuance of dimissorial letters, and has been giving indults whereby superiors in Missionary Societies can issue dimissorial letters for the ordination of their subjects. In 1947, immediately after the recommendations of the Code Commission mentioned above, the Sacred Congregation for the Propagation of the Faith granted by way of indult the faculty to issue dimissorial letters both to the Foreign Mission Society of the Province of Quebec, *ad quinquennium,*[103] and to the Foreign Mission Society of

[101] *Iuris Pont. de Prop. Fide,* Pars I, Vol. I, pp. 173-174; cf. S. C. Consist., responsum, 6 nov. 1920—*AAS,* XIII (1921), 259.

[102] *CpRM,* XXVIII (1949), 16-18.

[103] S. C. de Prop. Fide, litterae, 28 oct. 1947, Prot. n. 4093/47—from private communication.

Bethlehem in Switzerland.[104] In 1948, the Missionaries of Africa obtained an indult whereby the Superior General could issue dimissorial letters for the ordination of his subjects. The faculty was to last for five years and could be delegated to the provincials of the Society.[105] In the year 1950, the Society of Missionaries to Africa received the privilege of issuing dimissorial letters for the ordination of its members.[106] The same privilege is enjoyed at the present time by the Society of Maryknoll for Foreign Missions, by the Pontifical Institute of the Holy Apostles Peter and Paul and of Saints Ambrose and Charles for the Foreign Missions, and by the Scarboro Foreign Mission Society.[107] The Spanish Institute of Saint Francis Xavier has also received an indult whereby the Superior General can grant dimissorial letters for the ordination of his subjects.[108] Finally, the Constitutions of the Yarumal Institute for the Foreign Missions, which were approved, *ad septennium,* on January 16, 1953, in Article 44, contain the following provision:

> Quod attinet ad ordinationem sodalium, Superior Generalis sive per se sive per Superiores Provinciales, facultatem habet dandi suis subditis, litteras dimissorias ad primam clericalem Tonsuram et ad Ordines minores post eorum iuramentum temporarium, atque ad Ordines maiores post eorum iuramentum perpetuum.[109]

[104] S. C. de Prop. Fide, litterae, spet. 1947, Prot. n. 3207/47—from private communication.

This indult was renewed in 1952, *ad decennium.* Prot. n. 3883/52—from private communication.

[105] S. C. de Prop. Fide, litterae, 16 iun. 1948, Prot. n. 2335/48—from private communication.

[106] S. C. de Prop. Fide, 13 iul. 1950, Prot. n. 2938/50—from private communication; cf. *Ordo Divini Officii Recitandi Missaeque Celebrandae ad usum Societatis Missionum ad Afros pro anno Domini 1951,* p. 6.

[107] This information has been obtained by way of private communication.

[108] Paventi, *Organización del Instituto Español,* p. 44.

[109] This has been learned by way of private communication.

It has been seen thus far in the present section that today the majority of Societies enjoy the privilege of issuing dimissorial letters. The question may now be asked by what laws are these Societies regulated in their use of this privilege. In general, it may be answered that these Societies are regulated by the same law which regulates the issuance of dimissorial letters in religious institutes.[110]

In the first place, the bishop to whom the superior must address the dimissorial letters is the bishop of the diocese wherein is located the house to which the ordinand belongs.[111] The superior may direct the dimissorial letters to another bishop only if the bishop of the diocese has given permission, or if he is of a rite different from that of the ordinand, or if he is absent, or if he will not hold ordinations on the next regular ordination days, or if the diocese is vacant and the one in charge lacks the episcopal character. In each of these cases it is necessary that the ordaining bishop be assured of the existence of the requisite condition by way of an authentic statement of the episcopal curia.[112] Superiors in Societies are forbidden to circumvent this law by sending ordinands to another house of the Society or by putting off the issuance of dimissorial letters to a time when the bishop will be away or will not have ordinations.[113] Superiors of Societies who have presumed to send their subjects to an outside bishop for ordination in contravention of these prescripts of canons 965, 966, and 967, are by that very fact suspended for a month from the celebration of Mass.[114] If young members of Societies are sent to a seminary immediately after their period of probation without being assigned to any house of the

[110] Stanton, *De Societatibus*, pp. 138-139; Berutti, *Institutiones Iuris Canonici*, III, 370-371; Goyeneche, *Summa Principia*, p. 236; Schaefer, *De Religiosis*, p. 994; Ristuccia, *Societies*, pp. 201-202; Rothoff, *Sociétés*, pp. 176-177.

[111] Cf. canon 965.

[112] Cf. canon 966.

[113] Cf. canon 967.

[114] Canon 2410; P. C. I., 3 iun. 1918—*AAS*, X (1918), 347.

Society, however, it seems that the superiors in the Society can address dimissorial letters to the bishop of the place in which the seminary is located, provided that the ordinands have spent at least a year in the seminary at the time the dimissorial letters are sent.[115]

Canon 995 states that the ordaining bishop needs no other testimonial letters in addition to the dimissorial letters, which, by prescript of the same canon, must testify to the fact that the ordinand is a member of the community in the house over which the one issuing the dimissorial letters is superior, to the completion of the required studies, and to the fulfillment of the other prescripts of law.[116] It should be noted that a superior who has the right to issue dimissorial letters is not bound to gather the testimonials mentioned in canons 993 and 994 and present these testimonials to the ordaining bishop. He will already have obtained most of these testimonials for his own archives, however, in compliance with other prescripts of the law. Here contemplated in particular are the testimonial from the ordinaries of places in which ordinands have spent some time. Members of Societies possessing dimissorial letters from their superiors are not obliged to bring testimonials from the bishops of all the places in which they have spent six months, or even three months while in military service.[117] Nevertheless, the Instruction

[115] Cf. S. C. Ep. et Reg., decr., 7 iun. 1899—*AAS*, XXXVII (1904-1905), 240-241; cf. *supra*, p. 171.

[116] Dimissorial letters for the ordination of members of Societies should contain all the essentials required in dimissorial letters for the ordination of religious. Cf. Quinn, *Documents Required for the Reception of Orders*, pp. 158-161; Coronata, *De Sacramentis*, II, 231-232; Cappello, *De Sacramentis*, IV, 234.

Notice should be taken of the difference in the requirements in the contents of dimissorial letters for the ordination of members of Societies when they are issued by superiors in virtue of a privilege as compared with the case wherein they are issued by a local ordinary according to the norms of the common law. Cf. *supra*, pp. 126-127.

[117] Cf. canons 993, n. 4; 994, § 1.

Quantum Religiones requires that superiors of Societies, before they admit candidates to the period of probation, obtain the testimonials required of candidates for religious institutes by canons 544 and 545, [118] and canon 544, § 2, requires that male candidates for a religious novitiate bring with them testimonial letters from the ordinary of their place of origin and from the ordinary of each place in which they lived for a year or more since their fourteenth year.

It has been seen thus far in the present section, first, that today the majority of Societies enjoy the privilege of issuing dimissorial letters; and, secondly, by what laws these Societies are regulated in the use of this privilege. It has been seen above that, when the Sacred Congregations grant the privilege of issuing dimissorial letters, they usually make provision for canonical affiliation with the Society according to the norm of canon 111, § 1, for excardination according to the norms of canons 115 and 585, and for juridical status in the event of egress from the Society according to the norm of canon 641. It may be asked, however, what would be the status of a member ordained upon the issuance of dimissorial letters by his superior should he legitimately and of his own free will leave a Society for which no such provisions were made.

In trying to answer this problem, it seems necessary to keep in mind two fundamental principles. First, the fundamental purpose of incardination seems to evince the fact that each and every cleric must be subject to some ecclesiastical authority.[119] Secondly, it is necessary to consider the case of a member who is tonsured in his Society separately from the case of a member who comes to his Society already incardinated in some diocese. For in the former case there is question of establishing a bond; in the latter, of dealing with a bond already in existence.

[118] S. C. de Rel., instr. *Quantum Religiones,* 1 dec. 1931, § 6—*AAS,* XXIV (1932), 74-81, cf. p. 76.

[119] Cf. *supra,* pp. 113-115.

Consider first the case of a man who, after his admittance into a Society, is tonsured upon the issuance of dimissorial letters by his major superior. According to law, the major superior must ordinarily send such a man to the bishop of the place in which is located the house to which the ordinand is attached.[120] Under certain conditions, the major superior can send the ordinand to any bishop.[121] The bishop to whom the dimissorial letters are sent can rightly be expected to ordain the ordinand, provided that he can be sure of the authenticity of the dimissorial letters,[122] and provided also that he can satisfy his conscience, by way of a separate examination if necessary, as to the fitness of the candidate.[123] Apart from this, however, he has nothing to say about the admittance of the member to Orders. It would seem unjust, therefore, to expect that such an ordaining bishop should be expected to incardinate such an ordinand into his diocese. *A fortiori* it would seem unjust to expect that any other bishop would do so. On the other hand, what appears properly to be the purpose of canonical incorporation, namely, subjection to ecclesiastical authority, is provided for by reason of the fact that the subject becomes subordinated to the authority of the major superior who issued the dimissorial letters. It seems, therefore, that in this case, whether there be question of a Society which is exempt or of a Society which is non-exempt, the privilege of granting dimissorial letters contains in it, virtually, the privilege of canonically affiliating a cleric, at the time of First Tonsure, with the Society, thus satisfying the law of canon 111, § 1, without the need of incardination in a diocese.[124] In this case, should such an affiliated cleric leave his Society, he would have to find a benevolent bishop willing to receive him, no matter what might have been the occasion of his leaving.

Consider secondly the case of a man who is already a

[120] Canon 965.

[121] Canon 966, § 1.

[122] Canon 962.

[123] Canon 997, § 2.

[124] Berutti, *Institutiones Iuris Canonici,* III, 370-371; Rothoff, *Sociétés,* p. 176.

cleric incardinated in some diocese at the time of his entry into the Society. Here arises the need of dealing with an already established bond. It seems that that bond cannot be dissolved except by authority of the legislator who instituted it. But nowhere, in the case under consideration, does the legislator give evidence that he intends that this bond be dissolved, either by incorporation in a Society or by the reception of higher Orders within the Society upon the issuance of dimissorial letters by a major superior in the Society. Therefore it seems reasonable to conclude that, although the authority of such a cleric's bishop of incardination is suspended to a great extent while the cleric remains in the Society, nevertheless this authority does remain radically. And should the cleric leave the Society, he would immediately become fully subject to his proper bishop by reason of incardination, except, of course, when the clerical member would be reduced from minor Orders to the lay state.[125]

It should be remembered in this connection, however, that when a member in major Orders requests a dispensation from the Holy See in order to leave his Society, the Holy See's practice is to grant the dispensation only on condition that the member remain suspended until he finds a benevolent bishop willing to receive him.

Article 2. Privileges Regarding the Title of Ordination

Section 1. Privileges Regarding Title in Societies Subject to the Sacred Congregation for Religious

From the Council of Trent until the time when the Code went into effect, members of Secular Congregations were held, by the common law, to the law of title applicable for secular clerics.[126] But it was often difficult for members of Secular Congregations to obtain one of the titles employed for secular clerics. For this reason the Holy See

[125] Vermeersch, "Incardinatio in Societatem sine votis," *Periodica*, XXIII (1934), 57*; cf. *supra*, pp. 87-88.

[126] Cf. *supra*, pp. 30-38, 49.

received frequent petitions for, and often granted, indults whereby members of Secular Congregations could be ordained to major Orders under the title of the common table, of the Society, the Institute, the Community, or the Congregation. These titles were very similar in character, consisting in the right to sustenance from the goods of the institute.[127]

In the seventeenth century, the Holy See granted sparingly any indults for the use of the title of the common table. The indult was granted to some Secular Congregations to be used only if the common law titles were not available. In this way the title of the common table was granted between 1578 and 1622 to the Oblates of Saint Charles Borromeo,[128] and in 1685 to the Secular Clerics Living in Common.[129] In 1659 the title of the common table was granted by indult to the Congregation of Priests of Christian Doctrine; but it could be used in favor of only three members in a house of twelve, and two in a house of less than twelve. It was further specified that superiors should not dispense a subject ordained under the title of the common table from his vows and oath before the subject had obtained some other title. And if a subject ordained under the title of the common table left the institute illegitimately, he would be automatically suspended.[130] In 1685, the Sacred Congregation of the Council declared that the Oblates of Ostuni did not enjoy the privilege of using the title of the common table in virtue simply of a participation in it along with the Oblates of Saint Charles Borromeo.[131] And just five years later the Congregation of the Mission asked the Sacred Congrega-

[127] Many, *De Sacra Ordinatione*, pp. 427-428; Moeder, *Proper Bishop*, p. 20.

[128] *Anal. J. P.*, VII (1864), 747.

[129] Innocentius XI, breve *Prospero felicique*, 9 febr. 1685—*Bull. Rom. Taur.*, XIX, 613-614.

[130] Alexander VII, const. *Sacrosancti*, 15 mart. 1659—*Bull. Rom. Taur.*, XVI, 445-447.

[131] S. C. C., *Ostunen.*, 17 febr. 1685—*Anal. J. P.*, VII (1864), 746-748.

tion of the Council for the privilege of having its members ordained under the title of the common table in Poland and Lithuania in view of the scarcity of priests there. The Sacred Congregation refused this petition.[132]

In the eighteenth and nineteenth centuries, the Congregation of the Mission obtained the privilege of having its members ordained under the title of the common table in geographical stages, as it were. The privilege was first granted in 1744 for members of the institute from England, Scotland, Ireland, Poland, Hungary, Moravia, Silesia, and Italy.[133] In 1790 the privilege was granted for members from Portugal and Sardinia.[134] And in 1853 the privilege was granted for members from Spain.[135]

In the nineteenth century and in the beginning of the twentieth century, the Holy See often granted the privilege of using the title of the common table in the same indult in which it granted the privilege of issuing dimissorial letters. The use of the title of the common table was not limited by these indults to special circumstances or to certain places. Indults were granted during this period to the Congregation of the Most Holy Redeemer in 1828,[136] to the Institute of Charity in 1839,[137] to the Congregation of Jesus and Mary in 1864,[138] to the Congregation of the Oratory of Jesus and Mary Immaculate in 1864,[139] and to

[132] S. C. C., *Poloniae seu Lituaniae Ordinationis*, 17 iun. 1690—Pallottini, XVI, 157.

[133] Benedictus XIV, const. *Aequa apostolica*, 5 apr. 1744—*Acta Ap. in gratiam C. M.*, pp. 144-151.

[134] Pius VI, breve *Piis Christifidelium votis*, 22 ian. 1790—*Bull. Rom. Cont.*, X, 2148-2150.

[135] S. C. Ep. et Reg., 27 maii 1853—*Anal. J. P.*, XIII (1874), 691.

[136] Leo XII, const. *Inter religiosas familias*, 11 mart. 1828—*Bull. Rom. Cont.*, XIII, 659-661.

[137] Gregorius XVI, bulla *In sublimi*, 20 sept. 1839—*Acta Gregorii Papae* XVI, II, 361-373.

[138] This indult was limited to thirty cases.—Stanton, *De Societatibus*, pp. 139-140, nota (95).

[139] This indult was limited to twenty cases.—*Anal J. P.*, VII (1864), 763.

the Society of Saint Joseph of the Sacred Heart.[140]

No change was made by the Code in the common law of the ordination title for members of Societies. Today, members of Societies, just as members of Secular Congregations before the Code, are bound, by the common law, to the law of the title applicable for secular clerics.[141] The Sacred Congregation for Religious, however, has continued to grant to Societies subject to it the privilege of using the title of the common table. At first, the Sacred Congregation for Religious often granted this privilege by special indult. This was the case, for example, with regard to the Congregation of Jesus and Mary in 1932,[142] and with regard to the Congregation of the Most Precious Blood in 1938.[143] More recently, however, the Sacred Congregation for Religious has seen to it that the privilege of using the title of the common table be inserted in the Constitutions of a number of Societies. In this way, the Societies obtain the privilege in virtue of the approbation given to their Constitutions. This was the case, for example, with regard to the Constitutions of the Institute of the Oratory of Saint Philip Neri, approved in 1943,[144] and with regard to the Constitutions of the Congregation of the Most Precious Blood, approved *ad septennium* in 1946.[145] Insertion of the privilege of using the title of the common table in the Constitutions of a Society was not unknown, however, in the years immediately following the promulgation of the Code. Thus, for example, the Constitutions of the Society

[140] S. C. de Rel., 23 febr. 1910—from private communication.

[141] Cf. *supra*, pp. 134-138.

[142] S. C. de Rel., 15 mart. 1932—Stanton, *De Societatibus*, pp. 139-140, nota (95), cf. p. 140.

[143] S. C. de Rel., 25 mart. 1938—from private communication.

[144] "Alumni post triennium probationis Congregationi legitime aggregati, titulo mensae communis ex privilegio ordinari valent." —*Constitutiones Instituti Oratorii Sancti Philipi Neri*, § 109—from private communication.

[145] "Alumni perpetuo aggregati ordinantur titulo mensae communis."—*Regula et Constitutiones Congregationis Missionis a Pretioso Sanguine D. N. J. C.*, § 149, pp. 50-51.

of the Catholic Apostolate, which were definitively approved on March 1, 1910, and approved again after revision on March 2, 1922, make the following statement: "Finally professed students are ordained on the title of maintenance in the Community (*mensae communis*)."[146]

Finally, the Code Commission, in the year 1947, recommended that the Sacred Congregation for Religious continue in the practice of granting major superiors of Societies subject to it the faculty of promoting their subjects to Orders under the title of the common table, and that this privilege be inserted in the Constitutions of Societies of pontifical approval. This recommendation was approved by Pope Pius XII.[147]

SECTION 2. PRIVILEGES REGARDING TITLE IN SOCIETIES SUBJECT TO THE SACRED CONGREGATION FOR THE PROPAGATION OF THE FAITH

As a preface to the discussion of privileges regarding the title of ordination in Missionary Societies, something should be said about the origin and development of the title of the mission.

At the Council of Trent it was decreed that no secular cleric could be ordained unless he possessed a title of benefice, patrimony, or pension.[148] None of these titles was available, however, to those secular clerics who studied at Rome towards the end of the sixteenth century in preparation for priestly labor in the mission fields. In 1578, therefore, Pope Gregory XIII granted to the students at the English College in Rome the privilege of being ordained without a title.[149] Between 1578 and 1638, the Sovereign Pontiffs extended this privilege to the members of a number of other missionary colleges and seminaries subject to the

[146] *Constitutions of the Pious Society of Missions*, § 174, p. 44; cf. *Directorium Piae Societatis Missionum*, § 411.

[147] P. C. I., litterae, 24 iul. 1947—*CpRM*, XXVIII (1949), 16-18.

[148] Conc. Trident., sess. XXI, *de ref.*, c. 2.

[149] Gregorius XIII, const. *Quoniam divinae bonitati*, 23 apr. 1578—*Bull. Rom. Taur.*, VIII, 208-214, cf. p. 212.

Sacred Congregation for the Propagation of the Faith.[150] The expression "title of the mission" was used for the first time by Pope Urban VIII in 1631, when he granted the use of that title to the students of the Irish College in Rome.[151] In 1638 Pope Urban VIII extended the use of the title of the mission to all students in missionary colleges and seminaries subject to the Sacred Congregation for the Propagation of the Faith.[152] This title of the mission granted by Pope Urban VIII consisted in the very right of clerics ordained under this title to receive the necessities of life from the exercise of the ministry in the mission field to which they were assigned.[153]

Use of the title of the mission in these early years almost always presupposed that the cleric ordained under this title was destined for a *determined* mission as the scene of his life's labors. Sometimes, however, use of the title was allowed in favor of a cleric whose field of labor was still *to be determined.* In either case, however, the bond between the cleric and his mission was perpetual.[154] This bond always had to be strengthened with an oath. The papal privileges which allowed the use of the title of the mission always specified that the cleric using it bind himself by oath to the perpetual service of the mission to which he was, or would be, assigned.[155]

From the seventeenth century to the year 1871, the title and oath of the mission remained essentially the same, although the oath became the subject of much debate in so far as it contained the promise not to enter a religious institute.[156]

[150] Paventi, *De Iuramento*, pp. 30-32.

[151] Urbanus VIII, const. *Sacrosancti*, 12 apr. 1631—*Iuris Pont. de Prop. Fide*, Pars I, Vol. I, pp. 128-129.

[152] Urbanus VIII, const. *Ad uberes*, 18 maii 1638—*Iuris Pont. de Prop. Fide*, Pars I, Vol. I, pp. 173-174.

[153] Many, *De Sacra Ordinatione*, p. 150.

[154] Paventi, *De Iuramento*, p. 33.

[155] Paventi, *De Iuramento*, pp. 8-25.

[156] This aspect of the oath has no direct bearing on the subject matter of this dissertation. Cf. Paventi, *De Iuramento*, pp. 35-50,

In the year 1871, the Sacred Congregation for the Propagation of the Faith issued its famous Instruction on the title of the mission. In this Instruction, the Sacred Congregation, after giving a brief resumé of the various titles of ordination, stated that those who were ordained under the title of the mission were entitled to sustenance to be derived from the mission to which they were assigned. The title, however, was extraordinary, and outside the common law, and therefore it could not be enjoyed by anyone without an apostolic indult. This indult was ordinarily given to the superiors of missions, of colleges or of congregations serving the missions; but the indults were given only for a certain length of time or for a fixed number of cases. Before being ordained under the title of the mission, each and every one enjoying this privilege had to promise under oath that he would labor perpetually in the mission to which he was, or would be, assigned. And after being ordained under the title of the mission, a missionary who deserted the mission to which he had been assigned lost his title, and became bound to provide himself with some other title. But use of the title of the mission with reference to another mission called for a new apostolic indult.[157]

The instruction of 1871 carried with it the formula of the oath that was to be taken as a prerequisite for ordination under the title of the mission. It was clear from the wording of the oath that the ordinand promised to serve a particular diocese or vicariate.[158] He could not be transferred to any other diocese or vicariate apart from a previous relaxation of this oath by the Sacred Congregation.[159]

57-69; S. C. de Prop. Fide, instr. *Cum indecorum*, 27 apr. 1871, § 8—*Fontes*, n. 4878.

157 S. C. de Prop. Fide, instr. *Cum indecorum*, 27 apr. 1871, §§ 6, 7, 8, 13—*Fontes*, n. 4878.

158 S. C. de Prop. Fide, instr. *Cum indecorum*, 27 apr. 1871: "Voveo pariter et iuro quod in hac dioecesi, aut vicariatu ... perpetuo ... laborem meum ac operam ... impendam."—*Fontes*, n. 4878.

159 S. C. de Prop. Fide, 4 febr. 1873, ad 5—*Collectanea S. Congregationis de Propaganda Fide* (2 vols., Romae, 1907), n. 1394 (here-

In the year 1885, the bishops of England, which country then constituted a single ecclesiastical province, obtained from the Holy See a relaxation of the oath of service in the mission to the extent that those who had been ordained under the title of the mission could be transferred from one diocese to another without a special permission of the Holy See, provided that they remained within the province.[160] A few months later, the bishops of the United States obtained from the Holy See the same relaxation of the oath of service in the mission.[161]

This is a brief summary of the law regarding the title of the mission from its institution until the time when the Code went into effect. It was under this title that members of missionary Societies were very frequently ordained in the seventeenth, eighteenth and nineteenth centuries.

It should be noted that the Missionary Societies which today are Societies of the Common Life were not always Secular Congregations with moral personalities of their own distinct from the moral personalities of the missions whose personnel they supplied. From the time of the foundation of the Paris Foreign Mission Society in the year 1660 until the latter half of the nineteenth century, this Society, and others like it, such as the Foreign Mission Institute of Milan, were simply missionary seminaries which were conducted in the homeland under the authority of a number of vicars apostolic who were actually on the missions.[162] During this period there was no difficulty about the fact that men ordained under the title of the mission were bound by oath to serve one particular diocese or vicariate for life.

In the latter half of the nineteenth century, however,

after cited as *Coll. S. C. P. F.*); Vromant, *Ius Missionariorum de Personis* (Paris-Bruxelles, 1929), p. 211.

[160] S. C. de Prop. Fide, decr., 18 aug. 1885—*Coll. S. C. P. F.*, n. 1641.

[161] S. C. de Prop. Fide, decr., 30 nov. 1885—*Coll. S. C. P. F.*, n. 1641, nota (1).

[162] Paventi, *De Iuramento*, pp. 104-105.

Missionary Societies began to be converted into Secular Congregations with their own superiors distinct from the vicars apostolic, and with their own separate moral personalities. Thus, for example, the Constitutions of the Paris Foreign Mission Society were approved by the Sacred Congregation for the Propagation of the Faith *ad decennium* in 1874, *ad aliud quinquennium* in 1884, and *definitive* in 1890.[163] After the conversion of these institutes into Secular Congregations, the faculty to promote to Orders under the title of the mission, which the Holy See had previously vested in the vicars apostolic, or in the superiors of the missionary seminaries, who were the delegates of the vicars apostolic, were now vested by the Holy See in the new superiors of the missionary Secular Congregations. The faculty was still a privilege, enjoyed only by way of grant from the Holy See, but it was granted under slightly different terms than it had been granted previously. If it had been granted exactly as specified by the Instruction of 1871, the following difficulty would have arisen. The superiors of the missionary Secular Congregations would, at times, desire to recall certain missionaries to participate in administration or in education; or they would desire to transfer members from one mission to another in order to fulfill their obligation of staffing numerous missions with missionary personnel. But they would not have been able to recall or transfer their subjects without a special relaxation by Rome of the oath that these subjects would have taken to serve one mission for life. To obviate this difficulty, the Holy See usually granted to these missionary Secular Congregations, together with the privilege of using the title of the mission, the additional privilege whereby the members, in taking the oath required as a prerequisite for the use of this title, could promise, not indeed to serve any one particular mission, but to serve in any house or mission of their respective institutes to which their respective superiors might assign

[163] Paventi, *De Iuramento*, pp. 104-105.

them. This left the superiors free to transfer their subjects without a special relaxation of the mission oath in each particular case.[164] Thus, for example, the members of the Parish Foreign Mission Society took an oath referred to as a *"iuramentum domorum et missionum."*[165] A similar privilege was granted to the Foreign Mission Institute of Milan.[166] These privileges were analogous to the ones granted in favor of the missions in England and the United States in 1885.[167]

The Code brought about a change in the position of the title of the mission. Whereas before the Code this title could not be used without the permission of the Holy See,[168] since the Code has gone into effect the title of the mission is a common law title which can be used by any cleric without the permission of the Holy See, in a territory subject to the Sacred Congregation for the Propagation of the Faith.[169] There is also a pertinent difference in the mission oath required by the Code as compared with the mission oath which had been required by the Instruction of 1871. The Instruction of 1871 permitted a cleric to promise to serve perpetually a mission *to be determined* at a time after the pronouncing of the oath.[170] The Code, on the other hand, demands in every case that the mission be *determined* before the oath is taken.[171]

Since the Code has gone into effect, Societies of the Common Life may, in harmony with the common law, make use of the title of the mission as it is delineated in canon

[164] Vromant, *Ius Missionariorum de Personis*, pp. 207-209, 211-212; Paventi, *De Iuramento*, pp. 72, 77.

[165] Vromant, *Ius Missionariorum de Personis*, p. 209.

[166] Paventi, *De Iuramento*, p. 77.

[167] Cf. *supra*, p. 193.

[168] S. C. de Prop. Fide, instr. *Cum indecorum*, 27 apr. 1871, § 7—*Fontes*, n. 4878.

[169] Canon 981, § 1.

[170] Cf. the formula appended to the Instruction. S. C. de Prop. Fide, instr. *Cum indecorum*, 27 apr. 1871—*Fontes*, n. 4878.

[171] Canon 981, § 1; cf. Paventi, *De Iuramento*, p. 82.

981.[172] But such a use of the title of the mission by members of Societies presents to their superiors the same problems regarding transfer and recall that would have been presented if members of Secular Congregations had pronounced the oath of service in the mission in the form in which it was appended to the Instruction of 1871. For this reason it has after the promulgation of the Code been the preference of superiors that their subjects be promoted to Orders under a title of the mission different from the one delineated in canon 981, a title of the mission that would allow the recall and transfer of those who had been ordained under this title. But the use of such a title, even after the promulgation of the Code, requires the permission of the Holy See. This permission has, as a matter of fact, been granted in certain instances, either by way of indult or by way of approbation of Constitutions in which such usage is outlined.[173] In 1946 Paventi recommended that this particular title of the mission be called *"titulus missionum."*[174] And, as a matter of fact, in the above reported letter in which the Code Commission outlined recommendations approved by Pope Pius XII for the ordination of members of Societies, it was recommended that major superiors of Societies be given the privilege, either by way of indult or by way of approved Constitutions, of having their subjects ordained under the title of the common table or under a title referred to as *"titulus missionum."*[175]

The title of the mission, or the title of the missions, is not, however, the only title under which by privilege members of missionary Societies are ordained. In recent years, the Sacred Congregation for the Propagation of the Faith

[172] Cf. *supra*, pp. 134-138.

[173] Vromant, *Ius Missionariorum de Personis*, pp. 207-209, 211-212.

[174] *De Iuramento*, p. 113.

[175] P. C. I., litterae, 24 iul. 1947—*CpRM*, XXVIII (1949), 17; cf. *supra*, pp. 178-180.

has granted a number of missionary Societies the use of the title of the common table.[176]

Of twelve missionary Societies subject to the Sacred Congregation for the Propagation of the Faith, five still retain the title of the mission or the title of the missions. These Societies are the Paris Foreign Mission Society, the Society of Missionaries to Africa, the Pontifical Institute of the Holy Apostles Peter and Paul and of Saints Ambrose and Charles for the Foreign Missions,[177] the Spanish Institute of Saint Francis Xavier for the Foreign Missions,[178] and the Yarumal Society for the Foreign Missions.[179] The other seven Societies today use the title of the common table.

The Missionaries of Africa obtained an indult granting them the use of the title of the mission *ad decennium* on August 13, 1893. This indult was renewed *ad aliud decennium* on September 11, 1903. In 1913 the Society was granted *in perpetuum* the privilege of using the title of the common table.[180]

The Society of Missionaries of Saint Joseph of Mill Hill obtained the privilege of using the title of the mission in the indult in which the Society received the privilege of granting dimissorial letters. This indult was dated June 7, 1927, and the privilege was granted *ad triennium.* On January 25, 1935, the privilege of granting dimissorial letters was renewed. But on this occasion the Sacred Congregation for the Propagation of the Faith, instead of renewing the privilege of receiving major Orders under the title of the mission, granted the privilege of being

[176] Stanghetti, *Prassi,* p. 41; Paventi, *De Iuramento,* p. 108.

[177] This information about these three Societies has been obtained from private communication.

[178] *Organización del Instituto Español,* p. 44.

[179] "Clerici sodales ordinantur titulo missionis."—*Constitutiones Seminarii Pontificii pro Missiones de Yarumal* (approbatae 16 ian. 1953), art. 44—from private communication.

[180] S. C. de Prop. Fide, 2 sept. 1913, Prot. n. 1550/913—from private communication.

ordained under the title of the common table. Again, the grant was *ad triennium.*[181]

The Society of Maryknoll for Foreign Missions received the following grant from the Sacred Congregation in 1923:

> "... Tibi facultas fit ... Sodales ... ordinantur vel titulo Mensae Communis si in Seminario remanent, vel titulo Missionis, quoties determinatae cuidam Missioni destinati iam fuerint. Sodales ... iam sacerdotio initiati ... iuramentum ... emittant, quo ... in perpetuum cooptati maneant. Pro quibus, si necessarium videatur, titulus ordinationis, quo iam ordinati antea fuerant, in alium titulum sive Mensae Communis, sive Missionis, iuxta diversos casus, uti supra, commutari poterit."[182]

Today, however, all the members of this Society are ordained under the title of the common table.[183]

The Society of Saint Columban for the Missions in China used the title of the mission from 1919 until 1934, when it received *in perpetuum* the privilege of using the title of the common table.[184]

The Foreign Mission Society of the Province of Quebec, from the time of its foundation in 1921 until the year 1938, had its members ordained under the title of the service of the diocese. Since the year 1938, in which year the effect of excardination was given to the perpetual oath pronounced in this Society, the Society has enjoyed the privilege of using the title of the common table.[185]

The Foreign Mission Society of Bethlehem in Switzerland uses at present the title of the common table.[186]

Finally, the Scarboro Foreign Mission Society enjoys the

[181] From private communication.

[182] S. C. de Prop. Fide, 12 iun. 1923, Prot. n. 1523/23—from private communication.

[183] From private communication.

[184] From private communication.

[185] From private communication.

[186] "Sodales ordinantur titulo mensae communis."—*Constitutiones Societatis Missionum Exterarum de Bethlehem in Helvetia,* n. 63, § 2—from private communication.

privilege of using the "*titulum Societatis Scarborensis pro Missionibus ad Exteras Gentes.*"[187]

SECTION 3. THE RELATIONSHIP BETWEEN THE PRIVILEGE OF GRANTING DIMISSORIAL LETTERS AND THE PRIVILEGE OF USING THE TITLE OF THE COMMON TABLE

When the Holy See grants to a Society the privilege of issuing dimissorial letters, almost invariably it grants along with this privilege the additional privilege of using the title of the common table,[188] provided, of course, that the latter privilege is not already enjoyed by the Society.

One may raise the question, however, whether the privilege of using the title of the common table would be included implicitly in the privilege of granting dimissorial letters, if the latter privilege were granted to a Society without any mention of the former privilege, and the former privilege were not already enjoyed by the Society.

An affirmative answer to this question is given by Goyeneche,[189] Schaefer,[190] and Ristuccia.[191]

A number of other authors may *seem* at first sight to give an affirmative answer to this question, and some of these authors are even cited in defense of an affirmative stand on the problem. But after a careful reading it will be seen that they are either merely stating that the privilege of using the title of the common table is usually given along with the privilege of issuing dimissorial letters, or simply stating that Societies possessing the latter privilege are considered as religious for ordination purposes in those things which pertain to the proper bishop and the dimissorial letters, or perhaps stating that the privilege of giving dimissorial letters is to be understood according to

[187] From private communication.

[188] In the case of missionary Societies, the privilege of using the title of the mission is still sometimes given. Cf. *supra*, p. 197.

[189] *Summa Principia*, pp. 236-237.

[190] *De Religiosis*, p. 994.

[191] *Societies*, p. 205.

the norms of canons 964 to 967, and that the privilege of using the title of the common table is to be understood according to the norm of canon 982. Some authors in point are Moeder,[192] Berutti,[193] McBride,[194] Vermeersch-Creusen,[195] and Rothoff.[196]

Many, on the other hand, denies that the privilege of issuing dimissorial letters carries with it automatically the privilege of using the title of the common table.[197]

Perhaps the best argument in defense of the opinion of Many is the historical fact that the privilege of granting dimissorial letters was enjoyed by a Secular Congregation which did not, at the time, enjoy the privilege of using

[192] "Bishops may refuse to ordain members of societies without vows or insist that the superiors obtain a papal indult to grant dimissorial letters. The indult generally removes all difficulties. It makes provision for a canonical title."—*Proper Bishop*, p. 114.

[193] ". . . sin autem . . . agatur . . . de alia Societate in qua sodales ex peculiari indulto seu privilegio ad sacros ordines promoveri valeant titulo missionis, vel mensae communis seu Societatis, et cum legitimis dimissoriis proprii Superioris, huiusmodi speciales concessiones intelligendae sunt secundum communia iuris praescripta de ordinatione religiosorum (cann. 964-967 et 982), nisi aliud in casu particulari expresse caveatur."—*Institutiones Iuris Canonici*, III, 370-371.

[194] "Some of these societies also have received an Indult to issue dimissorial letters to their members, and they, too, for ordination purposes are enumerated amongst the exempt Religious." In this place McBride is commenting on canon 956, and is in no way concerned with the problem of the title of ordination.—*Incardination*, p. 343.

[195] "Inde perspicitur peculiares S. Sedis praescriptiones frequenter esse necessarias. Potissimum usu venit indultum tituli specialis, atque etiam indultum concedendi litteras dimissoriales."—*Epitome*, I, 631.

[196] "L'indult [containing the privilege of issuing dimissorial letters] pourvoit au titre d'Ordination; ce sera par exemple *titulus mensae communis, vitae communis.*" Rothoff cites as his authority for this statement the quotation from Moeder referred to in the present paragraph.—*Sociétés*, p. 176.

[197] "Imo, licet institutis votorum simplicium haec duo privilegia, nempe concedendi dimissorias subditis suis, et eos promovendi titulo mensae communis, simul concedi soleant, attamen posterius non includitur in priore."—*De Sacra Ordinatione*, p. 429.

the title of the common table. Contemplated here is the case of the Congregation of the Mission, which enjoyed the privilege of issuing dimissorial letters from the year 1632, but which did not enjoy the privilege of using the title of the common table until the year 1744.[198]

The only argument offered in defense of the opinion of Goyeneche, Schaefer and Ristuccia seems to be the following. The "privilege of granting dimissorial letters to its subjects makes a quasi-religious society, in the legal obligations concerning ordination, similar to a religious institute."[199] But it seems that this equivalation to religious institutes should be extended in this matter only so far as is demanded by the principle enunciated in canon 66, § 3: *Concessa facultas secumfert alias quoque potestates quae ad illius usum sunt necessariae.* Now, it is evident that use of the title of the common table is not necessary as a prerequisite for the use of the privilege of granting dimissorial letters, for the titles of benefice, patrimony, pension, service of the diocese and the mission are by the common law available to all members of Societies.[200] It seems, then, that to consider the privilege of using the title of the common table as being contained implicitly in the privilege of granting dimissorial letters is to go counter to the fundamental principle of law enunciated in canon 67: *Privilegium ex ipsius tenore aestimandum est, nec licet illud extendere aut restringere.*

In conclusion, it seems that the only derogations from the common law for the ordination of secular clerics which the privilege of issuing dimissorial letters carries with it for Societies are those derogations that are necessary for the use of the privilege of granting dimissorial letters. That is to say, Societies enjoying the privilege of issuing dimissorial letters follow the whole law regulating the issuance of dimissorial letters in religious institutes. Thus,

[198] Cf. *supra*, pp. 165-167, 188.

[199] Ristuccia, *Societies*, p. 205; cf. Schaefer, *De Religiosis*, p. 994; Goyeneche, *Summa Principia*, pp. 236-237.

[200] Cf. *supra*, pp. 134-138.

for example, such privileged Societies are not bound to present to the ordaining bishop the testimonial letters mentioned in canons 993 and 994; they are required to present to the ordaining bishop only the dimissorial letters themselves, drawn up according to the prescript of canon 995, § 1.[201]

Article 3. Other Privileges Relating to the Law of Ordination

Section 1. Other Privileges in Exempt Societies

As seen above, there are two Societies of the Common Life in existence today which enjoy the privilege of exemption, namely, the Congregation of the Mission and the Society of the Catholic Apostolate.[202] The privilege of exemption was granted to the Congregation of the Mission by Pope Urban VIII in the Bull *Salvatoris Nostri*, on January 12, 1632. In this Bull, Pope Urban VIII also granted to the Congregation of the Mission all the privileges which other similar or dissimilar Congregations enjoyed or would enjoy, provided that these privileges were not contrary to the decrees of the Council of Trent or to other apostolic constitutions. These privileges were granted *in forma aeque principali.*[203] On July 3, 1805, Pope Pius VII, in a private audience, confirmed the concession of privileges made to the Congregation of the Mission by way of reciprocal interparticipation in the Bull *Salvatoris Nostri*, and stated explicitly that the institute participated by way of reciprocal sharing in the privileges of the Institute of the Oratory of Saint Philip Neri, of the Pious Workmen, of the Congregation of the Most Holy Redeemer, and of the Congregation of the Passion.[204] All the privileges of regulars were granted to the Congregation of the Passion in the year 1769,[205]

[201] Cf. canon 995, § 2.

[202] Cf. pp. 165-168.

[203] *Acta Ap. in gratiam C. M.*, pp. 3-9, cf. p. 8.

[204] *Acta Ap. in gratiam C. M.*, pp. 228-229.

[205] Clemens XIV, const. *Supremi apostolatus*, 16 dec. 1769—*Bull. Rom. Cont.*, VII, 73-79.

to the Pious Workmen in the year 1792,[206] and to the Congregation of the Most Holy Redeemer in the year 1807.[207] Consequently, since the year 1769, the Congregation of the Mission has enjoyed not only all the privileges of similar and dissimilar Congregations, but also all the privileges of regulars.[208]

In like manner, on September 2, 1847, Pope Pius IX granted to the Society of the Catholic Apostolate by way of reciprocal sharing all the privileges enjoyed by Orders and by regular and secular Congregations.[209] On May 19, 1904, the Sacred Congregation of Bishops and Regulars declared that the grant made by Pope Pius IX in 1847 included the privilege of exemption from the local ordinaries in all things save those matters in which even regulars were subject to the local ordinaries by the common law.[210]

On December 30, 1937, the Code Commission declared that the words of canon 613, § 1: *exclusa in posterum qualibet communicatione,* by which acquisition of privileges on the part of religious by way of interparticipation was elminated, are to be understood in the sense that privileges which were thus acquired through a reciprocal sharing, and were peacefully enjoyed by religious institutes before the Code went into effect, are not revoked.[211]

Canon 680 states that Societies enjoy those privileges which have been granted to them directly. The authors

[206] Pius VI, const. *Inter multiplices,* 14 dec. 1792—*Bull. Rom. Cont.,* X, 2569-2570.

[207] Pius VII, breve *Qui sicut boni Christi milites,* 9 ian. 1807—*Bull. Rom. Cont.,* XI, 887-888.

[208] *Collectio Privilegiorum et Indulgentiarum quae S. Sedes Congregationi Missionis benigne Concessit,* pp. 2-7.

[209] *Promptuarium Facultatum Piae Societatis Missionum iussu Sexti Capituli Generalis Editum,* p. 9; Goyeneche, "Consultationes," *CpR,* I (1920), 144.

[210] *Promptuarium Facultatum Piae Societatis Missionum iussi Sexti Capituli Generalis Editum,* p. 8; Goyeneche, "Consultationes," *CpR,* I (1920), 144.

[211] *AAS,* XXX (1938), 73.

interpret the words "*directe concessis*" in canon 680 in the sense of canon 613, § 1, that is *exclusa in posterum qualibet communicatione*. But authors also consider that the exclusion of a possible interparticipation in reference to Societies is likewise to be understood in the sense of the reply of the Code Commission mentioned above in the previous paragraph. And therefore any privileges which a Society has obtained by way of reciprocal sharing before the Code will, *ceteris paribus*, remain intact today.[212]

With a full application of this teaching to the Congregation of the Mission and to the Society of the Catholic Apostolate, the conclusion is drawn that these Societies retain today the privileges of regulars, and, in particular, the privileges of exemption, which they enjoyed before the Code. And, as a matter of fact, these privileges of the Congregation of the Mission and of the Society of the Catholic Apostolate are generally recognized today.[213]

As a consequence of the fact that the Congregation of the Mission and the Society of the Catholic Apostolate enjoy the privileges of regulars, and in particular the privilege of exemption, the major superiors in these Societies are ordinaries,[214] and have ordinary jurisdiction in both the internal and the external forum.[215]

In the law for ordination contained in canons 948 to 1011, special faculties are sometimes granted to ordinaries, without any restriction in consequence of which these faculties would be enjoyed only by local ordinaries. For example, ordinaries can, either personally or through a

[212] Stanton, *De Societatibus*, p. 149; Cappello, *Summa*, II, 101; Cocchi, *Commentarium*, IV, 243, 179; Beste, *Introductio*, p. 461; Schaefer, *De Religiosis*, pp. 995-996; Ristuccia, *Societies*, pp. 227-228; Rothoff, *Sociétés*, p. 187; Vermeersch-Creusen, *Epitome*, I, 632, 583-584; Fanfani, *De Iure Religiosorum*, pp. 715, 489.

[213] Cf. Stanton, *De Societatibus*, p. 149; Schaefer, *De Religiosis*, p. 996; Regatillo, *Institutiones*, I, 438; Rothoff, *Sociétés*, pp. 115, 187; Vermeersch-Creusen, *Epitome*, I, 632.

[214] Cf. canons 198, § 1; 488, nn. 2, 4, 8; 615; 618, § 1.

[215] Cf. *Constitutions of the Pious Society of the Missions*, § 241, p. 63.

delegate, dispense from all irregularities arising from an occult delict, with the exception of the delict of homicide or abortion, and with the exception of any delict regarding which some action has been taken in a court of law.[216] Again, ordinaries can reduce the retreat for the diaconate to three days whenever more than one major Order is to be conferred within a period of six months;[217] and it remains for ordinaries to judge whether a retreat is to be repeated if an ordination is postponed for a period of time less than six months.[218] Now, since major superiors in exempt clerical religious institutes are ordinaries for their subjects,[219] the authors are unanimous in asserting that these major superiors enjoy these faculties in reference to their subjects.[220] Since major superiors in the two exempt clerical Societies enjoy by privilege the capacity of ordinaries for their subjects, it seems logical to conclude that major superiors in these Societies, too, enjoy, in reference to their subjects, the faculties granted to ordinaries in the law touching ordination, as long as these faculties are not restricted to local ordinaries.

The privilege of participating by way of reciprocal sharing in all the privileges of regulars has been the source of many other ordination privileges for these exempt clerical Societies. For example, in the year 1826 the Society of Jesus obtained from Pope Leo XII (1823-1829) the privilege whereby its members could be ordained *extra tempora* and without the observance of the normally required interstices.[221] But from the year 1769 the Congregation of the

[216] Canon 990, § 1.

[217] Canon 1001, § 1.

[218] Canon 1001, § 2.

[219] Canon 198, § 1.

[220] Wernz-Vidal, *Ius Canonicum*, Tom. IV, Vol. I, p. 354; Vermeersch-Creusen, *Epitome*, II, 179, 184; Coronata, *De Sacramentis*, II, 209; Beste, *Introductio*, p. 542; Cappello, *De Sacramentis*, IV, 384, 409; Bouscaren-Ellis, *Canon Law*, pp. 440-446; Abbo-Hannan, *The Sacred Canons*, II, 140.

[221] Leo XII, const. *Plura inter*, 11 iul. 1826, § 2—*Bull. Rom. Cont.*, XIII, 437-440, cf. p. 438.

Mission enjoyed all the privileges of regulars by way of its reciprocal sharing in them. From the year 1826, therefore, the Congregation of the Mission enjoyed the privilege whereby its members could be ordained *extra tempora* and without the observance of the normally required interstices.[222] And, as a matter of fact, the privilege of having its members ordained *extra tempora* was confirmed by Pope Pius IX in the year 1859.[223] Again, from the year 1847 the Society of the Catholic Apostolate also enjoyed all the privileges of regulars by way of interparticipation. From the year 1847, therefore, this Society, too, enjoyed the privilege whereby its members could be ordained *extra tempora* and without the observance of the normally required interstices.[224]

One privilege enjoyed by some institutes of regulars before the Code was the privilege of sending dimissorial letters to any bishop in peace and communion with the Holy See.[225] But the Congregation of the Mission and the Society of the Catholic Apostolate do not enjoy this privilege by reason of their participation in it along with regulars. The reason is that this privilege is valid only if it was granted after the Council of Trent and only if it was granted directly.[226] The Congregation of the Mission, however, does enjoy this privilege in virtue of direct concession.[227]

[222] *Collectio Privilegiorum et Indulgentiarum quae S. Sedes Congregationi Missionis benigne Concessit,* p. 53.

[223] Pius IX, breve *Relgiosas familias,* 13 maii 1859—*Acta Ap. in gratiam C. M.,* pp. 201-202.

[224] *Promptuarium Facultatum Piae Societatis Missionum iussu Sexti Capituli Generalis Editum,* p. 11.

[225] This privilege was granted to the Society of Jesus in the year 1582. Gregorius XIII, breve *Pium et utile,* 22 sept. 1582, § 1—*Bull. Rom. Taur.,* VIII, 397-398.

[226] Cf. *supra,* pp. 162-163. Coronata, *De Sacramentis,* II, 58-59; Cappello, *De Sacramentis,* IV, 230-231.

[227] Pius IX, breve *Religiosas familias,* 13 maii 1859—*Acta Ap. in gratiam C. M.,* pp. 201-202; *Collectio Privilegiorum et Indulgentiarum quae S. Sedes Congregationi Missionis benigne Concessit,* p.

At this point it may be wondered why the Congregation of the Mission did not enjoy the privilege of having its members ordained under the title of the common table before the year 1744. On the one hand, the Congreation of the Mission enjoyed all the privileges of similar or dissimilar Congregations by way of interparticipation since the year 1632, and, on the other hand, the privilege of using the title of the common table was enjoyed by the Oblates of Saint Charles Borromeo before the year 1622, by the Congregation of Priests of Christian Doctrine in the year 1659, and by the Secular Clerics Living in Common in the year 1685.[228] And yet, the Congregation of the Mission was granted the use of this title only in geographical stages, as it were, in 1744, 1790 and 1853.[229] The reason for this apparent discrepancy can be found in the Constitution in which Pope Benedict XIV first granted the use of the title of the common table to a large part of the Congregation of the Mission in the year 1744. The Pontiff stated that the title of the common table resembled very closely the title of poverty, in virtue of which the burden of support rests upon the institute. But no one could be ordained under such a title if he could leave or be dismissed from the institute and return to the world. It made no difference whether he was a religious or whether he merely imitated the life of religious. In order that such a man could be allowed to use the title of the common table, a *special* indult was necessary; a general indult did not suffice.[230]

The question of the examination before ordination presents a special difficulty, because before the Code not all regulars were exempt from the law which required that ordinands undergo an examination by the ordaining bishop

50; Gasparri, *De Sacra Ordinatione,* II, 166-167; Coronata, *De Sacramentis,* II, 58.

[228] Cf. *supra,* p. 187.

[229] Cf. *supra,* p. 188.

[230] Benedictus XIV, const. *Aequa apostolicae,* 5 apr. 1744—*Acta Ap. in gratiam C. M.,* pp. 144-151, cf. pp. 147-148.

before the reception of Orders.[231] It is *probable* that canons 996 and 997 introduced a change in this law with regard to exempt religious. For although canon 996, § 1, states that *every* ordinand, secular or religious, must undergo this examination, canon 997, § 1, which designates the local ordinary who ordains in his own right or who issues dimissorial letters as the one responsible for the examination, does not make it clear that this is one of those exceptions, expressly stated in the law, in which the exempt are *not* withdrawn from the jurisdiction of the local ordinary.[232] It is therefore the opinion of men who have studied this question thoroughly that ordinands in exempt institutes are, in virtue of their exemption, to be examined not by the local ordinary who ordains in his own right,[233] but by their superiors.[234] It seems, then, that in exempt Societies the right to examine ordinands pertains, in virtue of the privilege of exemption, not to the local ordinary, but to the superiors of the exempt Societies.[235] It must be borne in mind, however, that the bishop to whom dimissorial letters are sent *always* has the right to institute an examination if he has any doubt about any candidate, even though the candidate be exempt.[236]

The law of the publication of the banns was promulgated by the Council of Trent, which ended in the year 1563.[237]

[231] Conc. Trident., sess. XXIII, *de ref.*, c. 12; S. C. C., decr., 15 mart. 1596—*Fontes*, n. 2294; Gasparri, *De Sacra Ordinatione*, II, 54; Many, *De Sacra Ordinatione*, pp. 392-394.

[232] Cf. canons 615; 618, § 1.

[233] Cf. canon 965. There can be no question here of a local ordinary who issues dimissorial letters. Cf. canon 964, n. 2.

[234] Gallagher, *The Examination of the Qualities of the Ordinand*, pp. 129-131; O'Brien, *The Provincial Religious Superior*, The Catholic University of America Canon Law Studies, n. 258 (Washington, D.C.: The Catholic University of America Press, 1947), p. 219; Cappello, *De Sacramentis*, IV, 403; Coronata, *De Sacramentis*, II, 234-235; cf. S. C. de Rel., instr. *Quantum Religiones*, 1 dec. 1931, § 12—*AAS*, XXIV (1932), 74-81, cf. pp. 78-79.

[235] Cf. *Constitutions of the Pious Society of Missions*, § 176, p. 44.

[236] Canon 997, § 2.

[237] Conc. Trident., sess. XXIII, *de ref.*, c. 5.

Only a few years later, the Sacred Congregation of the Council made it clear that regulars were not bound by the law of the publication of the banns.[238] But from the year 1769 until the year 1918 the Congregation of the Mission enjoyed the privilege of participating in the privileges of regulars; and from 1847 until 1918 the Society of the Catholic Apostolate enjoyed the same privilege. It seems, therefore, that during these years both of these exempt Societies acquired by way of interparticipation the privilege of exemption from the law of the publication of the banns, and that they still retain this privilege today in virtue of canon 4 and according to the response of the Code Commission mentioned above.[239]

Finally, with regard to the designation of the place where the retreat before ordination is to be made, it seems that this right pertains to the superiors in exempt Societies. For these Societies enjoy the privilege of exemption in the same way as regulars, and regulars are exempt from the jurisdiction of the local ordinary in all things save in those cases which are expressly excepted in the law.[240] But far from any express statement in the law that regulars must obey the local ordinary in the matter of designating where the retreat before ordination should be made, the law actually gives the right of designating the place not only to regular superiors, but even to superiors of non-exempt religious institutes.[241] It seems correct, therefore, to conclude that in exempt Societies this right pertains to the superiors in the Societies.

SECTION 2. OTHER PRIVILEGES IN NON-EXEMPT SOCIETIES

Of all the ordination privileges granted to Societies, the two most commonly granted by the Holy See, aside from

238 S. C. C., *Mediolanen.*, mense aug. 1587, ad 4—*Fontes*, n. 2185; *Mileten.*, 27 apr. 1595—*Fontes*, n. 2285; *Monopolitana*, 27 febr. 1602 —*Fontes*, n. 2345; *Regularium*, 28 febr. 1602—*Fontes*, n. 2346.

239 Cf. *supra*, p. 203.

240 Canon 615.

241 Canon 1001, § 4.

the privilege of issuing dimissorial letters and the privilege of using the title of the common table or of the mission, are the privilege of having ordinations *extra tempora,* even on feasts of semidouble or of simple rite, and the privilege of holding these ordinations apart from the observance of the normally required interstices.

In the year 1932 the Sacred Congregation for Religious included these two privileges in the indult in which it granted to the Congregation of Jesus and Mary the privilege of issuing dimissorial letters and the privilege of using the title of the common table.[242]

In the year 1951 the Society of Missionaries to Africa enjoyed the privilege of having ordinations *extra tempora* and the privilege of not needing to observe the normally required interstices.[243]

In the year 1952 the Sacred Congregation for the Propagation of the Faith granted the following privilege to the Foreign Mission Society of Bethlehem in Switzerland:

> 1. L'indulto della dispensa dagli interstizi fra Suddiaconato e Diaconato, o fra Diaconato e Presbiterato;
> 2. L'indulto di poter far conferire il Presbiterato in un giorno festivo, e il Suddiaconato e Diaconato in un giorno pure festivo, o nel precedente o conseguente giorno non festivo;
> 3. L'indulto di poter far ricevere i sacri ordini agli alunni dell'Istituto nel giorno precedente alla festa di S. Nicola de Flüe e nel giorno di detta festa, oppure nel giorno immediatamente seguente.[244]

In the year 1927 the Sacred Congregation for the Propagation of the Faith granted to the Superior General of the Society of Maryknoll for Foreign Missions the faculty of dispensing his subjects from the law of the interstices *ad*

[242] S. C. de Rel., 15 mart. 1932—Stanton, *De Societatibus,* pp. 139-140, nota (95), cf. p. 140.

[243] *Ordo Divini Officii Recitandi Missaeque Celebrandae ad usum Societatis Missionum ad Afros pro Anno Domini 1951,* p. 6.

[244] S. C. de Prop. Fide, 1952, Prot. n. 3583/52—from private communication.

triennium.[245] This indult was renewed in 1930 *ad biennium.*[246]

It should be noted here that a bishop who possess an indult whereby he can confer Orders *extra tempora* and without the observance of the normally required interstices can use this indult even when he ordains members of Societies coming to him with dimissorial letters from their superiors, though the latter should lack such a privilege.[247]

With regard to the privilege of omitting the publication of the banns in non-exempt Societies, it should be noted first of all that it is the unanimous teaching of canonists that members of non-exempt Societies are, by the common law, held to the law of the publication of the banns as contained in canons 998, 999 and 1000.[248]

Some non-exempt Societies have received by direct concession the privilege of omitting the publication of the banns. For example, on March 2, 1885, the Congregation of the Most Precious Blood received from the Holy See the following privilege *in perpetuum*: *Alumni Congregationis ad ordines promovendi dispensantur a denuntiationibus in locis ubi morantur.*[249] In recent years the Society of Missionaries to Africa received from the Sacred Congregation for the Propagation of the Faith the privilege of omitting the publication of the banns provided that there existed a just cause for so doing.[250]

Stanton stated that in Societies in which the members lose their dioceses at the time when they pronounce their perpetual oath, there can be no question of the publication of the banns, because the members have lost their dioceses

[245] S. C. de Prop. Fide, 29 mart. 1927, Prot. n. 1115/27—from private communication.

[246] S. C. de Prop. Fide, 29 ian. 1930, Prot. n. 440/1930—from private communication.

[247] Cf. S. C. de Sacr., *Friburgen.*, 15 aug. 1909—*Fontes*, n. 2098.

[248] Cf. *supra*, pp. 142-143.

[249] From private communication.

[250] Rothoff, *Sociétés*, p. 179.

and parishes. In Societies in which the proper diocese is not lost upon the taking of a perpetual oath, but in which the superiors issue dimissorial letters with the specification that if members leave the Societies they must find a benevolent bishop, he held that the members lose their dioceses upon their ordination to the subdiaconate, and as a consequence the publication of the banns is not called for before their ordination to the diaconate and the priesthood. He even held that in this case the publication of the banns cannot be demanded before the subdiaconate, since canon 995, § 2, states that the ordaining bishop may rest content with the dimissorial letters alone.[251] Rothoff agrees with Stanton in all save Stanton's contention that in Societies where one's diocese is not lost at the time of perpetual incorporation the publication of the banns cannot be demanded even before the subdiaconate. Rothoff pointed out that the very canon which states that the ordaining bishop may rest content with the dimissorial letters alone[252] requires also that the dimissorial letters themselves should contain an attestation from the superior to the effect that all the requirements of the law have been fulfilled,[253] one of which requirements is that which commands the publication of the banns.[254] The fundamental reasoning behind the principle contentions of both Stanton and Rothoff is this. Canon 998, § 1, exempts from the law of the publication of the banns all perpetually professed religious. The reason why canon 998, § 1, makes this exception, they contend, is that the religious lose their diocese and parish at the time of perpetual profession in virtue of canon 585.[255] Therefore, they concluded, whenever anyone loses his diocese and parish, he is automatically excused from the law of the publication of the banns. But diocese and parish

[251] Stanton, *De Societatibus*, pp. 137-138, nota (92).

[252] Canon 995, § 2.

[253] Canon 995, § 1.

[254] Rothoff, *Sociétés*, pp. 178-179.

[255] Rothoff, *Sociétés*, p. 178; cf. Cappello, *De Sacramentis*, IV, 406.

are lost by the members of those Societies in which the perpetual oath has been given the force otherwise deriving from canon 585. And since this oath must precede the conferral of major Orders,[256] members of these Societies are without a diocese and parish at the time of the subdiaconate, and, therefore, are not held to the law requiring the publication of the banns. A similar situation exists in Societies in which the force and effect ordinarily deriving from canon 585 is not attached to the perpetual bond, but which enjoy the privilege of granting dimissorial letters with the proviso that those who leave the Societies must find a benevolent bishop. (The situation exists after the subdiaconate according to both authors.) Rothoff and Stanton believed that this proviso produced the same effect which they felt is produced by the ruling contained in canon 585.

The first objection to this opinion of Rothoff and Stanton is this. As seen above, the present writer takes a different view of the meaning of canon 585.[257] The present writer feels that canon 585 has reference *only* to religious who were clerics incardinated in some diocese before their entrance into religion, and that consequently its counterpart in the Constitutions of some Societies also has reference *only* to members who were clerics incardinated in some diocese before their entrance into their Societies. Furthermore, it seems that members of Societies, at the time of their first incorporation into their Societies, lose the domiciles they had in the world and acquire necessary domiciles in the place in which is located the house to which they are attached.[258]

The second objection to the opinion of Rothoff and Stanton is this. The principal reason for the exemption of religious from the law of the publication of the banns was not, historically, the loss of the proper diocese. In the

[256] Cf. S. C. de Rel., instr. *Quantum Religiones*, 1 dec. 1931, § 15—*AAS*, XXIV (1932), 74-81, cf. p. 80.

[257] Cf. *supra*, pp. 85-93.

[258] Cf. *supra*, pp. 71-81.

case of regulars the reason was their exemption from the local bishop, by whose authority such publication was to be made. It was not a case of losing one bishop and being subjected to the authority of another, as is the case with members of non-exempt Societies; it was a question of being removed from the authority of *every* bishop.[259] In the case of non-exempt Secular Congregations before the Code, it was only *probable* that they were exempt from the law of the publication of the banns.[260] This probable opinion grew up in the years preceding the Code as the result of a decree of the Sacred Congregation for the State of Regulars of the year 1848. In that year the Sacred Congregation ordered that a complete investigation be made of all candidates for all institutes, regular or secular, at the time of their admission in the institutes.[261] It was the opinion of a number of the canonists that the end of the law of the publication of the banns was accomplished by the fulfillment of the prescripts of the Decree of 1848.[262]

It seems, therefore, that there is no justification for exempting non-exempt Societies from the law of the publication of the banns, either in virtue of a prescript in their Constitutions whereby they lose their proper diocese at the time of their perpetual incorporation, or in virtue of an indult to grant dimissorial letters with the proviso that, should one ordained with such dimissorial letters leave his Society, he must find a benevolent bishop to receive him.

Confirmation of this view seems contained in an indult granted to the Society of Missionaries to Africa. The Constitutions of this Society, approved definitively in 1928, contain the following statement: "The taking of the oath

[259] Cf. Many, *De Sacra Ordinatione*, p. 402.

[260] Cf. *supra*, p. 56.

[261] S. C. super Statu Reg., decr. *Romani Pontifices*, 25 ian. 1848—*Fontes*, n. 4375.

[262] Gasparri, *De Sacra Ordinatione*, II, 26; Many, *De Sacra Ordinatione*, pp. 426-427.

for life ends incorporation in a Diocese."[263] Yet, an indult in effect in the Society in the year 1949 contained the following words: "*etiam omissis ex justa causa ante Ordinationem consuetis publicationibus.*"[264] And Rothoff, when he quoted this indult, admitted that the Society of Missionaries to Africa could omit the publication of the banns *only* for a just cause.[265]

[263] *The Society of African Missions. Constitutions and Directory*, Constitutions, § 22, p. 5.

[264] Rothoff, *Sociétés*, p. 179.

[265] *Sociétés*, p. 179.

CONCLUSIONS

1. The proper bishop for the promotion of members of Societies to First Tonsure is, by the common law, the bishop of the diocese in which the members have a domicile, according to the norm of canon 956. But at the time of their first incorporation in their respective Societies after their period of probation, members of Societies, by reason of their subjection to the dominative power of their superiors, lose the domicile which they had in the world and obtain a necessary domicile in the place in which is located the house to which they are attached. Therefore, the proper bishop for the promotion of members of Societies to First Tonsure is, by the common law, the bishop of the place in which is located the house to which the members are attached.[1]

2. Clerical members of Societies must, by the common law, be incardinated in some diocese. Canon 585 is not among those canons referring to religious which are extended to members of Societies by the common law, and therefore a cleric who is already incardinated in some diocese at the time of his entry into a Society is not, by the common law, excardinated from his diocese at the time of his perpetual incorporation, but rather remains forever incardinated in his proper diocese.[2]

3. At the time of promotion to First Tonsure, the proper bishop can, by the common law, incardinate members of Societies in his own diocese perpetually, or can incardinate members of Societies in his own diocese with the intention of excardinating them at a future date and having them incardinated in some other diocese, or can incardinate them immediately into another determined diocese with the consent of the bishop of that other diocese.[3]

4. If a bishop intends to incardinate a member of a

[1] Pp. 66-102.
[2] Pp. 102-106.
[3] Pp. 106-117.

Society in his own diocese perpetually, and the member has in that diocese a domicile distinct from the place of his origin, the member must first, according to the norm of canon 956, declare under oath his intention of remaining perpetually in the diocese of incardination.[4]

5. The proper bishop for the promotion of members of Societies to higher Orders is, by the common law, the bishop of the diocese in which the members are incardinated, even though they have no domicile in that diocese.[5]

6. The status of members of Societies who have been promoted to Orders according to the norms of the common law and who are dismissed from their Societies is regulated completely by canons 646 to 672, which regulate the status of dismissed religious. Members of Societies who have been promoted to minor or major Orders according to the norms of the common law, and who leave their Societies legitimately and of their own free will, remain incardinated clerics and as such must return to their dioceses of incardination. They can never claim automatic incardination elsewhere in virtue of canon 641, § 2.[6]

7. Candidates for major Orders in Societies must, by the common law, possess a title of benefice, of patrimony, of pension, of service of the diocese, or of the mission, and may not, by the common law, use the title of poverty or the title of the common table. In order to make use of the title of service of the diocese or of the title of the mission, members of Societies must take a promissory oath to devote themselves perpetually to the service of the diocese or the mission in so far as they will be called upon by lawful authority to render such service. This oath of service must be distinct from the oath by which members of some Societies become incorporated in their Societies.[7]

[4] Pp. 106-117.
[5] Pp. 117-118.
[6] Pp. 118-120.
[7] Pp. 134-138.

8. Exempt Societies enjoy the privilege of granting dimissorial letters in virtue of their exemption.[8]

9. In the use of the privilege of granting dimissorial letters, whether this privilege is possessed in virtue of exemption or in virtue of an indult, Societies are bound by the same laws which regulate the granting of dimissorial letters in religious institutes.[9]

10. If a Society has received the privilege of granting dimissorial letters, but has not received privileges regarding incardination and excardination and status after egress, members who legitimately and of their own free will leave the Society must find a benevolent bishop if they received First Tonsure in the Society, and must return to their diocese of incardination if they came to the Society as incardinated clerics.[10]

11. The privilege of granting dimissorial letters does not include the privilege of using the title of the common table.[11]

12. Major superiors in those Societies which enjoy by privilege the exemption of regulars are ordinaries, and, as such, enjoy the faculties granted to ordinaries in the law for ordination whenever local ordinaries are not specified.[12]

13. Societies which enjoy the privilege of the exemption of regulars do not, by that fact alone, enjoy the privilege of sending dimissorial letters to any bishop in peace and communion with the Holy See.[13]

14. The examination before Orders in exempt Societies is in the hands of the major superiors, but the ordaining bishop is always free to examine the ordinands himself.[14]

[8] Pp. 171-173.
[9] Pp. 182-184.
[10] Pp. 184-186.
[11] Pp. 199-202.
[12] Pp. 204-205.
[13] P. 206.
[14] Pp. 207-208.

15. The place in which the ordination retreat is to be held is designated by the superiors in exempt Societies.[15]

16. If a bishop enjoys the privilege of having ordinations *extra tempora* or the privilege of not having to observe the normally required interstices, he can use these privileges in favor of members of Societies, even though the Societies in question do not enjoy these privileges.[16]

17. Non-exempt Societies, aside from a special privilege, are held to the law regarding the proclamation of the banns, even though they enjoy the privilege of issuing dimissorial letters.[17]

[15] P. 209.
[16] P. 211.
[17] Pp. 211-215.

BIBLIOGRAPHY

Sources

Acta Apostolica, Bullae, Brevia et Rescripta in gratiam Congregationis Missionis, Parisiis, 1876.

Acta Apostolicae Sedis, Commentarium Officiale, Romae, 1909-1929; Civitate Vaticana, 1929-

Acta Gregorii Papae XVI, cura ac studio Antonii Rariae Bernasconi, 4 vols., Romae, 1901-1904.

Acta Sanctae Sedis, 41 vols., Romae, 1865-1908.

Bizzarri, A., *Collectanea in Usum Secretariae Sacrae Congregationis Episcoporum et Regularium*, 2. ed., Romae, 1885.

Bouscaren, T. Lincoln, *The Canon Law Digest*, 2 vols. and Supplement through 1948, Milwaukee, Wis.: The Bruce Publishing Co., 1934-1943-1949.

Bullarii Romani Continuatio Summorum Pontificum Benedicti XIV, Clementis XIII, Clementis XIV, Pii VI, Pii VII, Leonis XII et Pii VIII, 14 vols., Prati, 1840-1856.

Bullarium Diplomatum et Privilegiorum Sanctorum Romanorum Pontificum Taurinensis Editio, 24 vols. et Appendix, Augustae Taurinorum-Neapoli, 1857-1872.

Codex Iuris Canonici Pii X Pontificis Maximi iussu digestus Benedicti Papae XV auctoritate promulgatus, Romae: Typis Polyglottis Vaticanis, 1917.

Codicis Iuris Canonici Fontes, cura Emi Petri Card. Gasparri editi, 9 vols., Romae (postea Civitate Vaticana): Typis Polyglottis Vaticanis, 1923-1939. Vols. VII-IX, ed. cura et studio Emi Iustiniani Card. Serédi.

Collectanea S. Congregationis de Propaganda Fide, 2 vols., Romae, 1907.

Collectio Privilegiorum et Indulgentiarum quae S. Sedes Congregationi Missionis benigne Concessit, 3. ed., Parisiis, 1900.

Concilium Tridentinum. Diariorum, Actorum, Epistularum, Tractatuum Nova Collectio, ed. Societas Goerresiana, 13 vols., Friburgi Brisgoviae: Herder, 1901-

Constitutiones Piae Societatis Missionum, Ratisbonae, 1922.

Constittuiones Societatis Sancti Columbani pro Missionibus apud Sinenses, Dublin: Sealy, Bryers and Walker, 1932.

Constitutions de la Congrégation de Jésus et Marie, Paris, 1928.

Constitutions de la Société des Prêtres de la Miséricorde, Rome, 1928.

Constitutions of the Catholic Foreign Mission Society of America, 2. ed., New York: Maryknoll, 1938.

Constitutions of the Pious Society of Missions, translated by order of the General Council, 1935.

Constitutions of the Scarboro Foreign Mission Society, Scarboro Bluffs, Ontario, 1941.

Constitutions of the Society of Missionary Priests of Saint Paul the Apostle, New York: The Paulist Press, 1940.

Constitutions of the Society of St. Joseph of the Sacred Heart, Rome: Vatican Polyglot Press, 1932.

Constitutions of the Society of the Priests of Saint Sulpice, There is no place or date of publication, but the decree of definitive approbation of July 8, 1931, is appended.

Corpus Iuris Canonici, editio Lipsiensis secunda post Aemilii Ludovici Richteri curas instruxit Aemilius Friedberg, 2 vols., Lipsiae, 1879-1881.

Corpus Iuris Civilis, 3 vols., Berolini, Vol. I, *Institutiones,* quas recognovit P. Krueger, ed. stereotypa 15, 1928; *Digesta,* quae recognovit T. Mommsen et retractavit P. Krueger, ed. stereotypa 15, 1928; Vol. II, *Codex Iustinianus,* quem recognovit et retractavit P. Krueger, ed. stereotypa 10, 1929.

Costituzioni dell'Istituto delle Missioni Estere de Milano, Milano, 1925.

Customary of the Society of the Precious Blood, American Province, Carthagena, 1949.

Decreta Authentica Congregationis Sacrorum Rituum, 5 vols. et 2 Appendices, Romae: Typis Polyglottis Vaticanis, 1898-1927.

Directorium Piae Societatis Missionum, auctoritate Capituli Generalis anni 1919 a Consilio generali editum, Ratisbonae.

Holstenius, L., *Codex regularum monasticarum et canonicarum,* 6 vols., ed. M. Brockie, Augustae Vindelicorum, 1759.

Institutionum ad Oblatos S. Ambrosii Pertinentium Epitome, Mediolani, 1716.

Iuris Pontificii De Propaganda Fide, 2 partes, cura ac studio Raphaelis de Martinis, Pars I, 7 vols. in 8, Romae, 1888-1897; Pars II, 1 vol., Romae, 1909.

Jaffé, Philippus, *Regesta Pontificum Romanorum ab condita Ecclesia ad annum post Christum natum MCXCVIII,* 2 ed. correctam et auctam auspiciis Gulielmi Wattenbach, curaverunt S. Loewenfeld, F. Kaltenbrunner, P. Ewald, 2 vols., Lipsiae, 1885-1888.

Liber Sextus Decretalium D. Bonifacii Papae VIII, suae integritati cum Clementinis et Extravagantibus, earumque Glossis restitutis, Romae, 1582.

Mansi, Ioannes, *Sacrorum Conciliorum Nova et Amplissima Collectio,* 53 vols. in 60, Parisiis, 1901-1927.

Marrier, Martinus et Quercetanus, Andreas, *Bibliotheca Cluniacensis,* Matiscone, 1915.

Pallottini, Salvator, *Collectio omnium conclusionum et resolutionum quae in causis propositis apud Sacram Congregationem Cardinalium S. Concilii Tridentini Interpretum prodierunt ab eius institutione anno MDLXIV ad annum MDCCCLX, distinctis titulis alphabetico ordine per materias digesta,* 17 vols., Romae, 1868-1893.

Pflugk, J.-Harttung, Iulius, *Acta Pontificum Romanorum Inedita,* 3 vols., Vol. I, Tübingen, 1881; Vol. II, Stuttgart, 1884; Vol. III, Stuttgart, 1886.

Pontificale Romanum, Summorum Pontificum jussu editum, et a Benedicto XIV. Pont. Max. recognitum et castigatum, 3 partes, Mechliniae, 1873.

Promptuarium Facultatum Piae Societatis Missionum iussu Sexti Capituli Generalis Editum, Romae: Ad. SS. Salvatorem in Unda, 1932.

Règles Complémentaires de la Congrégation de Jésus et Marie, Paris, 1931.

Regula et Constitutiones Congregationis Missionis a Pretioso Sanguine D. N. J. C. Carthagena, 1946.

Schwartz, Eduardus, *Acta Conciliorum Oecumenicorum,* 4 tomi, Tom. II, *Concilium Universale Chalcedonense,* Vol. II, Pars II, *Rerum Chalcedonensium Collectio Vaticana. Canones et Symbolum,* Berolini et Lipsiae: Walter de Gruyter & Co., 1936.

Société des Missionnaires d'Afrique, Constitutions, Namur, Grands Lacs, 1948.

Society of African Missions, Constitutions and Directory, The, Cork: Guy & Company Ltd., 1935.

Reference Works

Abbo, John A.-Hannan, Jerome D., *The Sacred Canons,* 2 vols., St. Louis and London: Herder, 1952.

Agnelli, Francesco, *The Excellencies of the Congregation of the Oratory,* translated from the Italian and abridged by Frederick Antrobus, London, 1881.

Alciatus, Andreas, *Parergon Iuris,* in *D. Andreae Alciati Mediolanensis Iurecos. Opera Omnia,* 4 tomi, Basileae, 1582, Tom. IV, cols. 279-582.

André, M., et Condis, P., et Wagner, J., *Dictionnaire de Droit Canonique,* 5. ed., 4 vols., Paris, 1901.

Annuario Pontificio per l'Anno 1952, Città del Vaticano: Tipografia Poliglotta Vaticana, 1952.

[Bachofen] Augustine, Charles, *A Commentary on the New Code of Canon Law,* 8 vols., St. Louis-London: Herder, Vol. III, *Religious and Laymen,* 2. ed., 1919.

Bachofen, Augustine, *Compendium Juris Regularium,* Neo-Eboraci—Cincinnati—Chicagiae: Benziger Brothers, 1903.

Badii, Caesar, *Institutiones Iuris Canonici,* 2 vols., Vol. I, 3. ed., Florentiae, 1921.

Bastien, Pierre, *Directoire Canonique à l'Usage des Congrégations à Voeux Simples,* 1. ed., Abbaye de Maredsous, 1904; 3. ed., Bruges, 1923.

Berutti, Christophorus, *Institutiones Iuris Canonici,* 6 vols. in 7, Vol. II, Pars I, *De Personis et de Clericis in Genere,* Taurini-Romae: Marietti, 1943; Vol. III, *De Religiosis,* Taurini-Romae: Marietti, 1936.

Beste, Udalricus, *Introductio in Codicem,* 3. ed., Collegeville, Minn.: St. John's Abbey Press, 1946.

Blat, Albertus, *Commentarium Textus Codicis Iuris Canonici,* 5 tomi in 7 vols., Tom. II, Vol. II, *Liber II, Partes II et III, Ius de Religiosis et Laicis iuxta Codicis Ordinem,* 3. ed., Romae: apud "Angelicum," 1938.

Bouix, D., *Tractatus de Jure Regularium,* 2 vols., Parisiis, 1857.

Bouscaren, T. Lincoln-Ellis, Adam C., *Canon Law, A Text and Commentary,* 2. ed., Milwaukee: Bruce, 1951.

Brys, J., *Juris Canonici Compendium,* 2 vols., olim a De Brabandère et Van Coillie et De Meester editum, Vol. I, 10 ed., 2. ed. post Codicem, Brugis: Desclée et Brouwer et Sii, 1947.

Cance, Adrien, *Le Code de Droit Canonique,* 3 vols., Vol. II, 7. ed., Paris: J. Gabalda et Fils, Éditeurs, 1946.

Cappello, Felix M., *Summa Iuris Canonici in Usum Scholarum Concinnata,* 3 vols., Romae: Apud Aedes Universitatis Gregorianae, Vol. I, 4. ed., 1945; Vol. II, 4. ed., 1945.

———, *Tractatus Canonico-Moralis de Sacramentis,* 5 vols., Vol. IV, *De Sacra Ordinatione,* 2. ed., Augustae Taurinorum-Romae: Marietti, 1947.

Catholic Encyclopedia, The, 15 vols., 2 Supplements and Index, New York: Appleton Co., 1907-1922.

Chelodi, Ioannes, *Ius Canonicum de Personis,* 3. ed. curavit Pius Ciprotti, Vicenza: Società Anonima Tipografica-Trento: Libreria Moderna Editrice, 1942.

Cicognani, Hamleto-Staffa, Dino, *Commentarium ad Librum Primum Codicis Iuris Canonici,* 2 vols., Vol. I, Romae: Ex Officina Typographica Romana "Buona Stampa," 1939.

Claeys Bouuaert, Ferdinandus-Simenon, G., *Manuale Juris Canonici ad Usum Seminariorum,* 3 vols., Vol. I, *Introductio, Libri I et II Codicis,* 5. ed., Gandae et Leodii: in Seminariis Gandavensi et Leodiensi, 1939.

Cocchi, Guidus, *Commentarium in Codicem Iuris Canonici ad Usum Scholarum,* 8 vols., Vol. IV, *Liber II De Personis, Pars II, De Religiosis-Pars III, De Laicis,* 4. ed., Augustae Taurinorum: Marietti, 1946.

Coronata, Matthaeus Conte a, *Institutiones Iuris Canonici ad Usum Utriusque Cleri et Scholarum*, 5 vols., Taurini: Marietti, Vol. I, *Normae generales, De Clericis, De Religiosis, De Laicis*, 2. ed., 1939.

———, *Institutiones Iuris Canonici ad Usum Utriusque Cleri et Scholarum, De Sacramentis Tractatus Canonicus*, 3 vols., Vol. II, *De Ordine*, Torino: Marietti, 1945.

Costello, John Michael, *Domicile and Quasi-Domicile*, The Catholic University of America Canon Law Studies, n. 60, Washington, D.C., 1930.

Crnica, Antonius, *Commentarium Theoretico-Practicum Codicis Iuris Canonici*, 2 vols., Vol. I, *Normae Generales et De Personis*, Sibenik: Typis Typographiae "Kačić," 1940.

Currier, Charles Warren, *History of Religious Orders*, New York, 1899.

D'Angelo, Sosio, *Del domicilio ecclesiastico e dei suoi effetti*, Giarre, 1916.

De Angelis, Philippus, *Praelectiones Iuris Canonici*, 5 tomi in 9, Romae-Parisiis, 1877-1891.

De Carlo, Camillus, *Jus Religiosorum*, Parisiis-Tornaci-Romae: Desclée, 1950.

Dumas, Auguste, *Les églises monastiques*, in Fliche-Martin, *Histoire de l'Église*, Vol. VII, *L'Église au pouvoir des laïques*, Paris: Bloud & Gay, 1948, Livre III.

Fanfani, Ludovicus, *De Iure Religiosorum ad Normam Codicis Iuris Canonici*, 3. ed., Rovigo: Istituto Padano di Arti Grafiche, 1949.

Fathers of Mercy, The, New York: The Paulist Press, 1920.

Ferraris, Lucius, *Prompta Bibliotheca Canonica, Iuridica, Moralis, Theologica, nec non Ascetica, Polemica, Rubristica, Historica*, ed. novissima, 9 tomi, Romae, 1885-1899.

Freriks, Celestine, A., *Religious Congregations in Their External Relations*, The Catholic University of America Canon Law Studies, n. 1, Washington, D.C.: Columbia Polytechnic Institute for the Blind, 1916.

Gallagher, Thomas Raphael, *The Examination of the Qualities of the Ordinand*, The Catholic University of America Canon Law Studies, n. 195, Washington, D.C.: The Catholic University of America Press, 1944.

Gasparri, Petrus, *Tractatus Canonicus de Sacra Ordinatione*, 2 vols., Parisiis-Lugduni, 1893-1894.

Gerster a Zeil, Thomas Villanova, *Ius Religiosorum in Compendium Redactum*, Taurini: Marietti, 1935.

Gillis, James, *The Paulists*, New York: Macmillan, 1932.

Goyau, Georges, *Les Prêtres des Missions Étrangères*, Collection "Les

Grands Ordres Monastiques et Instituts Religieux," dirigée par Edouard Schneider, Paris: Éditions Bernard Grasset, 1932.

Goyeneche, Servus, *Iuris Canonici Summa Principia, Libri II, Pars II, De Religiosis, Libri II, Pars III, de Laicis*, Roma: Commentarium pro Religiosis, 1938.

Grandclaude, Eugenius, *Jus Canonicum*, 3 vols., Parisiis, 1882-1883.

Hallier, Franciscus, *De Sacris Electionibus et Ordinationibus*, 2. ed., 3 vols., Romae, 1739-1740.

Heimbucher, Max. *Die Orden und Kongregationen der katholischen Kirche*, 3. ed., 2 vols., Paderborn: Verlag Ferdinand Schöningh, 1933-1934.

Helyot, Pierre, *Dictionnaire des Ordres Religieux*, in J. P. Migne, *Encyclopédie Théologique*, I Série, Tomes XX-XXIII, 4 vols., Paris, 1847-1859.

Honorante, Romualdus, *Praxis Secretariae Tribunalis Eminentissimi et Reverendissimi Domini D. Cardinalis Urbis Vicarii*, 2. ed., Romae, 1762.

Jombart, Émile, *Manuel de Droit Canon*, Paris: Beauchesne et ses fils, 1949.

Kapsner, Oliver, *Catholic Religious Orders*, Collegeville: St. John's Abbey Press, 1948.

Kurtscheid, Bertrandus, *Historia Iuris Canonici, Historia Institutorum ab Ecclesiae Fundatione usque ad Gratianum*, reimpressio, Romae: Officium Libri Catholici, 1951.

Lafontaine, Élie, *L'Évêque d'Ordination des Religieux des débuts du monachisme à la mort de Louis le Pieux (840)*, Universitas Catholica Ottaviensis, Dissertationes, Series canonica, Tomus 22, Ottawa: Les Éditions de l'Université d'Ottawa, 1951.

Lane, Raymond A., *The Early Days of Maryknoll*, New York: McKay, 1951.

Launay, Adrien, *Histoire Générale de la Société des Missions-Étrangères*, 3 vols., Paris, 1894.

Leherpeur, Michel, *L'Oratoire de France*, Paris, 1926.

Maire, Élie, *Histoire des Instituts Religieux et Missionnaires*, Paris, 1930.

Many, Seraphinus, *Praelectiones de Sacra Ordinatione*, Parisiis, 1905.

Maroto, Philippus, *Institutiones Iuris Canonici*, 2 vols., Vol. I, 3. ed., Romae: Apud Commentarium pro Religiosis, 1921.

McBride, James Tomas, *Incardination and Excardination of Secular Clerics*, The Catholic University of America Canon Law Studies, n. 145, Washington, D.C.: The Catholic University of America Press, 1942.

McLaughlin, Terence, *Le Très Ancien Droit Monastique de l'Occident*,

Archives de la France Monastique, Vol. XXXVIII, Vienne: Abbaye Saint-Martin—Paris: A. Picard, 1935.

Melo, Antonius, *De Exemptione Regularium*, The Catholic University of America Canon Law Studies, n. 12, Washington, D.C., 1921.

Michiels, Gommarus, *Normae Generales Juris Canonici, Commentarius Libri I Codicis Juris Canonici*, 2. ed., 2 vols., Parisiis-Tornaci-Romae: Desclée et Socii, 1949.

———, *Principia Generalia de Personis in Ecclesia*, Lublin, Polonia: Universitas Catholica-Brasschaat, Belgium: De Bievre, 1932.

Migne, Jacques Paul, *Patrologiae Cursus Completus, Series Latina*, 221 vols., Paris, Vols. I—CCXVII, 1844-1855, et 4 indices: Vol. CCXVIII, 1887; Vol. CCXIX, 1879; Vol. CCXX, 1863; Vol. CCXXI, 1864.

Mocchegiani, Petrus, *Iurisprudentia Ecclesiastica ad Usum et Commoditatem Utriusque Cleri*, 3 vols., Ad Claras Aquas-Friburgi Brisgoviae, 1904-1905.

Moeder, John M., *The Proper Bishop for Ordination and Dimissorial Letters*, The Catholic University of America Canon Law Studies, n. 95, Washington, D.C.: The Catholic University of America, 1935.

Monacelli, Fr., *Formularium Legale Practicum Fori Ecclesiastici cum Supplemento*, 4 vols., Vol. II, *Pars Secunda*, Romae, 1706.

Monval, Jean, *Les Sulpiciens*, Collection "Les Grans Ordres Monastiques et Instituts Religieux," dirigée par Edouard Schneider, Paris: Éditions Bernard Grasset, 1934.

Nabucho, Joachim, *Pontificalis Romani Expositio Juridico-Practica*, 3 tomi, Petropoli, Brasilia: Sumptibus Editôra Vozes Ltda., 1945.

Naz, Raoul, *Traité de droit canonique*, 4 vols., Vol. I, *Livres I et II, Introduction, Règles générales, des Personnes*, Paris: Letouzey et Ané, 1946.

O'Brien, Romaeus W., *The Provincial Religious Superior*, The Catholic University of America Canon Law Studies, n. 258, Washington, D.C.: The Catholic University of America Press, 1947.

Ojetti, Benedictus, *Synopsis Rerum Moralium et Iuris Pontificii*, 3. ed., 4 vols., Romae, 1909-1914.

Ordo Divini Officii Recitandi Missaeque Celebrandae ad usum Societatis Missionum ad Afros pro anno Domini 1951, Lugduni: Ex Typis Missionum ad Afros, 1950.

Panormitanus (Nicolaus de Tudeschis, Abbas Siculus, Abbas Modernus), *Commentaria in Quinque Libros Decretalium*, 5 vols. in 7, Venetiis, 1588.

Passerini, Petrus, *De Hominum Statibus et Officiis*, 3 tomi, Lucae, 1732.

Paventi, Xaverius, *De Iuramento ac de Titulo Missionis,* Bibliotheca Missionalis, n. 3, Romae: Officium Libri Catholici, 1946.

———, *Organización del Instituto Español del S. Francisco Javier para Misiones Extranjeras, Comentario y Exposición de las Constituciones,* Burgos: Aldecoa, 1950.

Petra, Vincentius, *Commentaria ad Constitutiones Apostolicas,* 5 tomi, Venetiis, 1729.

Piatus Montensis (J. J. Laiseaux), *Praelectiones Juris Regularis,* 2. ed., 2 vols., Tornaci, 1898.

Piontek, Cyrillus, *De Indulto Exclaustrationis necnon Saecularizationis,* The Catholic University of America Canon Law Studies, n. 29, Washington, D.C., 1925.

Pirhing, Ernricus, *Jus Canonicum,* 5 vols., Dilingae, 1722.

Pisani, Paul, *The Congregations of Priests from the Sixteenth to the Eighteenth Century,* Catholic Library of Religious Knowledge, n. 14, translated from the French by Mother Mary Reginald, O.P., London-St. Louis, 1930.

Powers, George, *The Maryknoll Movement,* Maryknoll: Field Afar Press, 1920.

Prümmer, Dominicus, *Manuale Iuris Canonici,* 4. et 5. ed., Friburgi Brisgoviae, 1927.

Quinn, Joseph James, *Documents Required for the Reception of Orders,* The Catholic University of America Canon Law Studies, n. 266, Washington, D.C.: The Catholic University of America Press, 1948.

Ramstein, Matthew, *A Manual of Canon Law,* Hoboken: Terminal Printing and Publishing Co., 1948.

Regatillo, Eduardus F., *Institutiones Iuris Canonici,* 2 vols., Santander: Sal Terrae, Vol. I, *Pars Praeliminaris, Normae Generales, De Personis,* 3. ed., 1948.

Register of the Paulist Fathers, The, October, 1951.

Reiffenstuel, Anacletus, *Ius Canonicum Universum,* 5 vols. in 7, Parisiis, 1864-1870.

Riganti, Joannes Baptista, *Commentaria in Regulas, Constitutiones et Ordinationes Cancellariae Apostolicae,* 4 vols. in 2, Coloniae Allobrogum, 1751.

Ristuccia, Bernard Joseph, *Quasi-Religious Societies,* The Catholic University of America Canon Law Studies, n. 261, Washington, D.C.: The Catholic University of America Press, 1949.

Romani, Sylvius, *Institutiones Juris Canonici,* 2 vols., Vol. I, *Jus Constitutionale,* Romae: Schola Typographica "Pio X," 1941.

Rothoff, H., *Le Droit des Sociétés sans Voeux,* Paris: Desclée de Brouwer, 1949.

Sägmüller, Joannes Baptista, *Lehrbuch des katholischen Kirchenrechts,* 4. ed., 1 Band in 4 Teile, Freiburg im Breisgau, Teil I, 1925; Teil II, 1926; Teil III, 1930; Teil IV, 1934.

Schaefer, Timotheus, *De Religiosis ad Normam Codicis Iuris Canonici,* 4. ed., Roma: Editrice "Apostolato Cattolico," 1947.

Schmalzgrueber, Franciscus, *Ius Ecclesiasticum Universum,* 5 vols. in 12, Romae, 1843-1845.

Schmitz, Philibert, *Histoire de l'ordre de Saint Benoît,* 7 tomes, Tom. I, *Origines, Duffusion et Constituion jusqu'au XII° Siècle,* Maredsous: Les éditions de Maredsous, 1942.

Schreiber, Georg, *Kurie und Kloster im 12. Jahrundert,* Kirchenrechtliche Abhandlungen herausgegeben von Dr. Ulrich Stutz, 65-68 Heft, Stuttgart, 1910.

Sipos, Stephanus, *Enchiridion Iuris Canonici,* Pécs: Haladás R. T., 1926.

Society of Saint Joseph of the Sacred Heart 1893-1943, Baltimore: The Josephite Press, 1943.

Stanghetti, Giuseppe, *Prassi della S. C. de Propaganda Fide,* Bibliotheca Missionalis, n. 1, Romae: Officium Libri Catholici, 1943.

Stanton, William A., *De Societatibus sive Virorum sive Mulierum in Communi Viventium sine Votis,* 2. ed., Halifaxiae: Apud Custodiam Librariam Maioris Seminarii a Sanctissimo Corde B.M.V., 1936.

Suarez, Franciscus, *Opus De Virtute et Statu Religionis,* in *Opera Omnia,* 26 vols., Parisiis, 1856-1866 (2 Indices, 1878), Vols. XIII-XVI.

Toso, Albertus, *Ad Codicem Juris Canonici . . . Commentaria Minora,* 2 libri in 5 toms., Liber II, *De Personis,* Tom. I, Taurini-Romae, 1922; Tom. IV, Romae, 1927.

Van Hove, Alphonsus, *Commentarium Lovaniense in Codicem Iuris Canocici,* 1 vol. in 5 toms., Mechliniae-Romae: H. Dessain, Tom. I, *Prolegomena,* 2. ed., 1945; Tom. II, *De Legibus Ecclesiasticis,* 1930.

Vermeersch, Arthurus, *De Religiosis Institutis et Personis Tractatus Canonico-Moralis,* 2 vols., Vol. II, *Supplementa et Monumenta,* 4. ed., Brugis, 1909.

Vermeersch, Arthurus-Creusen, Josephus, *Epitome Iuris Canonici cum Commentariis ad Scholas et ad Usum Privatum,* 3 tomi, Mechliniae-Romae: H. Dessain, Tom. I, *Libri I et II Codicis iuris canonici,* 7. ed., 1949; Tom. II, *Liber III Codicis iuris canonici,* 6. ed., 1940.

Vromant, G., *Ius Missionariorum de Personis,* Paris-Bruxelles, 1929.

Waters, Joseph L., *The Probation in Societies of Quasi-Religious,* The Catholic University of America Canon Law Studies, n. 306, Washington, D.C.: The Catholic University of America Press, 1951.

Wernz, Franciscus, *Ius Decretalium,* 6 vols., Romae et Prati, 1898-

1914, Vol. I, *Introductio in Ius Decretalium,* Romae, 1898; Vol. II, *Ius Constitutionis Eccles. Catholicae,* Romae, 1899; Vol. III, *Ius Administrationis Eccl. Catholicae,* Romae, 1901.

Wernz, Franciscus-Vidal, Petrus, *Ius Canonicum,* 7 tomi in 8 vols., Romae: Apud Aedes Universitatis Gregorianae, Tom. I, *Normae Generales,* 1938; Tom. II, *De Personis,* 3. ed. a Philippo Aguirre recognita, 1943; Tom. III, *De Religiosis,* 1933; Tom. IV, *De Rebus,* Vol. I, *Sacramenta, Sacramentalia, Cultus divinus, Coemeteria et Sepultura ecclesiastica,* 1934.

Woywod, Stanislaus, *A Practical Commentary on the Code of Canon Law,* revised by Callistus Smith, revised and enlarged edition, 2 vols., New York: Wagner-London: Herder, 1948.

ARTICLES

Cappello, Felix M., "De Litteris Dimissoriis," *Periodica, XVIII* (1929), 249-251.

"Congrégations Séculières," *Anal. J. P.*, XXIV (1885), 383-422.

"Congrégations séculières. Privilèges. Ordinations. Direction des séminaries," *Anal. J. P.*, VII (1864), 758-764.

Coussa, Acacius, "De Episcopo Proprio Sacrae Ordinationis," *Apollinaris,* XII (1939), 321-325.

De Naurois, Louis, "Le 'Propre Évêque' pour l'ordination dans le clergé séculier," *BLE,* LI (1950), 15-40.

"Des ordinations dans les Congrégations séculières," *Anal. J. P.*, VII (1864), 744-751.

Fallon, M. J., "Proper Bishop for Ordination—Reply of Code Commission," *IER,* 5. series, LIV (1939), 409-413.

Francia, Ennius, "Animadversiones circa incardinationem," *Apollinaris,* IX (1936), 216-218.

Gil, N., "Studium," *CpRM,* XXVIII (1949), 18-29.

Goyeneche, Servus, "Consultationes," *CpR,* I (1920), 144-145, 177-178.

———, "Consultationes," *CpR,* VIII (1927), 113-115.

Hannan, Jerome D., "The Ordination of Quasi-Religious," *The Jurist,* XII (1952), 443-456.

Heneghan, John J., "Episcopus Proprius," *The Jurist,* III (1943), 326-330.

Hüfner, August, "Das Rechtsinstitut der klösterlichen Exemtion in der abendländischen Kirche," *Archiv für katholisches Kirchenrecht,* LXXXVI (1906), 302-318; 629-651; LXXXVII (1907), 71-86; 270-284; 462-479; 599-636.

"Instituts Séculières," *Anal J. P.*, XXVII (1887-1888), 424-446; 689-710.

Kinane, J., "Necessary Domicile," *IER,* 5. series, XXVII (1926), 647-648.

Langogne, Pie, "Sur le Décret '*Auctis admodum,*'" *Le Canoniste Contemporain,* XVI (1893), 79-93; 193-207.

Larraona, Arcadius, "Commentarium Codicis: Can. 491," *CpR,* IV (1923), 172-173; 210-218; 273-280.

Maroto, Philippus, "De Litteris Dimissoriis," *Apollinaris,* III (1930), 232-236.

Martin, Thomas Owen, "Seminarian Changing Domicile," *The Jurist,* V (1945), 448-450.

Oesterle, Gerardus, "De domicilio Religiosorum," *CpR,* V (1924), 167-178.

———, "Weihekandidaten aus einer Diözesan-Priestergenossenschaft," *ThPrQs,* LXXXV (1932), 563-571.

Schaaf, Valentine, "Episcopus Proprius Ordinationis," *ER,* XC (1934), 352-365.

———, "Episcopus Proprius Ordinationis Religiosorum," *ER, XC* (1934), 491-509.

Toso, Albertus, "De Litteris Dimissoriis," *J. P.,* IX (1929), 193.

"Traité des Congrégations Séculières," *Anal. J. P.,* V (1861), 52-103; 147-217.

Vermeersch, Arthurus, "De Domicilio Regularium," *Periodica,* IV (2. ed., 1913), 189-195.

———, "De Domicilio Religiosorum," *Periodica,* IX (1921), (7)-(8).

———, "De ordinatione religiosorum qui 'iure saecularium' reguntur," *Periodica,* IX (1921), 16)-(18).

———, "Incardinatio in Societatem sine votis," *Periodica,* XXIII (1934), 57*.

———, "Vows," *CE,* XV, 511-514.

Vindex, "Domicilium et quasi-Domicilium Eorumque Effectus in Codice Juris Canonici," *J. P.,* VI (1926), 34-55; 112-126; 154-158.

Voltas, Petrus, "De Domicilio quoad Ordinationem Religiosorum," *CpR,* II (1921), 299-307.

Periodicals

American Ecclesiastical Review, The (from July, 1905 to December, 1943, *The Ecclesiastical Review*), Philadelphia, 1889-1943; Washington, D.C., 1944-

Analecta Juris Pontificii, Romae, 1855-1869; Paris, 1872-1891.

Apollinaris, Romae, 1928-

Archiv für katholisches Kirchenrecht, Innsbruck, 1857-1861; Mainz, 1862-

Bulletin de Littérature ecclésiastique, Paris, 1899-1908; Toulouse, 1909-

Canoniste Contemporain, Le, Paris, 1878-1926.

Commentarium pro Religiosis et Missionariis (from 1920 to 1934, *Commentarium pro Religiosis*), Romae, 1920-

Irish Ecclesiastical Record, The, Dublin, 1864-

Jurist, The, Washington, D.C.: The Catholic University of America, 1941-

Jus Pontificium, Romae, 1921-1940.

Periodica de Re Morali, Canonica, Liturgica (from 1905 to 1919, *De Religiosis et Missionariis Supplementum et Monumenta Periodica;* from 1921 to 1927, *Periodica de Re Canonica et Morali utilia praesertim Religiosis et Missionariis*), Brugis et Romae, 1905-1936; Romae, 1937-

Theologisch-praktische Quartalschrift, Linz, 1848-

Abbreviations

AAS—*Acta Apostolicae Sedis, Commentarium Officiale.*
Acta Ap. in gratiam C. M.—*Acta Apostolica, Bullae, Brevia et Rescripta in gratiam Congregationis Missionis.*
Anal. J. P.—*Analecta Juris Pontificii.*
Annuario—*Annuario Pontificio per l'Anno 1952.*
ASS—*Acta Sanctae Sedis.*
BLE—*Bulletin de Littérature ecclésiastique.*
Bull. Rom. Cont.—*Bullarii Romani Continuatio Summorum Pontificum Benedicti XIV, Clementis XIII, Clementis XIV, Pii VI, Pii VII, Leonis XII et Pii VIII.*
Bull. Rom. Taur.—*Bullarum Diplomatum et Privilegiorum Romanorum Pontificum Taurinensis Editio.*
CE—*The Catholic Encyclopedia.*
Coll. S. C. P. F.—*Collectanea S. Congregationis de Propaganda Fide.*
CpR—*Commentarium pro Religiosis.*
CpRM—*Commentarium pro Religiosis et Missionariis.*
Digest—T. Lincoln Bouscaren, *The Canon Law Digest.*
ER—*The Ecclesiastical Review.*
Fontes—*Codicis Iuris Canonici Fontes,* cura Emi Petri Card. Gasparri editi.
IER—*The Irish Ecclesiastical Record.*
Iuris Pont. de Prop. Fide—*Iuris Pontificii De Propaganda Fide.*
JL—Jaffé, *Regesta Pontificum Romanorum,* ed. curavit Loewenfeld.
J. P.—*Jus Pontificium.*
Mansi—Mansi, *Sacrorum Conciliorum Nova et Amplissima Collectio.*
MPL—Migne, *Patrologiae Cursus Completus, Series Latina.*
Pallottini—Pallottini, *Collectio omnium conclusionum et resolutionum quae in causis propositis apud Sacram Congregationem Cardinalium S. Concilii Tridentini Interpretum prodierunt ab eius institutione anno MDLXIV ad annum MDCCCLX, distinctis titulis alphabetico ordine per materias digesta.*
Panormitanus—Panormitanus, *Commentaria in Quinque Libros Decretalium.*
P. C. I.—Pontificia Commissio Interpretationis.
Periodica—*Periodica de Re Morali, Canonica, Liturgica; De Religiosis et Missionariis Supplementum et Monumenta Periodica; Periodica de Re Canonica et Morali utilia praesertim Religiosis et Missionariis.*
Pirhing—Pirhing, *Jus Canonicum.*
Reiffenstuel—Reiffenstuel, *Ius Canonicum Universum.*
Schmalzgrueber—Schmalzgrueber, *Ius Ecclesiasticum Universum.*
ThPrQs—*Theologisch-praktische Quartalschrift.*

BIOGRAPHICAL NOTE

John Gerard Nugent was born on May 22, 1922, in Brooklyn, New York. He received his elementary education at Our Lady of Victory Parochial School, and his high school education at Bishop Loughlin Memorial Diocesan High School, both in Brooklyn. In 1940 he entered Saint Joseph's College, the Minor Seminary of the Eastern Province of the Congregation of the Mission, located at Princeton, New Jersey. In 1942 he was received into the Internal Seminary of the Congregation of the Mission at Saint Vincent's Seminary in Philadelphia. In 1944 he began his Major Seminary training at Mary Immaculate Seminary, Northampton, Pennsylvania. He was ordained on May 26, 1949. In October, 1950, after serving for a year as instructor in Saint Joseph's College, Princeton, he entered the Graduate School of Canon Law of the Catholic University of America. He received the degree of Baccalaureate in Canon Law in June, 1951, and the degree of Licentiate in Canon Law in June, 1952.

ALPHABETICAL INDEX

CANON LAW STUDIES*

337. Bourque, Rev. John R., S.T.L., J.C.L., The Judicial Power of the Church—Canon 1553, § 1.
338. Cornell, Rev. Charles E., A.B., S.T.B., J.C.L., The Juridical Status of Heretics and Schismatics in Good Faith.
339. Fitzgerald, Rev. William Francis, A.B., S.T.L., J.C.L., The Parish Census and the *Liber Status Animarum.*
340. Kubik, Rev. Stanislaus J., S.T.D., J.C.L., Invalidity of Dispensations according to Canon 84, § 1.
341. Nugent, Rev. John Gerard, C.M., J.C.L., Ordination in Societies of the Common Life.
342. Peterson, Rev. Casimir Melvyn, S.S., A.B., S.T.L., J.C.L., Spiritual Care in Diocesan Seminaries.
343. Reiss, Rev. John Charles, A.B., S.T.L., J.C.L., The Time and Place of Sacred Ordination.
344. Sheehan, Rev. Joseph George, J.C.L., The Obligation of Respect and Obedience of Clerics toward Their Ordinary—Canon 127.
345. Shekleton, Rev. Matthew M., O.S.M., J.C.L., Doctrinal Interpretation of Law.
346. Viau, Rev. Roger, S.T.L., J.C.L., Doubt in Canon Law.
347. Walsh, Rev. Donnell Anthony, A.B., J.C.L., The New Law on Secular Institutes.
348. Fus, Rev. Edward A., A.B., J.C.L., The Extraordinary Form of Marriage according to Canon 1098.

www.ingramcontent.com/pod-product-compliance
Lightning Source LLC
LaVergne TN
LVHW050251080826
844660LV00012B/620
9780813225104